Scottish [Doric]-English/ English-Scottish [Doric] Concise Dictionary

SCOTTISH [DORIC]-ENGLISH/ ENGLISH-SCOTTISH [DORIC] CONCISE DICTIONARY

Compiled and edited by
Douglas Kynoch M.A. (Aberdeen)

HIPPOCRENE BOOKS, INC.
New York

First published 1996 by Scottish Cultural Press, Edinburgh.
Copyright © Douglas Kynoch 1996

This edition 1998 by Hippocrene Books, Inc.

For information, address:
HIPPOCRENE BOOKS, INC.
171 Madison Avenue
New York, NY 10016

Cataloging-in-Publication data available from the Library of Congress.

ISBN 0-7818-0655-0

Printed in the United States of America.

FOREWORD

Doric is a name given to broad and rustic dialect. Deriving from that spoken by the Dorians in ancient Greece, it has been applied in more recent times to the dialects of England and of Scotland, while in Scotland itself the term refers pre-eminently to the dialect of the Scots language which is spoken in the north-eastern corner of the country. The Doric of North-east Scots meets both the traditional qualifications. On the one hand, its broadness can present difficulty even for Scots in other parts of Scotland, while on the other, its richest manifestation has always been found in the rural hinterland, where the language has recorded and labelled all the trappings of everyday life in what was a largely farming and fishing community.

It may be useful to establish what we mean in the present context by the term 'North-east'. For the purposes of this dictionary, it has been taken to include the old counties of Moray and Nairn, Banffshire and Aberdeenshire, along with Kincardineshire, where there are language differences between North and South. Additionally, as the North-east has always claimed as its own such writers as Violet Jacob, Helen Cruickshank, Sir Alexander Gray and Marion Angus, their home county of Angus has been included, or at least that part of it, the east, which has strong linguistic ties with Kincardine. Certain forms appear in Angus which are unknown in, even alien to the rest of the North-east (for example *no* for *nae*); but the similarities are strong and argue for inclusion.

It should come as no surprise to anyone that over so extensive an area there should be a considerable number of linguistic differences. If language can change slightly from village to village, as it does, then changes from county to county may be expected to be even greater. It would be a rash man who would say that this or that expression was not Doric simply because it was not *his* Doric. The truth is that there is not one monolithic form of Doric but a multiplicity of forms, differing to a greater or lesser degree here and there. Not only is there a northern and southern Doric, a Banffshire and Mearns Doric, there is a farming and fishing Doric and a now somewhat diluted urban Doric. It is interesting to note how the word for a *scarecrow* changes from county to county and that for a *seagull*, from town to town.

A North-east born journalist recently took me to task for using the word *gae* in a Doric context, protesting that *gyang* was the only allowable rendering of the English verb, *to go*. This is, quite simply, untrue. It was certainly the form used in the area the speaker was brought up in; but, as is clear from the ensuing text, there are other widely used and acceptable forms such as *ging* (Aberdeen city) and *gang, gaan* (coastal) and *gae*. Individual Doric speakers appear to use more than one.

The vocabulary in this dictionary has been drawn from the works of North-east writers published between 1871 and the present day, while Helen Beaton's book, *At the Back of Benachie*, attempts to reproduce the speech of 100 years before its publication, taking us back approximately to 1815. Some may question the value of including words long obsolete; but they are part of the Doric heritage and are useful for reading older Doric texts. The list of writers is very far from exhaustive but contains as many as could be conveniently referred to by one individual over the six and a half month period in which the dictionary was compiled.

Of greatest value has been the work of writers of prose or dialogue, of which, sadly, there have been few. Into this category come not only Helen Beaton but Wm. Alexander, the creator of *Johnny Gibb*; James Alexander, the author of the dialogues, *Mains and Hilly*; several newspaper contributors from Wm. Donaldson's Victorian prose collection, *The Language of the People*; and the autobiographical work of the Rev. David Ogston. Alexander Smith's work was of invaluable service in pointing to the linguistic variants to be found in Kincardineshire, and, although he spent the latter half of his life in Buchan and his Doric could conceivably have got a little *throwder*, I was never myself aware of any confusion.

Poetry, though much more readily available than prose, can be something of a minefield for someone in search of purity of language, since purity of language need not the poet's first concern. For one thing, a poet uses language creatively and moves it on from its original sense to mean something imaginatively different. For another, he or she may borrow terms used in other parts Scotland, believing any Scots word to be fair game for the writer. Hugh MacDiarmid certainly subscribed to this view and various other writers were to follow his example in the Scottish Renaissance of the early 1920s. For this reason, I had, at an early stage, to abandon Helen Cruickshank, a devotee of MacDiarmid, as a reliable example of Angus dialect, when I found several intrusions of the kind described (although a few cullings from Miss Cruickshank survive to confirm some of the more basic differences of Angus speech). The work of other well-known poets has, for similar reasons, been avoided or used with similar circumspect. Even Charles Murray, that revered exponent of the Aberdeenshire tongue may on occasion have borrowed from outwith the Doric-speaking area. His use of *toom* rather than *teem* being one of the factors which suggests the possibility.

In using the dictionary, readers will occasionally find words marked with an initial letter. This points to the writer in whose work the word was found and is an indication either of the part of the North-east he or she comes from, or in what period the word was used. A list of authors and appropriate code signs is provided. This system of word identification is quite unscientific but may prove useful as a general guide for writers and readers alike.

It may be fairly pointed out that much of the vocabulary listed here is not, strictly speaking, Doric at all but merely a Doric form of English. *Suppersteeshun* for *superstition* for example. Yet if this is or was the way in which the word was commonly spoken in the North-east, then it is right that it should be recorded and preserved rather than that the pure English form should be used in the speaking of Doric. As for what is pure Doric and what is Doric slang, it is not within my competence to distinguish between the two.

A Doric Dictionary is offered to the people of the North-east, wherever they may be, in gratitude for having been nurtured by our shared culture.

Douglas Kynoch
Glasgow, August 1996

SPELLING

Despite signs of increasing standardisation, there is no generally recognised way of spelling Scots; and readers of the language will find considerable variation. This will become apparent in the first part of the dictionary, where, with a few exceptions, spelling is generally as I found it in the text from which the word was culled. In turning the dictionary around, however, and compiling the English to Doric section, I have thought it sensible to review the orthography to some extent and to reduce the number of spelling options. It is not uncommon, therefore, for a word to be spelt one way in Part One and another in Part Two, the latter being considered preferable for one reason or another.

There may, in fact, be more than one acceptable spelling in Part Two; and, as I have not eradicated the forms used in other parts of Scotland, a North-east Doric form may be followed by a more common all-Scotland form (e.g. *daad* and *daud*; *meen* and *mune*; *stoor* and *stour*). Both spelling forms are capable of being spoken in the Doric way, or alternatively, the latter (e.g. *daud* and *mune*) may sometimes be spoken using a vowel sound alien to the North-east but heard in other parts of Scotland. In writing, then, one has the choice of appealing to an exclusively North-east audience on the one hand or a wider Scots audience on the other. Charles Murray adopted the latter course and perhaps in consequence, won himself a national following. Few other North-east poets have followed suit.

Modern practice is to eradicate the apostrophe as far as possible and certainly in common words such as *an* meaning 'and' and *amo* meaning 'among'. This is understood by some to indicate that the word in question exists in its own right and is not a mere corruption of English. Whatever the validity of that view, I am happy to respect the convention and apostrophes have been eliminated as far as possible, surviving only occasionally in Part II, where the meaning of a word would otherwise be unclear.

PRONUNCIATION

Vowels and Dipthongs

a, aa and *aw* are pronounced as in the English *car.*

a before *bb, m, mp* and *nk,* however, is pronounced *u* in both English and Scots words (e.g. *cabbage, crabbit, stamp* and *bank*). Before *g, a* may be pronounced *u* (e.g. *bag, baggie*) or *a* as in *car* (e.g. *stag*).

ai and *ae* are pronounced as in the English *hate* (e.g. *mait, maet*).

a_e as in the English *seen* (e.g. *ane, bane, stane,* more usually rendered *een, been, steen*).

ee and *ei* (sometimes also *ie*) as in the English *feet.*

i is pronounced somewhere between the English *i* and *e.*

ie is sometimes pronounced as in *feet* and sometimes as in *fit.* Several words are spelt now *ie,* now *ei.* To attempt to clarify the situation, I have classified those in Part Two according to pronunciation, so that *speil, speir, sheilin, deil* and *neist* are spelt *ei,* the first letter indicating the pronunciation, while *fient* and *nieve* are spelt *ie,* the first letter pointing once more to pronunciation. As the *diphthong* in *bien, brier, chief, chiel, feish, neiper, reive, remeid* and *sheil* appears to be spelt only one way, I have left these as they stand, though there is obviously room for further standardisation.

oi as *i_e* or *y,* being rendered this way in Part Two, e.g. *dytit, doitit.*

oo as in *moon.*

ou may be pronounced either as in *moon* or as in *cow.* With a few words like *clout,* both pronunciations are possible, though generally with different meanings. For this reason, I have eliminated the *ou* spelling as far as possible in Part Two, replacing it either with *oo* or *ow* according to pronunciation. Where this was uncertain, I left *ou* untouched.

u is pronounced as in the English *ju.*

u_e as in *mune* is generally pronounced *ee.* Hence *meen* and *sheen.*

ui is problematic being susceptible to different pronunciations in different areas. In the words *buird* and *buirdly,* for example, *boord(ly)* would appear to apply to Angus and South Kincardineshire, with *beerd(ly)* or *byoord(ly)* applying in the rest of the North-east. The *ui* division line is said to run from Mount Battock to Skateraw on the Kincardineshire coast.

Consonants

ch is pronounced as in the Scots *loch.*

g and *k* should be pronounced before *n* (e.g. *knowe* and *gnap).*

ng in the middle of a word is followed by no *g* sound, so that the *ng* in the Doric *hunger* is spoken like the *ng* in the English *singer.*

s or the *s* sound is sometimes replaced by *sh* in such words as *vessel, officer* and *sew (shoo).*

wh at the start of a word is, with the exception of Angus, pronounced *f,* the words *whaar, whan* and *what* being rendered *faar, faan* and *fat.*

Diminutives

North-east Scots is much given to the use of diminutives. 'Bairn' can become *bairnikie;* 'babbie', *babbitie;* 'lass', *lassock* or *lassockie.* The most popular of the diminutive forms, however, is the simple *ie* ending which appears most commonly in one-syllable words such as *loonie*, though it can also be found in words of two-syllables *(boorrachie)* and, exceptionally, in longer words. Diminutives appear rarely in this dictionary; but, by the use of the *ie* ending, can be created from appropriate nouns.

BIBLIOGRAPHY
and
KEY TO CODE SYMBOLS

The code symbols shown here indicate the writer in whose work the word was found and may point either to the part of the North-east where the word came from or to the period in which use of the word was current, the home area and dates of the writer being given where known. The symbol usually indicates an unusual word or an unusual variant of a word. A commonplace word is coded, where it is one of several having the same meaning. The system offers no more than a rough guide to the provenance of the word.

A   **George Abel of Aberdeenshire** (1856–1916); brought up on farms in the parish of Kintore; minister of Udny Free Church for 35 years; author of the verse collection *Wylins fae My Wallet*, published 1916.

A1   **James Alexander of Ythan Wells, Aberdeenshire;** author of *Mains and Hilly*, a collection of dialogues in the Aberdeenshire dialect, originally published in the *Aberdeen Weekly Free Press* and brought out in book form in 1929.

A2   **William Alexander of Aberdeenshire** (1826–94); author of *Johnny Gibb of Gushetneuk*, first published 1871; ploughman, journalist and editor of the *Aberdeen Free Press*, in which *Johnny Gibb* was serialised.

B   **Peter Buchan of Peterhead** (1917–1991); a fisherman like his father; author of a collection of poems, *Mount Pleasant* and a collection of North-east tales, *Fisher Blue*. What has been drawn on here is his contribution to **Buchan Claik**, a compendium of North-east words and phrases which he compiled in collaboration with David Toulmin.

B1   **Helen Beaton of Aberdeenshire.** Mrs Beaton's account of life in the Garioch in the nineteenth century is based in particular on the parish of Rayne and relies on the stories and language of her grandmother. Entitled *At the Back o' Benachie*, it was published in 1915.

C   **J. M. Caie of Banffshire** (1879–1949). John Morrison Caie was born in Banchory-Devenick, the son of a Banffshire minister, he was brought up on a farm in the parish of Enzie. Trained both in law and agriculture, he spent much of his working life with the Board of Agriculture for Scotland. Of his two volumes of verse, it is *'Twixt Hills and Sea* which helps give the dictionary its Banffshire flavour.

C1   **Helen B. Cruickshank of Angus** (1886–1975). Helen Burness Cruickshank was reared at Hillside between Montrose and the North Esk. The greater part of her working life with the civil service was spent in the Department of Health in Edinburgh. A devotee of Hugh MacDiarmid, her Scots vocabulary, tends to be eclectic, so only the most basic terms are quoted as examples of Angus speech.

F   **Alexander Fenton of Aberdeenshire** (1929–   ). Director of the European Ethnological Research Centre in Edinburgh, Prof. Fenton, himself a native of Auchterless, has used a farm in that parish as the basis of a study of the words and expressions describing farm equipment and techniques in the second quarter of the twentieth century. This invaluable record of North-east farm practice, is described in his book, *Wirds an Wark 'e Seasons Roon*, published in 1987.

G   **Flora Garry of Aberdeenshire** (1900–   ). Of farming stock, Mrs Garry was brought up at Mains of Auchmunziel, New Deer. Trained as a teacher, she taught at Dumfries and Strichen, married R. Campbell Garry, Regius Professor of Physiology at Glasgow University and ultimately retired to Comrie. Her verse collection, *Bennygoak* was first published in 1974.

G1   **Sir Alexander Gray of Angus** (1882–1968). Gray was first Jeffrey Professor of Political Economy at Aberdeen University from 1921–34, to which period much of his Scots verse belongs. The linguistic variants of Angus become apparent in his verse collection, *Any Man's Life* which appeared in 1924.

J   **Violet Jacob of Angus** (1863–1946). Mrs Jacob (née Kennedy-Erskine) was sister of the 19th laird of Dun, the family having owned for centuries the Dun estate between Brechin and Montrose. Author of four books of verse, her *Scottish Poems* were published in 1944.

M   **Charles Murray of Aberdeenshire** (1864–1941). Born in Alford, Dr Murray was a civil engineer who spend most of his professional life in South Africa, where he was ultimately appointed the Union's Secretary for Public Works. He retired to the North-east, where several books of verse were published his lifetime, *Hamewith: the Complete Poems* appearing in 1979.

M1   **J. C. Milne of Aberdeenshire** (1897–1962). Another writer of farming stock, John Milne was born at Memsie near Fraserburgh. After a brilliant academic career at Aberdeen University, he turned to teaching, later becoming Master of Method at Aberdeen College of Education. His verse collection, *The Orra Loon*, was published in 1946; his collected *Poems* in 1963.

O   **David D. Ogston of Aberdeenshire** (1945–   ). In two volumes of autobiography, *White Stone Country* and *Dry-stone Days*, David Ogston, minister at St John's, Perth described in Doric his upbringing on farms in Buchan and the Garioch. *Dry-stone Days* was on the reading list for the dictionary.

R   **Elsie S. Rae of Banffshire.** Elsie Ray was the wife of the Rev. Robert Wilson. Her verse collections include *Private John McPherson* (1917) and *Hansel Fae Hame and other Scots Poems* (1927), the latter forming part of this bibliography.

S   **Alexander Smith of Kincardineshire** (1911–1993). Alex Smith is remarkable for having, in the years before his death, written three substantial books in Doric. Two of them, *Forty Years in Kincardineshire* and *Forty Years in Buchan and Banff,* are autobiographical; the third, *Fairmin the Wey It Wis* records farm life over the period of a year. As well as having what appears to be total recall, Smith had a keen ear, which discerned the differences between the Doric of Kincardineshire and that of Buchan and Banff.

T   **David Toulmin of Aberdeenshire.** This is the pen-name of John Reid (1913–   ) born at Rathen in Buchan, the son of a farm-worker. He himself spent his working life in farm labour but turned, in due course, to the writing of novels. He contributed the farming data to *Buchan Claik*, while his collaborator, Peter Buchan provided the fishing material.

Additional Bibliography

Sheena Blackhall of Aberdeen and Deeside: *The Cyard's Kist* (1984);
George Bruce of Fraserburgh and Edinburgh: *Perspectives* (1984);

A. M. Davidson of Midmar: *Tinkler's Whussel* (1981);
Joyce Everill of Torry, Aberdeen and Fife: *Granny's Button Box* (1989);
William Imray of Tarland: *Langstene Nou and Syne* (1991);
M. S. Lumsden of Rothiemurchus and Aberdeen: *Affirmations* (1990);
Liliane Grant Rich of Glenlivet: *White Rose of Druminnor* (1969);
Alexander Scott of Aberdeen (1920–1989): *Collected Poems* (1994);
Margaret Smith of Gardenstown and Banff: *Hard Graft* (unpub. dialogue);
Wm. Thom of Inverurie: *Rhymes and Recollections of a Hand-Loom Weaver* (1845);
Rev. James Wood of Portnockie and Aberdeen: *The Wind on the Hill* (1988);
The Living Doric verse anthology (1985);
The Language of the People: Scots Prose from the Victorian Revival edited by William Donaldson (1989).

Acknowledgements

Further vocabulary was provided by the late Mrs Bella Sandison of Adendale, Strachan. To Mrs Sandison, to the writers of all published work listed, to the compilers of the *Scottish National Dictionary*, the *Concise Scots Dictionary* and *Chamber's Dictionary*, the author is greatly indebted. For kindnesses rendered, thanks are due too to the Aberdeenshire Library and Information Service, to James Slater of Portsoy, Bill Middleton of Ardlair, Strachan, Anne MacWilliam of Stonehaven and Olivia Scott of Glasgow.

ABBREVIATIONS

Abdn.	Aberdeen	phr.	phrase
adj.	adjective, -ival	pl.	plural
adv.	adverb	ppl.	participle (present
aux.	auxiliary		or past)
cf.	compare with	pred. adj.	predicative
chf.	chiefly		adjective
conj.	conjunction	pr. n.	proper noun
contempt.	contemptous	prep. phr.	prepositional
corr.	corruption		phrase
def. art.	definite article	pro.	pronounced
deriv.	derivative of,	pron.	pronoun
	deriving from	obs.	obsolete
dim.	diminutive	ref.	reference
e.g.	for example	rel. pron.	relative pronoun
Eng.	English	v.	verb
esp.	especially	var.	variant
excl.	exclamation	vb. n.	verbal noun
f.	female	v. pr.	verb present tense
fig.	figuratively	v. pt.	verb past tense
gen.	generally	v. tr.	verb transitive
imp.	imperative	v. intr.	verb intransitive
incl.	including		
indef.	indefinite article		
int.	interjection		
interrog.	interrogative		
lit.	literary		
liter.	literally		
m.	male		
n.	noun		
naut.	nautical		
neg.	negative		
n. pl.	noun plural		
orig.	originally		
perf.	perfect		
perh.	perhaps		

PART ONE

Doric~English

A *pron.* I. *cf.* **Aw, I**
a *indef. art.* a
'a' *v.* (in perf. tense with *aux. v.*)
have; *e.g.* **mith 'a' been** might
have been
aa, a' *adj.* all, every; **aa come** in
one's right mind; **aa gate** everywhere; **aa his lane** all on his
own; **aa itherbody** everyone
else; **aa the airts** in all
directions; **an aa** also, too
aabody *n., pron.* everybody
aacre *n.* acre. *cf.* **awcre**
aafa, aafu *adj., adv.* awful
aagent *n.* agent
Aagist *n.* August
aal *adj.* old. *cf.* **aul; aaler** older;
aalest oldest
aam *v.* thrash. *cf.* **aum**
aat, 'at *adj., pron., conj.* that
aathing *n.* everything
aawye *adv.* everywhere
abeech, abeich *adv.* at a distance,
aloof
abeen *adv., prep.* above. *cf.* **abune**
ablach *n.* dwarf; insignificant
person
ablins *adv.* perhaps (B1). *cf.* **aiblins**
ablo(w) *prep.* below (S)
abody *pron., n.* everybody
aboot *prep.* about
abreist *adv.* abreast
abune *prep., adv.* above. *cf.* **abeen**
accep *v.* accept; *ppl.* **acceppit**
accommodat *v.* accommodate
accoont *n., v.* account

accoontable *adj.* accountable
acht *adj.* eight. *cf.* **aicht, echt** *n.*
ownership; *v.* own; owe. *cf.*
aucht, yacht
achteen *adj.* eighteen. *cf.* **auchteen**
ack *n.* action; *v.* act
ackir *n.* actor
acquant *ppl.* acquainted (G)
acquantance *n.* acquaintance
acquaint *ppl.* acquainted (B)
acquint *ppl.* acquainted (S)
adappit *v. pt.* adapted
adaya *n.* idea
adee *n.* a to-do; *v.* to do; **muckle
adee** much to do
ae *adj.* one, single
aefaul(d) *adj.* sincere (B1, O)
aenoo *adv.* now. *cf.* **ivnoo, eyvnoo**
aet *n.* a feed; **a gweed aet** a good
feed; *v.* eat; **aeten** *ppl.* eaten
afen *adv.* often. *cf.* **aft, aften**
aff *adv., prep.* off; **aff his stotter**
losing the thread of his thought
affa *adj., adv.* awful. *cf.* **aafa, yafa**
aff-cast *n.* anything cast off
affeckit *adj.* moved, touched
aff-go *n.* start
aff-han *adj.* blunt, plain; without
warning or preparation
affint *prep. phr.* off it; from it (S)
affint *adj.* upset (S)
afflat, an *n.* time off, leave of
absence
afflickit *adj.* afflicted
affoord *v.* afford
aff-pittin *ppl., adj.* procrastinating

affrontit *adj., ppl.* ashamed; embarrassed; **black affrontit** deeply embarrassed
afore *adv.* in front; *prep., conj.* before, in front of
afore-han *adv.* beforehand; **to be afore-han wi** to forestall
aft, aften *adv.* often. *cf.* **afen**
agee *adj.* awry; in a disordered state, out of order
agin *prep.* against
agley *adv.* off the straight, obliquely
aggravation *n.* irritation
a-gyaun *ppl.* going about; going on
aheid *prep., adv.* ahead
ahin *prep.* behind; *adv.* late
ahint *adv.* behind
Aiberdeen *pr. n.* Aberdeen
Aiberdour *pr. n.* Aberdour
aiblins *adv.* perhaps (M1). *cf.* **ablins**
aicht *adj.* eight (S)
aidder *n.* udder
aifter *prep., conj.* after. *cf.* **efter** *adv.* afterwards
aifterhin *adv.* afterwards
aifterneen *n.* afternoon
aifternin *n.* afternoon (S)
aig *n.* egg
aik *n.* oak
ail *v.* to be unwell, to be amiss; (with *at* to be dissatisfied with)
ain *adj.* own
aince *adv.* once (S). *cf.* **eence**
aipple *n.* apple
air *adv.* early (A)
airch *n.* arch; *adj.* (**ch** gutteral) anxious (A2); timorous. *cf.* **arch**
airels *n. pl.* musical tones

airish *adj.* chilly
airly *adv.* early. *cf.* **air**
airm *n.* arm
airm-cheer *n.* armchair
airmy *n.* army
airn *v.* earn
airt *n.* direction; art
airth *n.* earth. *cf.* **yird**
aise *n.* ease. *cf.* **aiss**
aishan *n.* generation; family connection (A2). *cf.* **ation**
aisp *n.* asp, serpent
aiss *n.* ash, ashes
aiss-backet *n.* ash-can
aiss-midden *n.* ash-heap
aisy *adj., adv.* easy (S)
ait, aits *n.* oats; **ait kyaaks** oat cakes (A1); **aitmeal** oatmeal
aiten *adj.* oaten
aith *n.* oath
aits *n.* oats
aiven *adv.* even
aiv(e)rin *n.* cloudberry
aivis *n.* trick; fad (B1)
aixle *n.* axle
ajee *adv.* to one side, off the straight; (of a door) ajar. *cf.* **agee**
Ake, Akie *pr. n.* Alexander
alairm *n.* alarm
alane *adj., adv.* alone. *cf.* **aleen**
alang *prep.* along
ale *n.* ale; lemonade etc.
aleberry *n.* oatmeal boiled in ale, sweetened with sugar (A2)
aleen *adj., adv.* alone. *cf.* **alane**
aleyven *adj.* eleven
alis(s) *excl.* sudden cry of pain, alas!
alist *in phr.* **come alist** recover consciousness

alloo, allou *n.* approval; *v.* allow,
  pt. **alloot**
Almichty *adj.* Almighty
alow, in alow *prep.* below (S)
alow(e) *adv.* on fire, ablaze
alunt *adv.* ablaze. *cf.* **alow(e)**
amang *prep.* among. *cf.* **amin, amo**
ameesement *n.* amusement
amin *prep.* among (S). *cf.* **amo**
amint, oot *prep. phr.* out of things
  (S)
ammuneetion *n.* ammunition
amnin *v.* am not; **amnin aw** am I
  not? (A2)
amo, amon *prep.* among. *cf.* **amin**
amous *n.* alms
amshach *n.* accident, mishap (B1)
amunt *n.* amount
amus *See* **amous**
an *conj.* and
ance *adv.* once (G1). *cf.* **aince,**
  eence
Andra *pr. n.* deriv. of Andrew
ane *n., numeral* one. *cf.* **een**
anent *prep.* opposite; in front of;
  over against
Anersmas *pr. n.* Andrewmas
aneth *prep., adv.* beneath (A, M,
  M1). *cf.* **ablow, alow**
aneu, aneuch *adj.* enough
angersome *adj.* annoying,
  provoking
anidder *adj., pron.* another. *cf.*
  ·**anither, anodder**
anint *prep.* opposite. *cf.* **anent**
anither *adj., pron.* another; **anither**
  kind much improved (B)
annwal *adj.* annual
anodder *adj., pron.* another (A2).
  cf. **anidder, anither**

anse *adv.* else (C)
antrin *adj.* occasional
apairt *adv.* apart
apen *v.* open
appale *n., v.* appeal
appearandly *adv.* apparently
appint *v.* appoint
appruv *v.* approve
arch (ch guttural) *adj.* timorous;
  anxious (A2). *cf.* **airch**
aready *adv.* already
argie *v.* argue
argie-bargie; argle-bargle (A2) *n.*
  argument; *v.* to argue, contend
argiement *n.* argument
arles *n.* earnest given on striking a
  bargain
arn-tree *n.* alder (J)
aroon *adv., prep.* around
arreenge *v.* arrange
as *in phr.* **as much** so much
ashet *n.* large serving dish
aside *adv.* close by; present; *prep.*
  beside
asklent *adv.* askance
(asser), asseer *v.* assure (B1)
asteer *adv.* astir
astonisher *n.* a big surprise (A1)
astonishment, an *n.* shock (A1)
atheen *prep.* above (B1). *cf.* **abeen**
athin(g) *n.* everything
Athole brose *n.* honey or meal
  mixed with whisky
athoot *prep., conj.* without
athort *adv.* all over; *prep.* across
ation *n.* generation; family
  connection (A2). *cf.* **aishan**
attrack *v.* attract
atween *adv., prep.* between; **atween**
  hans *adv.* between times (B)

atweesh *prep. See* **atween**
Auchmacoy bummer *n.* the
  Buchan bumble bee
aucht *adj.* eight; *n., pron.* anything;
  n. possession; *v.* owe; own;
  auchtin due; **aucht nor ocht**
  nothing at all; neither one thing
  nor another
auchteen *adj.* eighteen
audiscence *n.* audience; hearing
aul, auld *adj.* old; **auler, aulest;**
  aulder, auldest
aul-farran(t) *adj.* old-fashioned
Aul Nick *pr. n.* the Devil
Auld Kirk, the *n.* established
  Church of Scotland; whisky
aum *v.* thrash. *cf.* **aam**
aumrie *n.* cupboard (A); pantry;
  press above a press (B1)
auncient *adj.* ancient
Australya *pr. n.* Australia
ava *adv.* at all
aven *adv.* even
Aw, aw *pron.* I
awa *adv.* away; **awa forrin** away
  abroad; **hine awa** far away; **keep**

her awa change course to
  leeward (B). *cf.* **tee**
awaar *adj.* aware
awat *adv.* I wot, indeed, truly. *cf.*
  awyte
awcre *n.* acre
awe *v.* owe; **awin** owing
aweel *adv.* well
aweers o *adv.* on the point of, just
  about to
awfu *adj.* awful. *cf.* **afa, aafa**
awmous *n.* alms
Awprile *n.* month of April. *See*
  Prile eeran
awpron *n.* apron; leather covering
  for use in open carriage
Aw'se *pron. with v.* I'll
awyte *pron. with v.* I wot, know;
  adv. assuredly
ay *adv.* yes
ay, ay *int.* hello
aye *adv.* always; still
ayoke *adv.* at work
ayon, ayont *prep., adv.* beyond
ayven *adv.* even

— B —

ba *n.* ball
baabee *n.* halfpenny; *in pl.* money.
  cf. **bawbee**
Baabie *pr. n.* deriv. of Barbara
baal *n.* ball, dance
baathe *v.* bathe
babbity *n.* baby
babbity bowster *n.* (bab-at-the-
  bowster) an old country dance to
  end a ball etc.

bacca bree *n.* the spittle of a
  tobacco-chewer
back *n.* wooden vessel for carrying
  peat; outermost board of a sawn
  tree; **back o** *prep.* just after (of
  time); **at the back o beyond** *phr.*
  far off the beaten track
back-been *n.* back-bone
backbin *n.* back band in harness
back-birn *n.* back burden

back-cheyn *n.* chain over saddle supporting cart shafts
back-door *n.* tail board of cart
backet *n.* bucket; three-sided wooden box with hand-holes, used for carrying peats, sliced turnips or potatoes and pre-dating sculls; wooden scuttle for carrying ashes
backie *n.* back-green; back-garden
backin *n.* address on a letter
backlins *adv.* backwards
backs *n.* refuse of sawmill
backset *n.* setback; *v.* disgust (B1)
back-spier *v.* question a speaker
bad *v. pt.* bade
badder *v.* bother. *cf.* **bather**
bade *v. pt.* lived. *cf.* **bed**
baet *v.* beat; *ppl., adj.* beaten, defeated
baggerel *n.* worthless woman
bag-raip *n.* rope around eaves of stack
baignet *n.* bayonet
baikie *n.* short iron stake to hold tether for cattle and goats
bailie, baillie, bylie *n.* cattleman; alderman; water bailiff (M); **little bailie** under-cattleman
baird *n.* beard
bairn *n.* baby, child; **bairnikie** little child; *v.* make pregnant
bairnheid *n.* childhood
baith *adj., pron.* both
bajan *n.* first year student at Aberdeen University
baket *n.* bucket. *cf.* **backet**
bale-fire *n.* bonfire
ballant *n.* ballad
ballie *n.* ball

ban *v.* to scold; curse, swear
bandie *n.* minnow, stickleback
bandster *n.* one who binds sheaves. *cf.* **banster**
bane *n.* bone; **near the bane** tight-fisted. *cf.* **been**
banie *adj.* boney
bang *v.* hasten (M)
bangstrie *n.* violence to person or property
bannock *n.* round, flat cake (usually of oatmeal) baked on a girdle; oatcake (S)
banster *n.* one who binds the sheaves. *cf.* **bandster**
banter *v. tr.* scold; tease
bantin *n.* a bantam
bap *n.* floury breakfast roll; *v.* walk in a plodding, flat-footed way
bapteese *v.* baptise
bapteesement *n.* baptism
bar *n.* a joke, funny story; *v.* fix door with a bar (B1)
barbet *n.* arrow; **bow an barbet** bow and arrow
barbit-weer *n.* barbed wire
barfit *adj.* barefooted
bark *n.* the skin; preservative for fishing nets; *v.* skin
bark-an-bowff *n.* scolding
barkit *adj., ppl.* skinned; encrusted with dirt, dirty
barleys-on *See* **parley**
barm *n.* yeast; ferment
barra *n.* barrow
barrie *n.* a baby's flannel coat (B1)
barritchfu *adj.* harsh (G)
bass *n.* doormat
batchie *n.* bachelor
bather *v.* bother (S). *cf.* **badder**

Baubie *pr. n.* deriv. from Barbara. *cf.* **Baabie**

bauch *adj.* shy, bashful; timid

bauchle *n.* old shoe; *v.* shamble; trouble (B1); defeat (B1)

bauchle-ban *n.* shoe-tie (B1)

bauk *n.* uncultivated strip of land between fields; cross-beam between rafters

baukie *n.* bat

baul *adj.* bold (A2); strong (B1)

bauld *adj.* bold (J)

bauldie-heidit *adj.* bald-headed. *cf.* **beld**

bau(l)drins, bawdrons *n.* ref. to a cat, puss

bawbee *n.* halfpenny; *in pl.* money

bawd *n.* hare (M). *cf.* **maukin**

baxter *n.* baker

bear *n.* four- or six-rowed barley

beardie *n.* good-natured rubbing of a man's beard on a child's face

beas' *n. pl.* animals in general, cattle in particular (C)

beat *v.* lash a hook to a fishing line

beck *v.* curtsey; do obeisance

bed *v.* spread straw for animals for the night

bed-claes *n. pl.* bed clothes

bed(d) *v. pt.* lived. *cf.* **bade**

beddal *n.* a bedridden person

beddie *n.* (small) bed

beddies *n.* hopscotch

beddit *ppl.* in bed, put to bed

bed-lids *n. pl.* doors of box-bed

bedraigle *v.* to bedraggle

beed *v. pt.* must, had to. *cf.* **beet**

beef *n.* beef; the term used on board fishing boats for all butcher meat (B)

beek *v.* warm before the fire

beelin *n.* whitlow. *See* **futlie**

been *n.* bone. *cf.* **bane**

beerial *n.* interment, funeral

bee-ruskie *n.* simple form of bee-hive, covered in ropes of twisted straw (T)

beery *v.* bury, *ppl.* **beeriet**

beesom *n.* a broom; untidy woman (A1); disparaging term used of a woman. *cf.* **besom**

beesom-ticht *adj.* swept-clean (B1)

beet *n.* boot. *cf.* **buit**; *v.* bet; replace lost hooks on a fishing line. *cf.* **beat**

beet tae *v. pt.* (**be tae** by wrong division) had to; **that beet tae be gran** that must have been grand; sometimes used as *v. pr.*

beezer *n.* something of huge size

befa *v.* befall

begeck *n.* disappointment; trick; shock

begood *v.* begin; *v. pt.* began

begowk *v.* trick, fool

begrutten *adj.* tear-stained

behauden *adj.* beholden

beheef *n.* behoof

beheeld *v. pt.* beheld

beheeve *v.* behove

beil, beilin *n.* boil, sore

bek (B1) *See* **beek**

belaabour *v.* belabour

belang *v.* belong; belong to a place; **he belangs Aiberdeen**

beld *adj.* bald

Beldie *pr. n.* deriv. of Isabella

belike *adv.* perhaps, likely

bellas, bellaws *n.* bellows

belly-ban *n.* harness belly-band

belly-rive *n.* indigestion
belly-thraw *n.* colic, stomach-ache
belt *n.* narrow plantation
beltie *n.* water-hen (G1)
belyve *adv.* by-and-by, before long
ben *adv., prep.* inside, through; **far ben wi** intimate with, esp. with God; *n.* hill, mountain
bencape *adj.* first rate
benmaist, benmost *adj.* innermost
Ben(n)achie *n.* well-known hill near Monymusk, Aberdeenshire
bennin *n.* bend (T)
bent *n.* coarse grass growing near sea; hillock covered in such grass; sand dune
bere *See* **bear**
besom *n.* broom; term of reproach for woman. *cf.* **beesom**
besom-shaft *n.* broom-handle
bess *n.* bass; *v.* sing bass
bestial *n.* cattle (A2)
beuk *n.* book. *cf.* **buik**
bevie *n.* large fire (B1)
bewotifie *adj.* beautiful (B1)
bibblie-nibbit *adj.* snotty-nosed
bick *n.* bitch
bicker *n.* scrimmage; wooden brose basin; *v.* move quickly and noisily; ripple; laugh heartily
bid *v.* invite; **bidden** *ppl.* asked; invited; told; stayed; **bidden gang** asked to go
bide *v.* wait; remain; live; tolerate; **bide ye** *excl.* wait
bidie-in *n.* a live-in lover
biel, bield *n.* shelter; **bieldy** sheltered
bien *adj.* well-to-do; comfortable; **bienless** *adj.* comfortless

big, bigg *v.* build; **biggit** *pt., ppl.* built
bigger *n.* builder
biggin *n.* building, house
biggit oot *ppl.* having abundance of (B)
bigsie *adj.* conceited
bike *n.* nest of wild bees
bikk *See* **bick**
bile *v.* boil; **bilt egg** boiled egg. *cf.* **bylt**
biler *n.* kettle
bilin *n.* a boiling (e.g. of rhubarb)
billet *n.* lot; situation (A)
billie, billy *n.* fellow; comrade
billie *n.* notice posted in seaports with news of herring fleet catches (B)
bin *v.* to bind (rhymes with tin)
bin *n.* humour, mood
bin' *v.* to bind. *cf.* **bin**
binch *n.* bench
binder *n.* tall story; an outstanding thing of its kind (B)
bing *n.* crowd; heap; bin for corn, turnips etc.
bink *n.* hob (B)
binna *v. neg. imp.* (of 'be') don't be
binner *n.* a quick movement; sounding blow; *v.* move rapidly and noisily
binnin *n.* binding for cattle
bird-alane *adj.* quite alone (B)
birdies' eenies *n. pl.* sago pudding (T)
birk *n.* birch tree
birken *n.* birch tree (C)
birkie *n.* lively, smart fellow
birl *n.* twirl; brisk dance; *v.* twirl
birn *n.* burden; large collection

birr *n.* force, energy, passion; whirr. *cf.* **virr**

birse *n.* bristle; bristle on cobbler's thread; beard; bruise; pressure, *esp.* of crowd

birse, birss *n.* fit of bad temper; **get yir birse up** to get angry; **set up your birss** make you angry; **birse** *v.* press, squeeze, push; bruise; **birse ben a bit** move along a bit; **birse tee** push to. *cf.* **birze**

birsel, birstle *v.* toast, roast; **birslet, birslin** *adj.* scorched, scorching

birsin *ppl., adj.* out of breath

birst *n.* over-exertion causing injury; *v.* burst, split

birze *v.* squeeze, press. *cf.* **birse**

bishop *v.* beat down earth or stones; *n.* device for doing this

bit *conj.* but; *n.* crisis; **at the bit** in a crisis

bittock *n.* small bit

bizz *v.* buzz; hiss

bizzar *n.* jade (J) probably from **bizzard** buzzard

bizzin *n.* buzzing

blackguaird *v.* to blackguard, abuse

blackie *n.* blackbird

black yarn *phr.* empty herring nets (B)

blad *v.* spoil. *cf.* **blaud**

bladderskite *n.* foolish, noisy talker

blae *adj.* blue; bluish; black and blue (B1)

blaeberry *n.* bilberry

blaewort *n.* blue cornflower

blaffert *n.* blast of wind (C). *cf.*

bluffert

blaik *v.* blacken

blaiken *v.* blacken

blain *n.* bare patch in field where grain has not sprung

blainy *adj.* covered with bare patches

blake *n.* black polish

blate *adj.* bashful

blatter *n.* sharp shower (C); *v.* dash noisily

blaud *v.* spoil. *cf.* **blad**

blauve *See* **blyaav**

blaw *v.* blow; brag; *n.* braggart

bleart *ppl.* bleary-eyed

bleat *adj.* dull, stupid. *cf.* **blate**

bleb *v.* sip; tipple (A)

bleck *adj.* black

bleck, bleckin *n.* blacking

bleck *n. joc.* blackguard, scoundrel (M2). *cf.* **blake**

bleck *v.* puzzle; defeat; beat, prove too much for

blecken *v.* blacken. *cf.* **blaik**

bledder *n.* bladder; *v.* talk idly

bleed *n.* blood. *cf.* **bluid; bleedy cooter** bleeding nose, nosebleed

bleed-jeelin *adj.* blood-chilling, blood-curdling (G)

bleed-reid *adj.* blood-red

bleery *adj.* bleary

bleeter *n.* blethering person, gasbag

bleeze *n., v.* blaze

bleezin *adj.* very drunk

blether *n.* a talk, chat; *v.* chat; talk nonsense

blewart *n.* bluebell (B1)

blibber *v.* sip a small amount of liquid (T)

blicht *n.* blight

blickers *n. pl.* nonsense
blin *adj.* blind
blin-bridle *n.* bridle with blinkers
blin lump *n.* boil
blin sieve *adj., n.* sieve with solid base
blin tit *adj., n.* blind teat
blink *n.* beam, ray; *v.* wink
blinter *v.* blink weakly or sorely
blithe(some) *adj.* cheerful, merry
blobbie-like *adj.* humid
blocher *v.* cough with phlegm in the throat
bloiter *n.* blast of wind. *cf.* **blouter**
blon *n.* blonde; girlfriend
blood *v.* bleed (S)
blouter *n.* blast of wind. *cf.* **bloiter**
blue *adj.* downcast (A1)
Bluemoggener *pr. n.* native of Peterhead
bluffert *n.* blast of wind
blyaav *v.* blow, pant; boast
blythe *adj.* glad, cheerful. *cf.* **blithe**
boakie *See* **bokie**
bob *v.* curtsey
bobbie, bobby *n.* policeman
bobbinjohn *n.* tin cylinder perforated at one end for sowing turnip seed by hand where it has failed in the drills
bocht *v.* bought
bockie *n.* hobgoblin
Boddam Coo *pr. n.* fog horn at Boddam Head (B)
boddom *n.* bottom
bode *n.* bid at a sale
bodie *n.* person
bodle *n.* small coin (J)
bodsie *n.* short, dapper person
body bulk *quasi-adv.* physically

bog *v.* stick in the mire or bog; confuse, dumbfound; **boggit** bamboozled
bogie *n.* two-wheeled open wagon
bogie-rowe *n.* bogie-roll tobacco
bogjavelt (B1), **bogshaivelt** *adj.* knocked out of shape, distorted
boiler *n.* kettle. *cf.* **biler**
bokie *n.* bogie, scarecrow; fisher term for small boy (B)
bondy *n.* bonfire (O). *cf.* **bale-fire**
bone *in phr.* **in richt bone** in fine fettle (M2)
bone davie (davy) *n.* horse-drawn manure distributor, spreading fertiliser including bone-meal (S, T)
bonnet *n.* a man's cap
bonnet-laird *n.* yeoman farmer; proprietor of the land he farms
bonnie, bonny *adj.* lovely, pretty; handsome; attractive
bonspeil, bonspiel *n.* contest, especially curling
boo *v.* bow; **boot, boo't** *ppl., adj.* bent; **boot twa faal** bent over
boodie *n.* ghost (B1); scarecrow (M1). *cf.* **tattie-boodie** etc.
booet, booit *n.* hand-lantern (without glass)
bool, bowl *n.* a marble
bools *n. pl.* marbles; bowls
boons *n. pl.* bounds; **oot o kent boons** in unknown territory; off the beaten track
boorach(ie) *n.* group, crowd
boortree *See* **bourtree**
boo't *See* **boo**
bore *n.* crevice, chink, hole
borra *v.* borrow; **borrat licht**

indirect light

bosie *n*. bosom

bosky *adj*. wild, unfrequented

boss *adj*. hollow

bossie *n*. large wooden bowl used for oatmeal in baking (B1)

bothy *n*. cottage where farm servants were lodged and cooked their own food

bouch *v*. bark; cough

bouk *n*. size, build; **boukit** large, bulky; **sma boukit** of small build, bulk; **muckle-boukit** pregnant (B1); **nairra-boukit** of lean build

boun *n*. boundary

bourach(ie) *See* **boorach**

bourtree, boortree *n*. elder tree

bout *n*. swathe cut by scythesman, corn or hay cut by a scythe and lying in rows

bow *n*. boll, an old Scottish dry measure of not more than six bushels; the part of the harness bent under the neck of an ox to fasten the yoke; **ower the bows** in a disorderly way (A2); **go through the bows** misbehave (A2)

bow-cheer *n*. armchair

bowden *v*. to fill; **bowdent** replete (after eating)

bowe *n*. fishing float

bowel-crappit *adj*. (hair) cut with a bowl

bowff *n., v*. bark (of dog)

bow-hoched *adj*. bow-legged

bowie *n*. barrel

bows *See* **bow**

bowsell *n*. iron cattle-binding (F)

bowster *n*. bolster

bowsterous *adj*. boistrous

box *phr*. **i the same box** in the same boat, or position

bracken *n*. fern. *cf*. **breckan**

braddie *n*. meat pie. *cf*. **bridie**

brae *n*. hill, slope, steep road

braeset *adj*. situated on a slope

braid *adj*. broad

braig *v*. brag

braird *n*. first sprouting of young grain

braith *n*. breath (G). *cf*. **breith**

braivity *n*. show, splendour; finery

brak *v*. break

brakfast *n*. breakfast

brak-fur *v*. plough shallow furrows (F)

bramble *n*. blackberry

brammle *See* **bramble**

brander *n*. gridiron; drain-cover

branert *adj*. baked on **brander**

branks *n*. halter of wood or metal

braw *adj*. fine, handsome, excellent; *in pl*. fine clothes

brawlies *adv*. well, finely. *cf*. **brulies**

brawly *adv*. well, splendidly

braxy *n*. internal inflammation in sheep; sheep that has died a natural death (M)

break *n*. hollow in a hill

brecham *n*. collar for a draught horse

breckan *n*. fern. *cf*. **bracken**

bree *n*. liquid, juice; liquor. *(See* **snaw-bree**); *v*. to drain boiled solids *e.g.* **tae bree the tatties; throwe the bree** (of potatoes) overboiled

breed *See* **breid**
breeder *n.* brother. *cf.* **bridder**
breeks *n.* trousers. *cf.* **briks**
breem *n.* broom; a thatch of broom
breem-buss *n.* broom bush
breenge *v.* rush forward impetuously; batter, bang
breer *n.* briar; first sprouting of a crop (A1); *v.* sprout. *cf.* **braird**
breest *n.* breast. *cf.* **breist**
breet *n.* brute (not always unsympathetic)
breid *n.* oatcakes taken as dessert in bowl of milk (F, T); bread; breadth
breist *n.* breast. *cf.* **breest**
breith *n.* breath (J)
brench *n.* branch
brent *ppl.* burned (G1). *cf.* **brunt**
bress *n.* brass
brevity *n.* fine show or display
brichen *v.* brighten
bricht *adj.* bright
bridder *n.* brother. *See* **breeder, brither, broder**
bridegreem *n.* bridegroom
bridie *n.* beef or mutton pie (S)
brier *n.* eyelash; **by the briers o the een** by the skin of his teeth (T)
brig *n.* bridge
briks *See* **breeks**
brinch *n.* branch
britchin *n.* breeching, the piece of harness that passes round the hind-part of a horse in shafts, to let it push backwards; **intae the britchin** into reverse
brither *n.* brother. *See* **bridder**
broadcast *n.* broadcast sowing

machine (F)
brob *v.* to prick; **brobbit** *pt., ppl.* pricked
Broch, the *pr. n.* nickname for Fraserburgh
broch *n.* burgh; halo round sun or moon (round moon, predicting storm); Pictish tower
brochan *n.* oatmeal boiled thicker than gruel, with butter and honey
Brocher *pr. n.* nickname for native of Fraserbugh
brocht *v. pt.* brought
brod *n.* board; collecting box in church
broder *n.* brother (A2). *cf.* **breeder, bridder, brither**
brodmell *n.* brood (B1, A2)
broke *v. pt.* became bankrupt
broncaidis *n.* bronchitis
Broo *n.* Employment Office
broo *n.* brow
broobin *n.* harness brow band
brook *n.* soot on pots; *v. pt.* broke. *cf.* **bruik**
brookie *n.* blacksmith (A); *adj.* sooty, grimy
brookit *adj.* (of cattle, sheep) speckled
broon *adj.* brown
brose *n.* oatmeal or peasemeal mixed with boiling water, milk etc; a meal
brose-caup *n.* wooden bowl for oatmeal dish
brosy *adj.* stout, well-fed
brow *adj.* handsome (M, R). *cf.* **braw**
browst *n.* a brew
bruckle *adj.* brittle, crumbly (C1)

11

bruik *v. pt.* broke. *cf.* **brook**
bruise-box *n.* corn-chest (F)
bruised corn *n.* pounded oats
bruk *v. pt.* broke (R). *cf.* **brak,
  bruik**
brulies (B1) *See* **brawlies**
brulzie *n.* brawl
brunt *v., ppl.* burned. *cf.* **brent**
bubble *v.* blubber, snivel
bubbly *n.* paraffin torch used at sea
bubbly-bairn *n.* cry-baby
bubbly(jock) *n.* turkey-cock
Buchan *pr. n.* Buchan's *Domestic
  Medicine*
Buchaner *n.* native of
  Buchanhaven, now part of
  Peterhead
Buchanie, the *pr. n.* the *Buchan
  Observer*
bucht *n.* a sheep-, cattle-fold
Bucker *pr. n.* native of Buckie
bucker *n.* annoyance; nuisance (A);
  v. botch, bungle (B1)
buckie *n.* refractory, mischievous
  person; periwinkle; spiral shell of
  winkle; **as fou's a buckie** drunk
buckle *v.* dress (for a journey) (R)
bucklins *n. pl.* paraphernalia of
  marriage (A2)
buddick *n.* small useless fish found
  in harbours (B)
buff *n.* nonsense
buffet steel *n.* square stool (B1)
buik *n.* bulk; book; *v.* book,
  register; record names of
  betrothed couple in church
  register before marriage. *cf.* **beuk,
  byeuck**
buikin-nicht *n.* the night on which
  the names of persons about to be

married are given to the church
  Session Clerk to have the banns
  proclaimed
buird *n.* board; table. *cf.* **brod**
buirdin-squeel *n.* boarding-school
buirdly *adj.* burly; fine-looking
buit *n.* boot. *cf.* **beet**
bul(l) *n.* bull; bill; *v.* serve a cow
bullaments *n. pl.* outer garments
  usually ragged or untidy (B1)
bullyrag *v.* scold, hector, treat in a
  bullying manner
bum *v.* hum, drone
bumbee *n.* bumble-bee
bummer *n.* anything outstandingly
  large
bun, bunt *v. pt., ppl.* bound. *See*
  bin; bun-bed wooden bed shut
  in with folding or sliding doors
buncher *n.* machine attached to
  mill for making straw bunches
bung *n.* ill-humour; huff (A); **on
  the bung** in the huff
bunkert *n.* obstacle
burn *n.* stream
burn the witchie *v.* to burn effigy
  on a boat deck to change bad luck
  (B)
buroo *n.* bureau
burr *n.* the uvular 'r'; *v.* pronounce
  the letter 'r' in the throat
burssen *ppl.* bursting
burssen-ile *n.* discarded lubricating
  oil used to soothe the skin of pigs
  (B) and prevent rust on farm
  machinery (T)
bushle, bussle *n.* bushel measure
busk *v.* dress; adorn
buss *n.* bush
but-an-ben *n.* two-roomed cottage;

12

from end to end; **but-bed** the bed
in the semi-parlour end of the
cottage
but-the-hoose *n.* kitchen
butt *n.* tail of a sheaf
butterflee *n.* butterfly (R). *cf.*
buttery
buttery (-rowie) *n.* flat morning
roll
buttery *n.* butterfly (M1)
buttock mail *n.* a spanking
buzness *n.* business
buzzle *n., v.* (of grain, indicating
ripeness) rustle
by, by wi't *adv.* over, past; **by the
warst** past the worst
byaakin *n., ppl.* baking

byes *prep.* compared with; besides
byeuck *n.* book. *cf.* **beuk, buik**
bygaein, bygaun, bygyaun, i the
phr. as you go by; incidentally
bygane *adj.* (of time) past
byle *n., v.* boil. *cf.* **bile**
bylie *See* **bailie**
bylin *n.* a boiling
byock *v.* vomit (B1)
byordnar *adj.* extraordinary
byous *adj.* extraordinary; *adv.*
exceedingly
byowty *n.* beauty
byowtifu *adj.* beautiful
byre *n.* cowshed
bywye *n.* byway

— **C** —

ca, caa *v.* call; drive; knock; **ca for**
head for; **ca** (a person) **for
aathing** defame; **on the ca** on
the move; **ca canny** take care; **ca
the crack** chat; **ca the door tee**
shut the door. *cf.* **caw**
caal *adj.* cold; **caal roch shooers**
cold blustery showers. *cf.* **caul**
caav *v.* give birth to a calf
cack *v.* defecate. *cf.* **kich**
cackie-stammackit *adj.* having
imperfect digestion; squeamish
(T)
caddis *n.* cotton-wool; flock;
padding; (cotton- or wool-) fluff;
any kind of fluff
cadge *n.* shake, jog; *v.* carry loads;
peddle wares; shake roughly,
knock about; sponge

cadger *n.* carrier; itinerant dealer,
hawker; sponger
caff *n.* chaff; **caff-bed, caff-seck**
mattress filled with chaff. *cf.*
cauff
caip *n.* cap
caird *n.* tinker; *v.* card (wool)
cairn *n.* loose heap of stones; *v.*
form a cairn or heap
cairry *v.* carry
cairry-on *n.* carry-on
cairt *n.* cart; *v.* carry
cairter *n.* carter
cairtin *ppl.* playing cards
cairts *n. pl.* playing-cards
caithick *n.* monkfish
calfie's mooie *n.* small cowrie shell
(B). *cf.* **Johnny Groatie, kysie**
callant *n.* stripling, lad

13

caller *adj.* fresh; cool, refreshing
cam *v. pt.* came; **cam in aboot** approached
camsteerie *adj.* perverse, quarrelsome
can *n.* ability
cankert *adj.* ill-humoured, fretful; (of weather) stormy, threatening; gusty
canle *n.* candle
Canlemas *n.* Candlemas
canna *v. neg.* cannot
cannas *n.* canvas, esp. that used in winnowing grain
canny *adj.* prudent, cautious; gentle; frugal; safe; moderate in price
cantle *v. intr.* brighten up; recover one's health or spirits
cantle (up) *v.* brighten (up), recover health
cantrip *n.* mischievous trick
canty *adj.* cheery, good-humoured
capawcity *n.* ability
capawshus *adj.* capacious
caper *v.* dance
capernicious *adj.* short-tempered; fretful
capital *adj.* excellent
capshon, caption *n.* lucky acquisition, windfall, prize
captire, in *phr.* in suspense (B1)
car *n.* calves. *cf.* **caur;** *v.* care
carefu *adj.* careful
carena *v. neg.* do not care; **carena doit** do not care in the least
cargie *n.* cargo
cark *n.* care, anxiety; **nae cark nor care** not a care in the world
carl *n.* churl; man; old man

carl-doddie *n.* stalk of rib-grass
carlers *n.* heavy seaweed. *cf.* **tangles**
carlie *n.* a little old man
carlin(e) *n.* old woman; witch
carn *n.* cairn (also in placenames)
carritch(es) *n.* catechism; *in pl.* the Shorter Catechism (M)
cartil *n.* cartload (B1)
carvel-biggit *adj.* (boat) built with planks edge to edge. *cf.* **clinker-biggit**
carvy, carvey, carvie *n.* caraway
case be *conj.* in case
cassen *See* **cast**
cassie *See* **causey**
cast *v.* cut with a spade (e.g. peat); dig; to throw off (e.g. coat); **casen, cassen** *ppl.* cast; (of colour) faded
castell *n.* castle
castock *n.* stalk of kail or cabbage
cast-oot *n.* quarrel; fall-out
catcher *n.* truant officer (S); townkeeper at weekends (F)
catch her (*phr.* used by fishermen) fall asleep; **he's catched her**
catecheese *v.* catechise, instruct by question and answer by use of the Church Catechism
catechis *n.* catechism (A)
cat's dicht *n.* quick wipe or wash
cattie's tailie *n.* plaything made from scraps of knitting wool on makeshift loom, using a cotton reel and pins (B)
cattlie *n.* cattleman (S)
cauf(ie) *n.* calf
cauk *v.* to chalk; challenge for repayment of a debt; calk, fix

guard on horse's hoof to prevent
slipping

caul(d) *adj., n.* cold; **caul steer**
sour milk or cold water and meal
stirred together

cauldrife *adj.* cold, chilly

caulker *n.* iron rim fixed on shoe to
minimise wear

caum *n.* mould for ball, spoon etc.

caunle *n.* candle. *cf.* **canle**

caup *n.* wooden bowl; **cauper**
maker of caups, wood-turner

caur *n.* calves. *cf.* **car**

cause *conj.* because

causey *n.* causeway, paved area; the
granite sett or cobblestone it is
paved with. *cf.* **cassie**

caw *v.* to drive. *cf.* **ca**

cawpable *adj.* capable

ceety *n.* city

ceevil *adj.* civil

'cep, 'cepin *prep., conj.* except

cert, certie *in phr.* **my cert, my
certie!** surely, certainly

chaamer *See* **chaumer**

chack *n.* chalk; chequered linen or
calico

chackie *n.* farm worker's bag (T)

chackie-mull *n.* death-watch beetle

chackit *adj.* of a checked pattern;
chequered

chad *n.* compacted gravel

chaddy *adj.* gravelly

Chae *pr. n.* deriv. of Charles

chaep *adj.* cheap

chaetry *n.* cheating

chaff *v.* chafe

chafts *n.* chops; cheeks

chaip-john *adj., n.* cheapjack

chairge *n., v.* charge

chairity *n.* charity

Chairlie *pr. n.* deriv. of Charles

chait *v.* cheat; *ppl.* cheated. *cf.*
chate

chalder *n.* dry measure, of grain =
16 bolls

chancy *adj.* lucky, fortunate; safe

changefu *adj.* changeable

change-hoose *n.* alehouse, inn

chanter *n.* the part of the bagpipes
on which the tune is played

chantie, chanty *n* chamber-pot

chap *n.* knock; *v.* to knock, to
pound, mash; chop; (of clocks)
strike; **the clockie chappit** the
clock struck; **chappin** *ppl., n.*
knocking

chape *adj.* cheap. *cf.* **chaep**

chapper *n.* utensil for mashing
potatoes; **chappit tatties** mashed
potatoes

chaps me *excl.* (when a person
chooses a particular thing) give
me…

charge *n.* oath

chate *n., v.* cheat. *cf.* **chait**

chatter *v.* shatter

chaumer *n.* chamber; best room;
sleeping-place for farm workers
in Banff and Buchan. In the
Mearns, the bothy was more
common. Unlike the bothy, no
food was eaten in the chaumer
(A, M1); *v.* to live in a chaumer

chaw *v.* chew

cheekie-for-chowie *adv.* cheek by
jowl; side by side

cheena *adj., n.* china

cheenge *v.* change. *cf.* **chynge**

cheengeless *adj.* changeless

15

cheeper *n.* young or half-fledged bird
cheer *n.* chair
cheerman *n.* chairman
cheery-pyke *n.* tasty morsel, treat
chessel, chesset *n.* cheese vat or press
chief (wi) *adj.* intimate, friendly
chiel *n.* man; fellow
chik *n.* cheek
chilpit, chilpy *adj.* chilled
chim(b)ley, chimbly *n.* chimney
chimbley-chik *n.* hearth
chine *n.* chain
chine-gaird *n.* (on a bicycle) chain-guard
chingle *n.* shingle
chirm *v.* complain; fret (A); sing, murmur (C1)
chirr-wirrin *n.* chatting back and fore, chin-wagging (S)
chirry *n.* cherry
chitter *v.* tremble, shiver; **chittering-chow** bread eaten after open-air bathing; **chit-chow** good things to eat (B1)
chop *n.* shop
chouk *n.* cheek
choup *n.* a cheep; **didna get a choup oot o im**
chowks *n.* the jaws
chowter *n.* term of endearment, mostly for children (B)
chucken, chucknie *n.* chicken
chucken-hertit *adj.* faint-hearted
chuckenwort *n.* chickweed
chuckie-steen *n.* granite chipping; pebble
chuddy *n.* chewing-gum
chuff *adj.* chummy

chumla, chumlay *n.* mantel-shelf. *cf.* **chimbley**
chunner *v.* murmur plaintively
chuntie *n.* chamber-pot
chynge *v.* change. *cf.* **cheenge**
chyse *n.* cheese; *v.* choose
chyser *n.* team-picker in games
cla *n., v.* claw, scratch
clachan *n.* hamlet
claes *n.* clothes. *cf.* **clyse**
claggieleerum (T) *See* **claggum**
claggum *n.* treacle toffee
claik *n., v.* gossip, tittle-tattle. *cf.* **clash**
clair *adj.* clear; distinct; ready
claith *n.* cloth; **aa ae claith** all the same
claithe *v.* clothe
clam(b) *v. pt.* climbed
clamjamfrey, clanjamfry *n.* noisy crowd, mob; company of people
clamp *v.* walk noisily, as with hobnailed shoes
clap *n., v.* pat, fondle
clart *v.* daub, smear
clash *n.* gossip, tittle-tattle
clapper *n.* butter-hand
clashmaclavers *n.* idle discourse, silly talk
claught *v.* clutch, lay hold of
claw *v.* scratch; **clawed the caup** cleaned the dish (the last to rise in the morning had to clean the common bowl); *fig.* came to the end; **clawin post** scratching post for cattle, usually a stone (T)
clead *v.* clothe. *cf.* **claithe**
cleadin *n.* clothing
clean-lan *adj.* (field) cleared of turnips and ready for ploughing (T)

16

clear *adj.* undamaged, in good condition (S)

cleathin *n.* mould-board (F)

cleck *v.* give birth to young (of rabbits)

cleckin *n.* brood, litter

cled *adj.* clad

cleek, cleik *n.* hook; device to set gird spinning (S); golfing iron; *v.* seize (with the claws); hook, catch up by or fasten (on a hook)

cleekit shalt *n., ppl.* pony suffering from string-halt

cleg *n.* gadfly, horsefly

clench *v.* clinch, settle; limp (A2)

cless *n.* class

cleuch *n.* narrow glen, ravine

clew *v. pt.* clawed; *n.* ball of straw-rope used in thatching. *cf.* **cloo**

clim *v.* climb. *cf.* **sclim**

clink *n.* resounding blow; *v.* mend by rivetting; hammer; weld

clinker-biggit *adj.* (boat) built with planks overlapping. *cf.* **carvel-biggit**

clip *n.* pert girl; *v.* cut

clipe *n.* tell-tale; *v.* to tell tales. *cf.* **clype**

clish-ma-claver *n.* idle talk

clivver *adj.* clever; *n.* clover

clocher *v.* cough, wheeze

clockin *ppl., adj.* (of hen) brooding, broody

clod *v.* pelt

cloddie *n.* clod of earth; a peat

clog(gie) *n.* log; block of wood

clog-fit *n.* club-foot

cloo *n.* ball of rope, cord or wool, etc. *cf.* **clew**

clood *n.* cloud

clook *n., v.* claw

cloot *n.* cloth; blow; *v.* mend. *cf.* **clout**

clootch *v.* clutch (A)

clootie-dumplin *n.* sweet dumpling cooked in a cloth

clootie-rug *n.* rug made from old cloths

Cloots *pr. n.* the Devil

clort *n.* mud; anything soft and sticky; *v.* to besmear

clortit *ppl.* smeared

clorty *adj.* dirty; messy

close, closs *n.* enclosure; farmyard; passage; alley

close-han't *adj.* tight-fisted

closen-in *ppl.* closed in

clossach *n.* a mass; hoard of money

clour *v.* strike, indent

clout, cloutie *n.* a cloth

clout *n., v.* mend, patch *(e.g.* a kettle). *cf.* **cloot**

clout *n.* blow; *v.* beat, strike. *cf.* **cloot**

clouty-rug *See* **clootie-rug**

clum *v. pt.* climbed. *cf.* **clim**

clyack *n.* end of harvest; **clyack shafe** the last sheaf cut in harvest

clype *n.* tell-tale; *v.* to tell tales. *cf.* **clipe**

clyse *n.* clothes. *cf.* **claes**

clyte *n.* a sudden or heavy fall; **cam clyte** fell suddenly

coach *n.* pram

coal-coom *n.* coal-dust

coble *n.* pond for watering cattle

cock *v.* swagger, show off

cock-a-leekie *n.* chicken and leek soup

cockernony *n.* starched crown of a

17

woman's cap

cockit on *ppl., prep.* perched, mounted on

cockit up *ppl., prep.* dressed up showily

cockle-ee *n.* an eye with a squint (B)

Cock o the North *phr.* nickname for the Marquises of Huntly

coff *v.* buy (G1); *ppl.* **coft**

cog, coggie, cogue *n.* wooden pail for milking, or herring-guts

cog *v.* feed from the cog or pail

coggit *ppl.* fed from the **caufie's cog** (T)

colcannon *n.* dish of mashed potato and chopped cabbage served with meat

cole, coll *n.* haycock; *v.* to make haycocks

colleague (wi) *v.* associate, consort with

colleeginer *n.* student at college (A1)

collieshangie *n.* uproar (C)

collogue *v.* converse; *n.* intimate chat

come *in phr.* **come hairst** when harvest comes; **come ower** *v.* befall

commeenicant *n.* communicant

compleen *v.* complain

compleent *n.* complaint

concairn *n.* concern

concaited *adj.* conceited

condeeshun *n.* condition

conduck *n.* conduct

confeerin tae *ppl.* corresponding to, accordant with

confoon, confoun *v.* confound

congregat *v. pt.* congregated

connach *v.* spoil; destroy; **connacht** *ppl.* destroyed, wasted

conneck *v.* connect; *ppl.* **conneckit**

constiteetion *n.* constitution

conteena *v.* continue (B1); *v. pt.* **conteenit**

conteenwal *adj.* continual

conten *v.* contend

conter, contar *v.* contradict; *adj.* opposite. *cf.* **cwanter**

contermashious *adj.* contrary

contermin't *adj.* contradictory; contrary, perverse

contreebit *v.* contribute

convainience *n.* convenience

convoy *v.* convey, escort

coo *n.* cow; **coo's lick** hair overhanging the brow at one side

cooch *n.* dog's kennel (A)

coof *n.* coward (M)

coonjer *v.* scold; intimidate. *cf.* **counger**

coont *v.* count

coontenance *n.* countenance

coonter *n.* (shop) counter

coonter-louper *n.* shop-assistant

coontin *n.* arithmetic

coor *v.* cower

coord(ie) *n.* coward

coordy-lick *n.* coward's blow

coorie *See* **coory**

coorse *adj.* coarse; cruel (A); evil, bad (M1); *n.* course; **an coorse, of coorse** of course

coort *v.* court; *n.* cattle-court

coory *v.* cower, crouch

cooter *See* **couter**

corbie *n.* crow

core *n.* company, corps

corkit *adj.* constipated
corn *n.* oats; *v.* feed with oats
corn-laft *n.* grain-loft
corn-kist *n.* corn-chest
cornkister *n.* farm-workers' song
corn-yard *n.* stack-yard
corp *n.* corpse
correck *v.* correct
corrie *n.* circular hollow on mountainside; *v.* cower, crouch. *cf.* **coorie**
corrieneuchin *ppl.* conversing intimately
corter *n.* quarter; quarter of oatcake. *cf.* **korter**
cottar *n.* farm worker occupying tied cottage; *v.* to lead the life of a cottar
cottar-hoose *n.* farm worker's house
cotts *n. pl.* petticoats
counger *See* **coonjer**
coup *See* **cowp**
coup-the-ladle *n.* the game of see-saw
couper *n.* one who deals in horses or cattle
couple *n.* rafter (S). *cf.* **cupple**
couter *n.* coulter, iron cutter at front of plough; nose; **bleedy couter** nosebleed. *cf.* **cooter**
couthie, couthy *adj.* kindly; pleasant
covin-tree *n.* trysting tree; tree in front of an old mansion-house, where the laird met visitors
cow *v.* beat, outdo, surpass; **yon cows aa** that beats everything
cowe *n.* twig of a shrub or bush; *v.* to surpass

cower *v.* recover from, get over
cowk *v.* retch; vomit (A)
cowp *v. tr.* upset; *intr.* fall over, overturn; bargain, exchange; **cowp the creels** upset a plan; **cowpit sheep** overturned sheep. *cf.* **coup**
cowshus *adj.* cautious
cowt *n.* colt
coy *n.* heifer. *cf.* **quaik**
crabbit *adj.* bad-tempered, cross
crack *n.* talk, gossip; *v.* to chat
crackie *adj.* chatty, talkative
crackit *ppl., adj.* cracked
craft *n.* croft
craggin *n.* jar, pitcher
craig *n.* throat
craighle *v.* cough huskily
craighly *adj.* husky
craik *n., v.* croak
craiter, craitur *See* **cratur**
crame *n.* cream (S). *cf.* **ream**
crannie *n.* the little finger
cran-the-net, a *n.* a good catch
crap *n.* crop; bird's crop; throat; highest part of anything; **craw in his crap** annoy, give cause for regret; **shook their craps** expressed their grievances and feelings; **crap o the wa** highest part of an inside wall; *v.* crop land; *v. pt.* crept
crater, cratur *n.* creature; **the cratur** whisky
craver *n.* creditor; dun
craw *n.* crow; *v.* boast, exult; **a craw tae pluck** a bone to pick
creel *n.* basket for fish, used by fishwives
creenge *v.* cringe

creep doon *v.* shrink, bend with age
creepie *n.* low stool
creepin-eevie *n.* convolvulus; a very slow person (T)
creesh *v.* thrash, beat; *n.* fat, grease
creesis *n.* crisis
creetick *n.* critic
cries *n. pl.* banns (giving notice of impending marriage)
crine *v.* shrink; shrivel
criticeese *v.* criticise
crive *n.* enclosure (for poultry)
crochle *n.* disease in the hindlegs of cattle; *v.* limp
crochle, crochly *adj.* crippled
crockeneetion, crockaneeshin *n.* destruction; smithereens
crood *n., v.* crowd
crood-brakker *n.* curd-breaker (F)
croodit *adj.* crowded
croodle *v.* huddle together
croods *n. pl.* curds; **croods an fy** curds and whey
crook *n.* iron hook from which pots and kettles were hung by chain over fire; twist. *See* **links**
croon *n.* crown; the head; *v.* crown
croose *adj.* lively, bold, bright, confident; **croose i the craw** brisk and confident in conversation. *cf.* **crouse**
croup *v.* croak. *cf.* **crowp**
crouse *adj.* lively, bold, bright. *cf.* **croose**
crowdy *n.* meal and water mixed cold (M)
crowp *v.* croak; complain. *cf.* **croup**
cruisie *n.* old-fashioned oil lamp, with rush wick

crulge (doon) *v.* cower, crouch
crummie *n.* cow; cow's name
crunkle *v.* crease, crinkle
crusie *See* **cruisie**
cry in by *v.* visit briefly
cry on *v.* to call (on); visit; shout for
cry tee *v.* call in by (B)
crydit *n.* credit
crynt *adj.* stunted. *cf.* **crine**
cud *v.* could; **cudna** *v. neg.* could not
cuddy *n.* donkey
cuff *v.* winnow for the first time
cuffins *n. pl.* rough husks and hairs after first winnowing
cuist *v. pt.* cast, threw. *cf.* **ceest**
cuitikins *n.* gaiters. *cf.* **queetikins**
Cullen skink *n.* fish soup made with smoked haddock, onion and mashed potato
cupple *See* **couple**
curduddoch *adv.* close together (J)
curlie-wurlies *n.* hair in curl papers (B1)
curn, a *n.* a quantity; company; **a gweed curn** considerable number
currack *n.* coracle
curran *n.* currant; **curran daad** fruit slice
curran-bap *n.* currant bun
currieboram *n.* confused, noisy crowd
cushie (doo) *n.* wood-pigeon
cut *v.* reap; castrate
cutchack *n.* small blazing coal or peat fire; the clearest part of the fire; the side of the fire
cutter *n.* small whisky bottle

cuttins *n. pl.* encouragement; **ye'll get nae (short) cuttins fae him**
cuttit *v. pt.* cut
cutty *n.* short tobacco pipe; knife
cutty steel *n.* stool with short legs
c'wa *imp.* come away
cwanter *v.* contradict. *cf.* **conter**

cwanter-kine *adj.* contrary
cweel *adj., v.* cool
cwid *v. pt.* could
cyaard, cyaurd *n.* tinker
cyacks *n.* oatcakes
cyarn *n.* cairn

— D —

daachter *n.* daughter (A2). *cf.* **dother, dochter**
daar *adj.* dear, expensive
Daavit *pr. n.* David
dab *v.* poke; *in phr.* **let dab** give hint, give sign, let on; **dab han** skilled exponent
dacent *adj.* decent. *cf.* **daicent**
dachle, dackle *v.* hesitate, dawdle; (of the weather) let up; cause to hesitate, discourage (C)
dad *n.* lump; *v.* pelt; spatter. *cf.* **daud**
dae *v.* do *(gen. pro.* **dee**; *pro.* **day** by S, J); *ppl.* **daen; dae awa** do not so badly. *cf.* **dee, deen**
daff *v.* flirt (J)
daffie *n.* daffodil
daft *adj.* foolish; frolicsome
dag *v.* confound; **dag it** *excl.* confound it; **dag the bit** not a whit (B1); **dag the grain** not at all (B1)
daicent *adj.* decent. *cf.* **dacent**
daidle *v.* dirty (S)
daily-day *adv.* every day
dainner *n.* dinner. *cf.* **denner**
dairk *adj.* dark (J)
daith *n.* death

daivert *adj.* fatigued; confused; benumbed
dale *v.* deal
dall *n.* doll
dallies' cleysies *n. pl.* doll's clothes; coloured seaweed (B)
dambrod *n.* draught board
dammer *v.* confuse; astonish (R)
damn the bit *excl.* mild expletive
dander *n.* temper; **tae get yer dander up** to get angry
dandy *adj.* fine, light-hearted (J)
dane *ppl.* done. *cf.* **daen, deen**
dang *v. pt.* dashed down. *cf.* **ding**
dang *n., v.* used for *damn*
darg *n.* a day's work; *v.* work
darger *n.* a day-labourer; worker
darksome *adj.* melancholy, dismal
dask *n.* desk
dassint *adj.* decent. *cf.* **daicent, dacent**
dauchle *v.* dangle
daud *n.* stroke, blow; a large piece; **daud aboot** *v.* bump, bounce; jolt; pelt; spatter
daunder, dauner *v.* stroll
daur *v.* dare; **daurna** dare not; **daursna** dares not
daut *n.* caress. *cf.* **dawt**

21

daver *v.* stun, stupify; benumb
daw *n., v.* dawn
dawt *n.* caress; *v.* dote, fondle. *cf.* **dawt**
dawtie *n.* darling, pet
dazzle *n.* any fizzy drink
deave *v.* deafen; pester with entreaties. *cf.* **deeve**
dee *v.* do; die; **dee doon** do down; **dee wintin** do without. *cf.* **dae**
deece *n.* wooden seat or settle, which could be used as table or bed; turf seat out-of-doors; **haud doon the deece** rest, take it easy. *cf.* **deese**
deed *in phr.* **to be the deed o' t** to be responsible for (B); *adv.* indeed
deef *adj.* deaf. *cf.* **deif**
deegnity *n.* dignity
deelt (wi) *v. pt.* dealt (with)
deem(ie) *n.* a young girl; servant-girl
deen *ppl.* done; *adj.* exhausted; **caad himsel deen** wore himself out
deese *See* **deece**
deester *n.* (often contemptuous) doer; promoter; agent
deet *v. pt.* died
deeth *n.* death (A2). *cf.* **daith, deith**
deeve *v.* deafen; pester with entreaties. *cf.* **deave**
deevil *n.* devil; potato digger
deevilock *n.* imp, demon
defait *n., v.* defeat; *ppl.* defeated
defarred *v. pt., ppl.* deferred
defate *See* **defait**
defiet *v. pt.* defied
deft *adj.* bold; hard up

deg *See* **dag**
degraad *v.* degrade, *ppl.* **degraadit**
degraadin *ppl.* degrading
deid *adj.* dead
deidly *adj.* deadly
deid-thraw *n.* death-throe; **i the deid-thraw** between one state and another, undecided
deif *adj.* deaf. *cf.* **deef**
deil, Deil *n.* devil, Devil; *adv.* no, not, *e.g.* **deil-ma-care** no matter; **deil the bit** not at all
deist *See* **dyst**
deith *n.* death (J). *cf.* **daith**
deleebrate(ly) *adj., adv.* deliberate(ly)
deleer *v.* intoxicate; render delirious
deleerit *ppl.* demented, gone mad
dell *n.* goal or base in children's games; **nae great dell** no great shakes, not of great quality (T)
dell *v.* dig, delve; **dellt** *ppl.* dug
delt *v.* fondle, cuddle (M2)
delve *v. in phr.* **delve the bank** argue out the matter (B1)
dem *v.* dam
denner *n.* dinner; *v.* provide dinner. *cf.* **dainner**
denty *adj.* dainty (J)
dert *n.* dart
descrive, descryve *v.* describe
designtly *adv.* deliberately
deteen *v.* detain
deuk *n.* duck
devall *n.* a pause, ceasing; *v.* to cease, stop
deydie *n.* grandfather
deykon *n.* deacon. *cf.* **dykon**
dibber-dabber *n.* wrangle (B)
dicht *v.* clean; wipe up

diddle *v.* sing in a low tone without words; dandle a child (B)
didnin *v. neg. interrog.* didn't?
diffeekwalty *n.* difficulty (accent the second syllable) (A2)
dilet *adj.* stupid; crazed; confused. *See* **dylt**
dilse *n.* dulse, edible seaweed
dince *n.* dance (S)
dindeerie *See* **dundeerie**
ding *v.* beat, over-come, excel; (of rain, snow) to fall heavily
dinna *v. neg.* don't
din-raisin *adj.* quarrelsome, trouble-making; **din-raiser** trouble-maker
din-skinnt *adj.* weather-beaten, sunburned (T)
dip *v.* challenge; discuss
dipthairy *n.* diphtheria
dird *n.* a thud, thump, blow; heavy fall; *v.* beat, thump
dirdin *n.* onslaught
dirdum *n.* loud noise, uproar
dirk *n.* long dagger
dirl *v.* tingle; vibrate
dirler *n.* chamber-pot
dirrum-dicht *n.* vigorous wipe (B)
dirry *n.* ash on top of a pipe (T)
dirten *ppl.* dirtied; mean, contemptible
diry *See* **dyrie**
dis *v.* does
disadvise *v.* warn against (A1)
disappint *v.* disappoint
discoont *n.* discount
discoorse *n.* discourse
dish-cloot *n.* dish-cloth
disjaskit *adj.* downcast, dejected (J, M2)

disjeest *v.* digest
disna *interrog.* doesn't
disnint *interrog.* doesn't it?
dispeace *n.* trouble, discord
displenish, displinis *v.* disfurnish; to sell off goods and stock on leaving farm; **displenishing sale** *n.* sale by auction of farm stock etc.
dist *n.* dust; fine particles of meal and husk (F)
dister *n.* duster
districk *n.* district
dit *v.* close, shut up; shut the mouth
dite *See* **doit**
div *v. pr.* do (I, you, we, they **div**)
divert *n.* entertainment, diversion
divnin *v. neg. interrog.* don't?
divot *n.* piece of turf
dixie *n.* severe scolding (A); **she gya him his dixie** she gave him a dressing-down
dizzen *n.* dozen
doag *n.* dog (J). *cf.* **tyke**
dochter *n.* daughter (A1). *cf.* **daachter, dother**
dock *n.* buttocks; bottom. *cf.* **doke**
docken *n.* common dock plant
dockiment *n.* document
docknail, docknell *n.* mainpin; nail used to fix handle on a scythe or plough; very experienced farmservant
Dod *pr. n.* nickname for George
dodd *v.* to be, or be made, hornless
doddit *ppl., adj.* without horns
doddy mitten *n.* worsted glove without separate division for the four fingers
dog-birdie *n.* storm petrel (B)

dog-dirder *n.* whipper-in; kennel attendant

doit *n.* old coin of little value; **he caredna a doit**

doit *v.* to grow feeble in mind; **doitit** *ppl.* in dotage; stupid

dome *n.* press-stud

dominie *n.* schoolmaster

done *ppl.* outwitted

donal(ie) *n.* glass of spirits (from Donald)

donnert *adj.* in dotage; stupid

Dons, the nickname of Aberdeen football team

doo *n.* dove, pigeon

dooble *adj.* double; two-faced (A1)

dooble-jintit *adj.* double-jointed

dooble-legs *n. pl.* crutches

doocot *n.* dovecot

dook *n., v.* bathe

dooker *n.* bather

dool *adj.* sorrowful; *n.* woe; grief

doolsome *adj.* sad

doomsil *n.* domicile (B1)

doon *adv., prep.* down; *adj.* depressed, fed up; **doon i the moo** disconsolate, dejected

doonby *adv.* down yonder

dooncome *n.* fall

doonfa *n.* downfall

doonpoor *n.* downpour

doonricht *adj.* downright

doon-sit *n.* home (B1). *See below*

doon-sittin *n.* settlement, usually at marriage

doorie *n.* (small) door; a game of marbles played against a door

doosht *n.* bump, heavy fall or throw

doot *n., v.* doubt; **dootfu** *adj.* doubtful

dorb *(of birds) n.* a peck; *v.* grub, peck (R)

dorty *adj.* fastidious, hard to please, *e.g.* **dorty wi their maet**

dose *n.* large number of anything

doss *n.* bow, or knot

dossie *n.* small quantity in the form of a cluster or heap

dother *n.* daughter (A, M). *cf.* **daachter, dochter, douther**

dottle *n.* the unconsumed tobacco left in a pipe; *v.* become stupid and fretful; **dottelt** mentally confused; in dotage

douce *adj.* respectable, decent; gentle, kind; circumspect

Doup *pr. n.* nickname for village of Boddam

doup *n.* buttocks. *cf.* **dowp**

dour *adj.* grim, austere

dover (ower) *v.* doze (off)

dowf *adj.* melancholy, gloomy

dowie *adj.* sad; dismal

dowp *n.* buttocks. *cf.* **doup**

dozen *v.* to benumb, stupify, daze

dozent, dozin *ppl.* in a benumbed state; stupid

dozen't *excl.* confound it!

draaght *See* **dracht**

dracht *n.* a load; two or more cartloads brought at one time; draught, drink

draars *n. pl.* long underpants

draavers *n. pl.* long drawers for men

drabble *v.* make wet or dirty, to besmear

drabbly *adj.* (of weather) wet, disagreeable

drablich *n.* muddy person (B1)

draff-hurlie *n.* iron trolley filled with distillery draff for feeding cattle
draigon *n.* child's paper kite (J)
drap *v.* drop
drappie *adj.* rainy
drate *v. pr., pt.* defecate; *ppl.* **dritten**
draucht *See* **dracht**
drauchtit *ppl., adj.* (of a horse) harnessed for work
drauchts *n. pl.* draughts
dree *v.* endure; **dree yer ain weird** endure your fate
dreeble *v.* dribble
dreed *n., v.* dread. *cf.* **dreid**
dreel *n.* drill, small furrow for sowing seed; ridge with such furrow on top; scolding
dreep *n.* drip; dripping condition; *v.* drip; empty to last drop
dreepin *n.* dripping
dreepin-pen *n.* enclosure, where newly dipped sheep were held for dripping (T)
dreeve *v. pt.* drove
dregie *n.* refreshment given at a funeral
dreich *adj.* dull, wearisome
dreid *n., v.* dread. *cf.* **dreed**
dribble, driblach *n.* drop, usually of alcohol
dribbly *adj.* drizzly
drift *n.* driving or driven snow
drog *n.* drug
droggie, droggist *n.* druggist
drook *v.* drench
drookit *adj.* drenched
droon *v.* drown; **droont** drowned
drooth, drouth *n.* drought; thirst;

drunkard, tippler. *cf.* **drucht**
droothy, drouthy *adj.* thirsty
drow *n.* fit of illness (A, A1)
drucht *n.* drought. *cf.* **drooth; druchtit** *ppl.* in a state of drought; dehydrated (G)
drucht *n.* drying effect of air; **a gran drucht** (B)
drucken *adj.* drunken
druckenness *n.* drunkenness
drumly *adj.* thick, muddy, gloomy (of water); sullen
drumster *n.* town drummer
drush *n.* peat dust (R)
dry-darn *n.* constipation
dryster *n.* man who dried the grain before grinding
dubs *n.* mud; **dubby, dubbit** *adj.* muddy
ducksie *adj.* dull; lazy (A)
duddie *adj.* ragged
duds *n. pl.* rags; clothes
Duffer *pr. n.* native of Macduff
dule *See* **dool**
dumfoonert *adj.* dumbfounded
dummie *n.* a mute
dumplin *n.* plum (or Christmas) pudding
dundeerie *n.* a great noise (M2)
dunderheid *n.* an outstanding fool
dune *ppl.* done. *cf.* **deen**
dung *v. pt.* (of **ding**) dash down, smash. *cf.* **dang**
dungers *n. pl.* dungarees
dunt *n., v.* thump; **the very dunt** the very thing needed
dursna *See* **daursna**
durstna *v. pt. neg.* did not dare
dusht *ppl.* struck dumb, silenced
dutch *n.* ditch (G, M1)

dwaal, dwall v. dwell; **dwallin-hoose** dwelling-house
dwam, dwaam, dwalm, dwaum n. a faint, fit of sickness; **tae tak a dwam**
dwebble, dweeble, dweebly adj. feeble
dweemly-dwamly adj. feeble (M1)
dwine v. languish, pine; waste away
dyester n. dyer
dyke n. wall of stone or turf; **dry stane dyke** made without mortar

dyker n. builder of dykes
Dyker pr. n. native of Cellardyke
dykon n. deacon
dylt ppl. wearied, fatigued
dyod excl. euphemism for God
dyow n. dew; **dyowie** adj. dewy
dyrie n. dairy
dyst(e) v. fall, sit down or throw with a thud or bump; go up and down bumping
dytit ppl. in dotage; stupid. cf. **doitit**

—— E ——

e, 'e def. art. the
each n. adze
ear, ear' adj., adv. early
ear, 'ear n. year
ear v. plough
earer adj. earlier
earin n. ploughing (A2)
Earl o Hell pr. n. the Devil; **blaik as the Earl o Hell's weskit**
earock n. a fowl of the first year
easedom n. ease; relief; comfort
easin n. eaves. cf. **eezen**
easin-gang n. row of sheaves projecting at the eaves of a stack to keep the rain off
easy adv. easily
easy-osy adj. easy-going
eave-raip n. rope around eaves of a stack
ebb land n. shallow soil
ebb-ploo v. to shallow plough (F)
echt adj. eight. cf. **aicht, aucht**
echt v. owe; own. cf. **acht, yacht**
echteen adj. eighteen

echty adj. eighty
edder, edderan conj. either (can be used at end of sentence as in Eng.)
edder v. to rope thatch with an edderin (F)
edderin n. shuttle-shaped ball of rope (F)
eddicat adj., ppl. educate
eddicashun n. education
edick n. edict
edifee v. edify; ppl. **edifeein**
ee n. eye; **hid a lang ee at** was attracted to (G). See **een**
eechie n. absolutely nothing (in phr. **eechie nor ochie**)
eediot n. idiot
eedle-oddle adj. easy-going, lacking character
eek v. add on or to; **eekin** ppl. adding to
eeksy-peeksy, -picksy adj. exactly equal
Eel pr. n. Yule. cf. **Eile, Yeel**

26

eel *adj.* dry, empty (used of cows which have stopped giving milk). *cf.* **yeld**

eely *adj.* oily

eemost *adj.* uppermost; **eemost wynin** upper part of field

eemur *n.* humour

een *n., numeral* one. *cf.* **ane**

een *n. pl.* eyes. *See* **ee**

eence *adv.* once. *cf.* **aince, ance;** **eence on a day** once upon a time, at one time

eenoo *adv.* just now. *cf.* **eyvnoo**

eeran *n.* errand

eesage *n.* usage; behaviour

eese *n. (pro.* **eece**) use; *v. (pro.* **eeze**) use; **eest wi't** used to it

eesefu *adj.* useful

eeseless *adj.* useless

eeshan *n.* small child (M2); small puny person (B1)

eeshich *n.* small, untidy person (B1)

eeswal(l) *adj.* usual; **eeswally** *adv.* usually

eevie *n.* ivy; **creepin eevie** convolvulus; a slow person

eezen(s) *n.* eaves. *cf.* **easin**

effeck *n.* effect

efter *prep., adv.* after; *adv.* afterwards; **efter-an-aa** after all. *cf.* **aifter**

efterhin *adv.* afterwards. *cf.* **efter**

efterneen *n.* afternoon (A1)

efternin *n.* afternoon (S)

egg shallies *n. pl.* egg shells; **aa egg shallies** feeling fragile, fretful (B)

eident *adj.* diligent; industrious

eik, eke *n.* addition; *v.* add; **eik him**

up egg him on (A2). *cf.* **eek**

Eile *pr. n.* Yule. *cf.* **Eel, Yeel**

eild *n.* old age; **eildit** aged

elbick, elbock, elbuck *n.* elbow; **elbick jam** runny jam

eld *n.* old age (C1). *cf.* **Eild**

eldritch *adj.* unearthly, uncanny

eleeven, eleiven *adj.* eleven. *cf.* **aleyven**

ell *n.* Scottish measurement, equal to 37.0578 inches

eller *n.* elder (of the church). *cf.* **elyer**

ellieson *n.* shoemaker's awl (B1). *cf.* **eshin**

ell-wan *n.* yardstick

elshin *n.* shoemaker's awl. *cf.* **ellieson**

elyer *n.* elder tree; church elder

emmers *n. pl.* embers

emmerteen *n.* ant

en *n.* end

enew *adj.* enough. *cf.* **eneugh**

engeen *n.* engine

enoo *adv.* just now

en-rig *n.* the land at the end of the furrow on which the plough is turned

enstinck *n.* instinct

enstrument *n.* instrument

enteetle *v.* entitle

enterdick *n., v.* interdict

enterfere *v.* interfere

enterin *adj.* favourable for beginning or entering on (S)

enterteenment *n.* entertainment

ere *prep., conj.* before. *cf.* **or**

errant *n.* errand (S)

erse *n.* arse, hind-quarters. *cf.* **doke**

esk *n., v.* hiccup; **tak the esk** get

hiccups
espeeshully *adv.* especially
ess *n.* ash, ashes. *cf.* **aiss**
essfu *adj.* useful. *cf.* **eesefu**
ether *n.* udder
etnach *n.* juniper (berry)
etsleel *n.* young child (B1)
etten *See* **aeten**
ettercap *n.* spider. *cf.* **nettercap**
ettle *v.* aim at, intend, be eager, to begin
ettlin *ppl., adj.* intending, eager
even *n.* evening. *cf.* **een; at even** in the evening
evendoon *adj.* sheer, downright
everlaistin *adj.* everlasting
excamb *n.* one piece of ground exchanged for another; *v.* exchange lands
exceesable *adj.* excusable
excep *prep.* except. *cf.* **'cep**
exerceese *n.* exercise; **exerceese-beuk** exercise-book

exhibeetion *n.* exhibition
exkeesable *adj.* excusable
expairience *n.* experience
expeck *v.* expect; **expeckit** expected
expoon(d) *v.* expound
exterordnar *adj.* extraordinary
eydent *See* **eident**
eyn *n., v.* end; *ppl.* ended; **the back eyn** the end of harvest; late autumn; **get eyns tae rug the gidder** make ends meet. *cf.* **en, eynt**
eynless *adj.* endless
eynrig *n.* end ridge
eyven *adj.* even, straight; **set yer tie eyven** straighten your tie
eyvnoo, eynoo *adv.* just now. *cf.* **enew, eenoo**
eyzle *n.* a live coal, hot ember; **eyzly ee't** with eyes like burning coals

— **F** —

fa, faa *pron.* who; *v.* fall, befall; *n.* fall, fate; **faa clyte** fall heavily; **fa tee** fall to, begin
faamous *adj.* famous
faar *adv.* where
faavour *n.* favour; **for ony faavour!** for goodness sake!
faavrit *adj.* favourite. *cf.* **fauvrit**
faceable *adj.* likely to be true; barely true (B1)
fack *n.* fact; *v.* make, shape, form (B1)
fader, fadder *n.* father (A)

faddom *v.* fathom
fae *n.* foe (A); *prep.* from. *cf.* **frae**
faem *n.* foam
faik, fayich, fyaak *n.* plaid
fail-dyke *n.* turf wall. *cf.* **feal-dyke**
faimly *n.* family
fain *adj.* eager, anxious
fair *adj.* fair; **fair hornie** fair play; *adv.* very, quite, completely
fair-furth-the-gate *adj.* honest and straightforward (R)
fairin *n.* treat, present bought at a fair

fairlie *See* **ferlie**
fairly *adv., excl.* quite, surely
fairm *n.* farm. *cf.* **ferm**
fairmer *n.* farmer
fairmhoose *n.* farmhouse
fairmin *n.* farming
fairm-servan *n.* farm-hand
fairn *n.* fern
fairrier *n.* farrier
faist *adj., adv.* fast. *cf.* **fest**
faisten *v.* fasten
faith *excl.* indeed!
faither *n.* father (C1, F). *cf.* **fader**
faithfu *adj.* faithful
Faithlie *pr. n.* Fraserburgh
fald *v.* fold
fan *adv.* when; *v. pt.* felt, found.
    See **fin**
fan, fanner *n.* winnowing machine
fancy *n.* fancy-cake
fang *n.* scamp; lout; large lump cut
    from something
fank *n.* sheepfold
fant *n.* fainting fit; *adj., v.* faint
fantoosh *adj.* very smart, grand
far *adv.* where. *cf.* **faur**
far *in phr.* **far ben wi** intimate
    with, esp. in favour with God
far-ben *adj.* in high favour
fardel *n.* a large piece (B1)
farder *adv.* farther
fardin *n.* farthing; butter biscuit,
    originally four a penny (B)
farever, farivver *adv., conj.*
    wherever
Farfar *pr. n.* Forfar
Farfar bridie *See* **bridie**
farlan *n.* a long box into which
    herrings are emptied for gutting
farrer *adj.* further; **farrest**

furthest; **farrest ootbye** furthest
    out
fas, fast *n., v.* fast; **fast day** day in
    week preceding half-yearly
    Communion in Presbyterian
    Churches, treated as holiday, with
    service of preparation for the
    Sacrament
fash *n., v.* trouble; **dinna fash yer
    thoom** don't trouble yourself
fashious *adj.* fussy, hard to please
Fasten's Een, Faster's Even *etc.*
    Shrove Tuesday. *cf.* **Festeren's
    Eve**
fat *adj.* what; **fat o** what a lot of;
    fatna what sort of a
fatever *adj., pron.* whatever
fat-hen *n.* weed growing among
    turnips
fattal *adj.* fatal
fattrels *n. pl.* ribbon-ends (B1)
fatty-bannocks *n.* fat person
fat-ye-ca't *n.* what-do-you-call-it
fauch *v.* rub; scratch, claw (B1);
    plough or harrow fallow land
fauchie *adj.* sickly-looking
faugh *n.* fallow land. **Fairmers'
    faugh gars lairds lauch**
    (Proverb)
faul(d) *n.* fold; sheep-fold; *v.* fold;
    fold sheep; **faul yer fit** sit down
    (R)
faur *adj., adv.* where. *cf.* **far**; *v.*
    fare; **faur-ye-weel**
faur idder *interrog. adv.* where
    else?
faured, faurt *adj.* favoured. *See*
    weel-faurt, ill-faurt
fause *adj.* false
faut *n.* fault

29

fauvrit *adj.* favourite. *cf.* **faavrit**

fawmous *adj.* famous

fawvour *n., v.* favour

fawvourt *adj., ppl.* favoured

feal dyke *n.* wall built of sods

fear *n.* fright; *v.* frighten (Abdn. and coastal)

fear, for *conj.* in case (in neg. context)

fearna *v. neg.* have no fear

feart *adj.* afraid

feart things *n. pl.* superstitious beliefs (A1)

feathers *n.* See **ploo**

fecht *n., v.* fight

feck *n.* the majority

fecket *n.* waistcoat, under-jacket

feckless *adj.* weak, feeble; useless, incapable

feckly *adv.* chiefly, mostly

fedder *n., v.* feather

fee *n.* a farm-hand's wage; *v.* engage a farm-hand; **fee't man** *n. with ppl.* hired hand

feech *excl.* of pain or distress. *cf.* **feich**

feeder *n.* an ox fattened for market

feedle *n.* field (A, A2)

feein-fair, -mairket hiring-fair, market for farm servants

feel *n.* fool; *adj.* foolish; **feel's eeran** fool's errand. *cf.* **fule**

feelish *adj.* foolish

feelness *n.* foolishness

feem *n.* state of sudden heat, a sweat; *v.* fume

feenal(ly) *adj., adv.* final(ly)

feenish *n., v.* finish

feer *v.* to set up the first furrow, when ploughing a field

feerich *n.* bustle; state (of excitement); fit of enthusiasm; *v.* bustle

feerin *n.* furrow drawn out to mark the rigs before ploughing the whole field; **feerin pole** pole used as marker in setting up the first furrow (F)

feerious *adj.* furious; *adv.* (used intensively for exceedingly)

feeroch See **feerich**

feese *v. pt.* fetched

feesick *n.* medicine

feesickle *adj.* physical

fegs *excl. of surprise or emphasis* faith!

feich *excl. of disgust. cf.* **feech**

feingie *v.* feign

feint See **fient**

feish *v. pt.* fetched

fell *adj.* deadly; dangerous; *adv.* exceedingly; clever, shrewd (J); *v.* kill; stun; knock down

fell-thocht *v. pt.* reconsidered, had second thoughts (B)

femisht *adj.* famished

fence-fed *adj.* (of animals) fed with titbits at the side of the fence; pampered

fen(d)less *adj.* shiftless, without energy

fere *adj.* strong, sturdy; **hale and fere** thoroughly healthy

ferich See **feerich**

ferlie *n.* oddity, wonder

ferm *n.* farm. *cf.* **fairm**

fer-nothing *n.* dreadnought coat

fernyear *n.* last year; **fernyear was a year** the year before last

fern(y)-tickles *n. pl.* freckles

ferny-tickled *adj.* freckled

ferr *n.* fear (S)
fersell *adj.* forceful, energetic
fesh, fess *v.* fetch, bring; **fess back**
bring to mind, recall; **fess up**
bring up (children); **fessen in**
ppl. established
fest *adj., adv.* fast
Festeren's, Festren's Eve *See*
Fasten's Een
feth *n.* faith; *excl.* faith!
feuch *v.* smoke a pipe (R); *n.* smoke
(B1)
fey *adj.* disordered in the mind;
clairvoyant; behaving in an
excited way, not oneself
feyther *n.* father (J). *cf.* **faither,**
fader
fiars *n.* prices of grain legally fixed
for the year
ficher *n.* slow awkward work; *v.*
fiddle about
ficket *n.* woollen garment with
sleeves and buttoned front, an
undervest worn under shirt
fidder *conj.* whether. *cf.* **fudder**
fiddley *n.* hatchway on a drifter (B)
fidge *v.* fidget; be eager (B1)
fidgick *n.* tufted vetch; **fidgick piz**
small peas growing at the
roadside
fiedle *n.* field (A1). *cf.* **feedle**
fie na *excl.* not at all
fient *n.* fiend; the devil (used in
strong negations); **fient a** not (a);
fient een not one; **fient a fears**
not likely; **fient haet** not a bit,
the devil a bit. *cf.* **feint, fint**
Fiersday *n.* Thursday
fifeteent *adj.* fifteenth
fifety *adj.* fifty

fikie *See* **fykie**
file *conj., n.* while; **files** sometimes;
v. dirty, soil. *cf.* **fool**
filget, filjit *n.* untidy, disreputable-
looking person
filie *n.* a little while
filk *pron.* which
fillies *n. pl.* felloes of wheel
fin *adv., conj.* when
fin *v.* find; feel
Finechty *pr. n.* local name for the
village of Findochty
fineerin *n.* fancy ornamentation
finger-eyns *n.* finger-tips
fingerin *n.* fine worsted from spun
wool
fint *See* **fient**
fir, fir-candle *n.* pine-torch; **fir-**
yowes fir-cones; **firwood** bog-
wood, formerly used for candles
fire *v.* to discharge any missile
firehoose *n.* dwelling house (M);
farmhouse
firewid *n.* firewood
firlit *n.* a corn measure, the fourth
part of a boll
firry *adj.* resinous
first fit *n.* the first person to meet a
marriage party or other
procession (A2); the first visitor
to cross the threshold on or after
New Year's day
fisher-loon *n.* fisher-boy
fisher-quine *n.* fisher-girl
Fishie *pr. n.* village of Fetterangus,
near Mintlaw
fist *v.* grasp with the hand (B1)
fit *n.* foot; *v.* to foot it; **first fit** first
visitor of a new year; **fit-an-mou**
foot-and-mouth disease

31

fit *adj., pron.* what; *rel. pron.* which
(S); **fit like?** how are you?; **fit
wye** how; why; **fit I leuch** how I
laughed
fitba *n.* football
fit-socks *n. pl.* short socks; the feet
of stockings
fitstep *n.* footstep
fite *adj.* white; *v.* whittle; **fite the
idle pin** pass the time away (M).
cf. **futtle**
fite-iron *n.* tin ware
fite-oot *n.* blinding snowstorm (S)
Fittie *pr. n.* Footdee. *cf.* **Futty**
fittie-fies *n. pl.* fault-finding;
quibbles
fittit *v. pt.* footed
fittock *n.* sock with the leg cut off
fivver *n.* fever; **fivvert** *adj.* fevered
flacht *n.* flash, gleam, flash of
lightning; **flacht o fire** streak of
lightning; **get the flacht** suffer
damage (B); flight. *cf.* **flaught**
flae *v.* flay, skin
flaesick *n.* spark from wood fire;
wood-shaving. *cf.* **flezick**
flaff, flaffer *v.* flap, flutter
flag *n.* large snowflake; *v.* snow in
big flakes
flagarie *n.* finery (esp. in dress); a
gewgaw, piece of frivolity;
dainty, delicacy
flaggit *ppl., adj.* (of floors) flagged
flake *n.* hurdle for penning sheep;
hurdle used as a gate (M2)
flan *n.* a gust of wind; sudden
down-draught in a chimney
flang *v.* flung
flannen *n.* flannel; **flannen broth**
saps (T)

flap *n.* a rest; *v.* flop
flate *v.* scolded. *cf.* **flite, flyte**
flaught *See* **flacht, flocht**
flaughter-spaad *n.* two-handed
spade for cutting turfs, peats
flech *n.* flea
flee *n., v.* fly; **flee aboot** dash
about; **flee up** *imp.* get lost!
fleech *See* **fleetch**
fleed *n.* head ridge on which the
plough is turned
fleein *adj.* wildly intoxicated
fleem *n.* fleam, lancet
fleep, flype *n.* lout
fleer *n.* floor; jeer (J)
fleerish *v.* flourish; **flint an fleerish**
flint and steel, used to strike a
spark
fleetch *v.* flatter
fleg *n.* fright; *v.* frighten; *ppl.*
fleggit
flench *v.* flinch
fley *v.* frighten, scare
fleyed, fleyt *ppl., adj.* frightened
(A1). *cf.* **fleggit**
flezick *See* **flaesick**
flicher *v.* flicker
flicht *n.* flight
flichty *adj.* flighty
flinrikin *n.* very thin cloth, a mere
rag
flit *v.* leave a place, go elsewhere;
move house
flite, flyte *v.* scold
flittin *n.* house removal
float *n.* lorry for carrying livestock
flocht *v.* excite, flurry; **flochtit** in a
state of excitement, worked up
flooer, floor *n., v.* flower
floor *n.* (wheaten etc.) flour

floorish *n.* blossom

flow *n.* very small quantity of powdery substance, *e.g.* meal, dust

flucht *v.* agitate; **fluchtit** *ppl.* in a state of excitement

fluffert *n.* (of snow) a light shower (T)

flum(mer)gummery *n.* any useless thing or action; vain adornment, trimming (B1)

fly, fly-cup *n.* sly cup of tea (but taken ritually)

flype *v.* turn inside out

foalie *n.* foal

fob *v.* pant with heat or exertion; **fobbit yowe** ewe panting from exertion

fochen *ppl.* fought; exhausted; **fochen deen** worn out

focht *v. pt.* fought

fodderin, foddrin *n.* fodder

fog *n.* long grass left standing in winter; moss, lichen; *v.* gather wealth

foggie-bee *n.* yellow humble-bee

Foggieloan *pr. n.* Aberchirder, Banffshire

foggit *ppl., adj.* moss-covered; well off

foggy *adj.* wizened, dry, sapless; mossy

foifteen *adj.* fifteen (A2)

folk (G, M). *cf.* **fouk, fowk**

folla *n.* fellow

folm *n.* a billow of mist; *v.* overturn

fond *adj.* foolish; *n.* fund

foo *adj.* full; *adv.* how; why

foodge *v.* (in marble-playing) to take unfair advantage; cheat

fooever *conj., adv.* however

fool *adj.* dirty. *cf.* **file**

fools *n. pl.* fowls (*dim.* **foolies**)

foon(d) *n.* foundation. *cf.* **founs**

foon *ppl.* found (J)

fooner *v.* founder; *ppl.* **foonert** exhausted, worn out

foont *n.* fount

foord *n., v.* ford

foorich *v.* work in a flurried manner

foort *adj.* fourth

foorty *adj.* forty

foosh up *v. pt.* fetched up; brought up

foosion *See* **fushen**

foostie, fooshtie, fooshtit *adj.* fusty, mouldy

footer *n.* bungler; silly, useless person; troublesome, fiddling job; *v.* fiddle with

footers term of contempt

foraneen *n.* forenoon. *cf.* **forenin**

forby(e) *adv.* besides; *prep.* in addition to; compared with

forbyes *prep.* besides; far less; not to mention; *conj.* whereas

forcie *adj., adv.* active(ly), forceful(ly); (of weather) warm, dry, good for crops

fordal, fordel, fordle *n.* progress, advancement; a store; *v.* store up for future use; **get fordalt wi** get ahead with (G)

forder *adj., adv.* further

forebreist *n.* front seat of a gallery; front of a cart

forenicht *n.* interval between twilight and bedtime

forenin *n.* forenoon (S). *cf.* **foraneen**

foreshaida *v.* foreshadow

foreslings *n. pl.* for attaching harness at front of cart shaft

foresta *n.* manger

forfecht (yersel) *v.* overburden (yourself), overdo

forfochen *adj.* exhausted, worn out

forgaither *v.* forgather

forgat *v.* forgot

forgettle *adj.* forgetful

forgie *v.* forgive

forgieness *n.* forgiveness

forgya *v. pt.* forgave (A)

forhooie *v.* forsake; **forhooiet** *ppl., adj.* forsaken

forjeskit *adj.* fatigued, worn out

forkie(tail) *n.* earwig

forl *n.* whorl, small wheel on a spindle steadying its motion

forleithy *n.* surfeit (B1)

fornent *prep.* over against, opposite, facing

forquant *v.* acquaint; intimate

forrit *adv.* forward(s)

fort *adj.* fourth. *cf.* **foort**

fortiet *adj.* fortieth

fortig *n., v.* fatigue

fortin *n.* fortune

fortnat *adj.* fortunate

fortnicht *n.* fortnight

forty-faal *adj.* deceitful (B)

foryet *v.* forget, *pt.* **foryat**

fossy, fosy *adj.* (often used of rotten vegetables) soft, spongy. *cf.* **fozie**

fou *adj.* full, drunk; *n.* stone crop, saxifrage

fouk *See* **fowk**

foumart *n.* pole-cat; term of abuse

founs *n. pl.* foundations

fousome *adj.* foul

fower *adj.* four

fowk *n.* people (A, A1, A2, C, J, M, R). *cf.* **fouk, folk, fock**

foy *n.* farewell feast on leaving a place or finishing a job (B1)

fraacht *See* **fraucht**

frae *prep.* from (J). *cf.* **fae**

fraikie *adj.* coaxing, wheedling

fraise *v.* speak flatteringly

fraisie *adj.* given to flattery

frap *n.* predicament (B)

fraucht *n.* freight or load; what can be carried or carted at one time (two pails-full, cartloads)

fraughty *adj.* liberal, generous

Freday *n.* Friday

freely *adv.* particularly; **freely fine** remarkably fine

freen *n.* friend

freest *n., v.* frost

freet *See* **fret**

freevolous *adj.* frivolous

fremt, fremmit *adj.* foreign; **the fremt** *n. pl.* strangers

fresh *adj.* (of weather) thawing; cold; open

fret *n.* superstition

freuch *adj.* brittle, dry

frichen *v.* frighten. *cf.* **frichten**

fricht *n.* fright

frichten *v.* frighten

froon *n., v.* frown

front shelvin *adj. with n.* movable board on front of box-cart

frost *v.* to fit frost nails (F)

frost-hole *n.* frost nail hole (F)

frostit *adj.* inflamed by cold

fry *n.* parcel of fish taken home by workers in the fishing industry

fu *adj.* full, tipsy; *adv.* very. *cf.* **fou**

fucher *See* **ficher**
fudder *v.* move hurriedly; run in excited or aimless fashion; *conj.* whether
fuffer *v.* (M1) prob. **fuffle** walk awkwardly, hobble, shuffle
fugie (*rhymes with budgie*) *n.* truant from school
fugle *v.* deceive (B1)
fuish *v. pt.* fetched, brought. *cf.* **feish, foosh**
ful, full (*rhymes with gull*) *adj.* full; puffed up, conceited; *v.* fill; **ful (up)** replete after food
fulage *adj.* foolish (B1)
fule *n.* fool. *cf.* **feel**
full *See* **ful**
fullt *ppl.* filled
fulp *n.* whelp
fulpie *n.* puppy, whelp
fummle *v.* fumble
fun, funn *n.* whin; **fun mull** whin mill for bruising whins for food for horses etc.
fun *v. pt., ppl.* found. *See* **fin**
fun *v.* to do something for fun; joke
fund *v. pt.* found (S)
fung *v.* throw
funk *n.* a breath (of wind) (B); *v.* sulk (B1)
funtain *n.* fountain
funtainheid *n.* fountainhead
fup *n., v.* whip; **fup-han** whip-hand. *cf.* **whup**
fur, furr *n., v.* furrow
fur-beast *n.* horse for walking in furrow. *cf.* **furrer**
furhooied *See* **forhooie**

furl *v.* whirl; **furly** whirly
furliefaa *n.* showy ornament(ation)
furligorum *n.* showy ornament (G)
furm *n.* form, bench without a back
furnitur *n.* furniture
furrer *n.* horse walking in furrow
furth *adv.* forth, away
furth, the *n.* the open air
furth-the-gait *adv.* honestly
fushach *n.* loose, untidy bundle; **I carena a fushach**
fushen, fushon *n.* pith, vigour
fushenless *adj.* lacking vigour
fusion *See* **fushen**
fuskers *n. pl.* whiskers
fuskert *adj.* whiskered
fusky *n.* whisky
fusome *adj.* disgusting. *cf.* **fousome**
fussle *n., v.* whistle
fut *pron.* what; **fut for nae** why not. *cf.* **fat, fit**
futher *conj.* whether. *cf.* **fudder**
futlie (beelin) *n.* whitlow
futrat, futtrat *n.* weasel; small, thin, hatchet-faced person
futtle *n.* short gutting knife; *v.* whittle
Futty *pr. n.* Footdee. *cf.* **Fittie**
fy *n.* whey
fyaach *v.* fidget. *cf.* **fyke**
fyaak *n.* plaid. *cf.* **faik, fayich**
fyke *n.* fuss; difficulty; *v.* fidget
fykie *adj.* troublesome, tricky; restless
fyle *n., v.* while; **fyles** now and then; *v.* to soil, make dirty
fyou, fyow(e) *adj.* few
fyower *adj.* fewer

— G —

gaad, gad *n.* goad, wand
gaager *n.* exciseman. *cf.* **gauger**
gaan *v.* go (coastal); *ppl.* going. *cf.*
 gaun
gaan-aboot hen *adj., n.* free-range
 hen
gaar *n.* oozing vegetable matter;
 green gaar growth seen on piers
 and low on the walls of houses
 (B)
gab *n.* prattling talk; one who talks
 incessantly; the mouth; *v.* to
 chatter, prate
Gab o Mey *phr.* the last days of
 April anticipating the weather of
 May
gabbin *n.* chattering
gaberlunzie *n.* beggar
gad *n.* goad for driving horses or
 cattle. *cf.* **gaud**
Gadie *pr. n.* stream at the hill of
 Bennachie, Aberdeenshire
gadsman *n.* person who drives
 horses or cattle with a gad; or
 uses gad to direct corn to the
 scythe (B1) or binder. *cf.*
 gaudsman
gae *v.* go (A, A1, A2, J, M, R). *cf.*
 gyang, gang, ging;
gae *v. pt.* gave (A2, M)
gaed *v. pt.* went; **gaed worth**
 became as nothing
gae-lattin *ppl.* letting go; *n.* the
 verge of bankruptcy
gaff *v.* laugh loudly, guffaw. *cf.*
 gauff

gager *n.* exciseman
gaidy *n.* the arm (A)
Gaimrie *pr. n.* local name for the
 village of Gardenstown; **Gaimrie
 knottie** biscuit
Ga'in *pr. n.* Gavin
gaird *n., v.* guard
gairden *n.* garden
Gairtly *pr. n.* Aberdeenshire village
 of Gartly
gait *See* **gate**
gaither *v.* gather. *cf.* **gedder,
 gether, gidder**
gaitherer *n.* one who gathers grain
 to make sheaves. *cf.* **lifter**
gaivel *n.* gable. *cf.* **gavel**
gale *n.* gable (M)
galliart *adj.* bright, gaudy (B1)
galluses *n. pl.* trouser braces
galore *adv.* in abundance
galshachs, galshochs *n. chf. in pl.*
 sweets, titbits; treats, goodies;
 junk foods
gamey, gamie *n.* gamekeeper
gane *v.* gone
gang *v.* go (A2, M, M1, R); **gang
 yer gait** go your way. *cf.* **gyang,
 ging, gae**
gangrel *n.* vagrant, tramp
ganjie *See* **gansey**
ganner *n.* gander
gansey *n.* guernsey, a seaman's
 jersey. *cf.* **ganjie**
gant *v.* yawn
gapus *adj.* stupid; *n.* fool
gar *v.* compel, cause to

garron *n.* small horse
gartens *n.* garters; **green gartens**
given by girl to her elder sister if
marrying before her
gash *adj.* ghastly, gruesome
gast *n.* fright; shock
gat *v. pt.* got
gate *n.* way, route; **the richt gate**
properly; **dee the richt gate** do
the right thing; **some gates** in
some places
gatefarrin *adj.* presentable; comely
gate-ganger *n.* wanderer, tinker
gaud *See* **gad**
gaudsman *See* **gadsman**
gaun *v.* go (coastal) *ppl.* going. *cf.*
gaan
gaup *v.* gape; eat voraciously (A1)
gavel *n.* gable. *cf.* **gaivel**
gawk, gawkie *n.* silly, clumsy
person
gawkit *adj.* stupid, clumsy
gawkitness *n.* stupidity; uncouth
silliness
gavel *n.* tail of sheaf (F)
gean *n.* wild cherry tree
gear *n.* property, wealth
geck *n.* disdainful toss of head; *v.*
toss the head in scorn; turn the
head in a foolish or coquettish
way; **geck-neck(it)** (having) a
twisted neck
gedder *v.* gather; **geddert** *v. pt.,*
ppl. gathered; *adj.* well-to-do. *cf.*
gaither, gether, gidder
gedderer *n.* (usually female)
gatherer in the harvest field
gee *n.* sullenness; stubbornness; **tak**
the gee wi take offence at
someone; whim, foolish notion;

gee up *imp.* forward! (command
for a plough-horse in Buchan)
geed *adj.* good (F)
Geery *pr. n.* Garioch (a district in
Aberdeenshire). *cf.* **Gerry**
geet *n.* child
genteelity *n.* gentility
Geordie *pr. n.* deriv. of George
Gerry *pr. n.* Garioch (a district in
Aberdeenshire). *cf.* **Geery**
gether *v.* gather (R). *cf.* **gaither,**
gedder, gidder
get on tae *v.* scold, *e.g.* **dinna get**
on tae them
gey *adj.* great, considerable
gey, geyan *adv.* very, somewhat,
rather
geylies *adv.* rather; nearly; pretty
well
ghaist(ie) *n.* ghost
gheelie *n.* man or boy attending
sportsman
gibbles *n.* wares
gid *See* **gaed, gied**
gidder *v.* gather. *cf.* **gaither,**
gedder, gether
gie *v.* give; **gie intae trouble** scold
gied, gid *v. pt.* gave
gif *conj.* if (B1). *cf.* **gin**
gilgal *n.* (hard g) hubbub; uproar
(B1)
gillieperous, gileepris *n.* (hard g)
fool; rough, ungainly person
(B1, T)
gilp *See* **jilp**
gimmer *n.* ewe from one to two
years old; or not yet having borne
young
gin *conj.* if, whether; if only (M2);
than, by the time that; *prep.* (used

of time) by
ginch-breid *n.* gingerbread
ging *v.* go (A, S). *cf.* **gyang**
ginkmen (B1) *See* **ginkum**
ginkum *n.* trick, dodge
gird *n.* child's hoop
girdin *n.* girthing, *e.g.* to secure
saddle, or lash a load to a cart
girdle *n.* circular iron plate with
bow handle for baking oatcakes,
etc.
girn *n.* snare; whimper; fretful
fault-finding; *v.* complain
peevishly, grumble; snarl
girnal, girnel *n.* meal chest
girnie, girnin *adj.* peevish
girse, girss *n.* grass
girse-hyeuk *n.* metal strut on scythe
girssy *adj.* grassy
gizzen *v.* dry up; shrivel; **gizzent**
adj. parched; shrivelled; warped
glack *n.* fork of a tree; ravine; point
where two things branch off
glaid *adj.* glad. *cf.* **gled**
glaik *n.* gleam
glaiket, glaikit *adj.* senseless;
stupid
Glaisga *pr. n.* Glasgow
glammach, glammoch *n., v.* grasp,
grab; **lat glammach at;** *n.* morsel
glamour, glamourie *n.* magic
glaur *n.* mud; ooze
gled, gledsome *adj.* glad
gled, gleed *n.* kite (bird of prey)
gleebrie *n.* large piece of (waste)
ground
gleg *adj.* keen, sharp; eager; *n.*
gadfly
glegsome *See* **gleg** *adj.*
glen *n.* narrow valley

glent *n.* glance
gless *adj.* glass; *n.* mirror
glesses *n.* spectacles
gley *n., v.* squint; **gleyed ee** eye
with a squint
gliberal *n.* large piece of waste
ground (B1). *cf.* **gleebrie**
gliff *n.* shock, scare (B1)
glint *n.* glimpse (M)
glive *n.* glove (A2)
gloam, gloamin, gloomin *n.*
twilight
glorious *adj.* highly stimulated by
alcohol (M2)
glowe *n., v.* glow
glower *n., v.* scowl
gluff *n.* shock; inhalation of air; *v.*
eat greedily (B)
glumf *v.* to look sulky
gnap *n.* bite, mouthful
gnappin *in phr.* **in gnappin
earnest** in dead earnest (B1)
gnauve *v.* gnaw
gnipper *n. in phr.* **gnipper for/and
gnapper** the very smallest
particle (deriv. from sound of mill
when grinding); every bit
go-ashores *n. pl.* fishermen's dress
for going ashore (B)
gobbinfae *See* **gowpenfu**
gock *n.* cuckoo; fool. *cf.* **gowk**
gockit *adj.* foolish
gog *n.* nestling (S). *cf.* **gorbel**
gollach, goloch *n.* beetle; **hornie-
gollach** earwig
gollar *v.* shout incoherently
gomeril *n.* fool, blockhead
good al meggins! *excl.* probable
euphemism for God Almighty
goodman *n.* husband (A2). *cf.*

guidman
goodwife *n.* wife (A2). *cf.* **guidwife**
goon *n.* gown
goor *n.* mud; slime
goranichy *adj.* complaining feebly (B1)
gorbel, gorblin *n.* unfledged bird. *cf.* **gog**
gorbellt *adj.* state of egg with young bird partially formed
goshie *excl.* gosh!
goup *v.* gawp, stare. *cf.* **gowp**
govie-dick(s) *excl. of surprise* (M1)
gow *n.* seagull (Buckie); *v.* induce, persuade; gull (A2). *cf.* **goy**
gowan *n.* daisy
gowd *n.* gold; **gowden** *adj.* golden
gowdie *n. in phr.* **heels ower gowdie** head over heels
gowf(f) *n.* ruin, destruction; golf
gowf(f)er *n.* golfer
gowk *n.* cuckoo; fool. *cf.* **gock**
gowkit *adj.* foolish. *cf.* **gockit**
gowp *v.* gawp, stare. *cf.* **goup, gype**
gowpenfu (fae) *n.* as much as two cupped hands can hold
gowsty *adj.* pale, sickly
gowt *v. pt., ppl.* got
goy (ower) *v.* allure, entice; convince (B1). *cf.* **gow**
graavit *n.* scarf; cravat. *cf.* **grauvit**
graen, grain *n., v.* groan
graip *n.* large fork used in farming; *v.* fork
graith *n.* accoutrements, harness; substance, riches; clothes
graivel *n.* gravel
gralloch *v.* disembowel the carcass of a deer
gran *adj., adv.* grand

granda *n.* grandfather
grane *v.* groan. *cf.* **graen, grain**
gran'eur *n.* grandeur
granfadder *n.* grandfather
Granny's John *n.* coddled boy
grape *v.* grope (J)
grat *v. pt.* wept; **roared an grat** wept noisily. *cf.* **greet**
grauvit *n.* cravat; scarf
grease *n.* disease affecting horses' legs
great-hertit *adj.* overcome by emotion; having a full heart
gree *v.* agree
green *n.* lawn; grassland
green (efter) *v.* long, yearn (for) (B1)
green-hoose *n.* greenhouse
greenichtie *adj.* greenish
greep *n.* open drain in cowshed; middle part of byre
greeshach *n.* flameless fire of red-hot embers (A1)
greet *v.* weep; **greetin fou** in an advanced stage of intoxication
greff *n.* grave (A)
greybeard *n.* earthenware bottle
grieve *n.* farm overseer
grimmy *n.* Grimsby boat or fisherman (B)
grindie, grindie tocher *n.* small greenish crab found in sea-shore pools (B)
grinsteen *n.* grindstone
grippit *adj., ppl.* seized with pain; hard up, pressed for cash (R)
grippy *adj.* stingy, tight-fisted
grizzelt *ppl.* turning gray (G)
grofe *adj.* coarse, rough
groncie *n.* anything large or fine of

its kind

groo *v. See* **grue**

growe *v.* grow; **growin shoorie** light rain good for plants and crops (T)

growthe *n.* growth; vegetation

growth-midden *n.* compost heap

growthy *adj.* (of weather) conducive to growth; (of a season) of good growth

grozart *n.* gooseberry

grubber *Eng. n.* agric. implement clearing ground of roots etc.

grubbit *ppl.* (land) cleared with a grubber

grue *v.* shudder

gruggle *v.* to render sub-standard by much handling; **grugglt** creased

grumlie *adj.* grumbling, fault-finding

grummle *v.* grumble

grun *n.* ground

grunny *n.* grandmother

grun offisher *n.* manager of an estate (A2)

grunter *n.* fisher word for the pig, where the word pig is taboo. *cf.* **Sandy Campbell**

gruntle *v.* grunt

grup *v.* grip

grutten *ppl.* wept; *adj.* tear-stained

gryte *adj.* great; **gryte lins** heavy fishing lines (B)

guaird *n., v.* guard. *cf.* **gaird**

Gude *See* **Gweed**

guddle *v.* catch fish with the hands by groping below the banks of a stream

gudge *n.* small, thickset fellow

guff *n.* smell

guffa *n.* guffaw

guid *adj.* good. *cf.* **gweed**

guid-brither *etc. See* **gweed-brither**

guidman *n.* master, head of household; husband (J)

guidwife *n.* female head of house, the mistress; wife (J)

guidwillie *adj.* generous (R)

guise *v.* to go mumming, masquerade. *cf.* **gyse**

guiser *n.* mummer; child in disguise who goes round doors at Hallowe'en offering entertainment in return for gifts or money

guizard *n.* mummer (J)

gull *n.* haze, mist

guller *n.* gurgling sound in throat

gullie *n.* large knife

gumbile *n.* gumboil

gumfleers, gumfloors *n. pl.* artificial flowers for ladies' bonnets (B1)

gumption *n.* common-sense

gundy *n.* candy; toffee

gunpouther *n.* gunpowder

Gurdon *pr. n.* Gourdon

gurk *n.* a short fat person

gurl *n., v.* growl

gurlie, gurly *adj.* (of weather, sea) stormy, threatening

gurr *n.* growl; drive, spirit; *v.* to growl

gurron *n.* strong, thickset person

gushet *n.* gusset; triangular piece of land; corner of a building

gutsy *adj.* greedy

gutter(s) *n.* mud, mire (S)

gutter *v.* work untidily, dirtily

g' wa *imp.* go away
gwana *n.* guano fertiliser
Gweed *pr. n.* God; **Gweed kens!**
  goodness knows!; **Gweed keep's**
  aa God keep us all; **Gweed**
  preserve's God preserve us!;
  Gweed send God grant
gweed *adj.* good; **gweed fegs** *excl.*
  good faith
gweed *n.* good; **tak the gweed o**
  take advantage of
gweed-brither, -breeder *n.*
  brother-in-law
gweed-dother *n.* daughter-in-law
gweed-father *n.* father-in-law
gweedlie *adv.* godly
gweed-mither *n.* mother-in-law
gweed-nicht *int.* goodnight
gweed-sin *n.* son-in-law
gweedwife *n.* wife
gweed-words *n. pl.* prayers
gweed-wull *n.* goodwill
gweed-wully *adj.* good-hearted;
  generous (B1). *cf.* **guid-willie**

gwestie, gweeshtie, gweeshtens
  excl. goodness!
gwite *n.* a narrow rocky inlet
gya *v. pt.* gave (A)
gyad(-sakes) *excl.* of revulsion,
  usually over food
gyana *v. neg.* did not give
gyang *v.* go (A, A1); *n.* a gang;
  row; **gyang forrit** attend
  Communion
gyangrel *See* **gangrel**
gyaun, gyaan *ppl.* going; **a-gyaun**
  going about
gyke-neckit *adj.* descriptive of
  someone whose neck is held
  slightly to one side (B). *cf.* **geck-**
  neckit
gype *n.* a fool; *v.* stare foolishly. *cf.*
  gowp
gypery *n.* foolishness, silly talk
gypit *adj.* foolish
gyse *See* **guise**
gyte *adj.* mad, crazy

— H —

ha *n.* hall
haach *n.* phlegm; *v.* hawk, clear the
  throat
haar *n.* (sea) mist
haaver *n.* half share; *v.* divide in
  two. *cf.* **halver**
habber *v.* stutter, stammer
hack *n.* chap, the effect of severe
  cold; notch
hack(ie) *n.* a certain amount, a bit;
  a hackie langer
had *v.* hold; **haddin hame** going

home. *cf.* **hud**
haddie *n.* haddock
hae *v.* have; **haed** *v. pt.* had; *ppl.*
  haen had; **haena** *v. neg.* have
  not. *cf.* **hinna**
haffets *n.* temples; sides of the head
hag *n.* brushwood
hagger *n.* wound (A)
haibit *n.* habit
haik *n.* rack for fodder; **living at**
  haik and manger living
  extravagantly; **on the haik for**

41

on the look-out for. *cf.* **hake**

hail, haill *adj., n.* whole. *cf.* **hale**

haill *v.* heal

haill Eel *n.* the old Christmas season which extended from Dec. 25th to Twelfth Night; *in phr.* **tae haud haill Eel** to make merry, to celebrate with abandon

haimal(t), haimil(t) *adj.* homely, plain; without ceremony

haimle *See* **haimal(t)**

haimmer *n., v.* hammer. *cf.* **hemmer**

haims *n.* curved pieces of iron attached to horse's collar; **pit the haims on** *(fig.)* bring someone into line

hain *v.* save, husband; hoard; **a great hainin** a great saving; *v.* spare

hair *in phr.* **nae a hair o't** not a bit of it

hairbour *n.* harbour. *cf.* **herbour**

hairm *n., v.* harm

hairmless *adj.* harmless

hairrial *n.* something that impoverishes, costly expenditure. *cf.* **herrial**

Hairry *pr. n.* Harry

hairse *adj.* hoarse

hairst *n.* harvest

hairt *n.* heart. *cf.* **hert**

hairth *n.* hearth (J). *cf.* **ingle**

hairy-tatties *n.* hash made with potatoes and dried, salted fish (B)

hait *n.* atom, particle; **fient hait** not a bit

haith *excl.* (of surprise) faith!

haive *v.* heave, throw

haiveless *adj.* careless; unmannerly (A2)

haiver *v.* talk nonsense. *cf.* **haver**

haivers *n.* nonsense. *cf.* **havers**

hake *n.* wooden frame for drying fish. *cf.* **haik**

hale *adj.* whole; **hale an fere** whole and entire. *cf.* **hail**

halesome *adj.* wholesome

half-hung-tee *adj.* irresponsible (T)

halfie *n.* half-holiday

halflin *adj.* half-grown; *n.* half-grown boy, youth; farm- or stable-boy

half roads *adv.* half-way

halla *adj.* hollow (C). *cf.* **boss**

halver *v.* divide in two. *cf.* **haaver**

hallyrackit *adj.* boistrous, romping

hame *n.* home; **fae hame** away from home

hame-drauchtit *adj.* selfish

hame-fairm *n.* home farm

hamel *adj.* belonging to home. *cf.* **haimal(t)**

hameowre, -ower *adj.* homely, humble

hamesick *adj.* homesick

hamespun *adj., n.* homespun

hameward *adv.* homewards

hamewith, -wuth *adv.* homewards

hammer *v.* work or walk in clumsy, noisy way

hamsh *v.* eat noisily, voraciously

han *n.* hand; **at aa hans** at every opportunity; **tak throw han** deal with, discuss

han-breed *n.* hand-breadth

hane *ppl.* had. *cf.* **haen**

hanfu *n.* handful

hangie *n.* hangman; a soft cheese (F); **hangman cheese** curds in cloth, salted and hung to dry (T)

hank *v.* fasten, secure; tie tightly, constrict
hankey *n.* handkerchief
hanle *n.* handle
han-leem *n.* hand-loom
hanlin *n.* going-over, critical assault (A1); hand fishing line (B)
hansel *n.* handsel; first money received (B1); *v. tr.* handsel
hantle *n.* large quantity or number
hap *v.* hop; cover; **happit** *ppl.* covered; *n.* cover
hape *n.* heap (S)
hap in/up *v.* cover over
happer *n.* basket or container, esp. of seed for sowing
hap-warm *n.* a warm wrap or covering
harassment *n.* fatigue (A2)
hard *v. pt.* heard
harden *(adj.), n.* (of) very coarse cloth made of **hards**
hards *n. pl.* the coarse refuse of flax or hemp separated by heckling
hard-vrocht *adj.* hard-worked
hare-shard *n.* hare-lip (B1)
harigals *n. pl.* animal entrails
harken *v.* listen
harle *v.* rough-cast a wall with mix of mortar and small gravel
harlin *n.* rough casting
harn *n.* coarse cloth, sackcloth
harns *n.* brains; **harn pan** the skull
harp *n.* (a mason's) wire screen for cleaning sand or gravel
harra *n.* harrow
harry *v.* plunder bird's nest, bee's bike. *cf.* **herry**
hash *v.* slice, cut up; work at high pressure, hustle; **hasht** *ppl.* pressed, harrassed
haste-ye-back *phr.* come back soon. *cf.* **hist**
hat *v. pt.* hit
haud *n., v.* hold; **haud awa** go on; **haud in wi** keep in with; **haud oot** maintain; **haud ootower** keep away; **haud redd o** keep clear of (R); **haud yer tongue** be quiet; say no more; **haud yer wheesht** be silent; **nae tae haud nor bin'/bin** not to be held down, out of control
haud *v.* continue, to go on
haud awa fae *prep. phr.* except for
hauden-doon inhibited, constrained (of husbands) hen-pecked
hauden in aboot *ppl.* constrained
haudin *n.* (small)holding (A, M)
hauf *adj.* half
haugh *n.* low-lying ground beside a river; clearing of throat
hauld *n.* stronghold
hault *See* **hult**
haumer *v.* stamp about noisily
haved *v. pt.* heaved
haveral *n.* half-witted person; fool; garrulous person
haw *adj.* bluish-gray or pale green
haythen *adj., n.* heathen
heapie-on, a *n.* boy's game
hearken *v.* listen
hearthsteen *n.* hearthstone
heater *n.* glazed, sugared bun
hech *v.* pant (J)
heck an manger, to live at to live extravagantly. *cf.* **haik**
hed *v. pt.* had (A2)
hedder *n.* heather

heediepeers *n. pl.* people of the same height
heelabalow *n. var.* of hullabaloo
heeld *v.* held; (of time) spent (A1)
heelster-gowdie *adv.* head over heels
heelster-heid *adv.* head first
heely, heely *excl.* of correction slowly! or wait!
heemlin *ppl., adj.* humbling
heepocreet *n.* hypocrite
heerican *n.* hurricane (G)
heerin *n.* herring
heese, heeze *v.* heave; lift; exalt; intensify
heesh *int.* make hissing sound to drive animals away. *cf.* **hish**
heepochondreech *adj.* listless, gloomy (B1)
heepocrat *n.* hypocrite
Heeven *pr. n.* Heaven (C)
heft *n.* haft, knife handle; *v.* lift up; carry aloft; **heftit coo** unmilked cow with full udder
heich *adj.* high; *adv.* aloud
heichen *v.* heighten
heicher, heichest *adj.* higher, highest
heich-heidit *adj.* haughty
heicht *n.* height. *cf.* **hicht**
heid *n.* head; headmaster; **ower the heids o** because of
heid-bummer *n.* leader
heid-hurry *n.* busiest time
heid-, heidin-shafe *n.* last sheaf on top of a stack
heidie, heidy *adj.* clever; head-strong; opinionative
heidiepeers *n.* (young) people of exactly the same height

heidmaister *n.* headmaster
heid-rig *n.* head ridge
heid-stall *n.* head-stall, part of halter
heir *v.* inherit
heirskip *n.* heirship, inheritance
heist *v.* lift with effort
helpender, helpener *n.* assistant; minister's assistant
helter *n.* halter
hemmer *n.* hammer
hems *See* **haims**
hench *v.* to launch missiles by striking the hand against the thigh
hennie *n.* familiar name for a henwife
henny-hertit *adj.* timid, faint-hearted
henshine *n.* party for females
henwife *n.* woman in charge of poultry
herbour *n., v.* harbour. *cf.* **hairbour**
herd *n.* herdsman, -boy, one who tends cattle or sheep; *v.* tend cattle, sheep
heretick *n.* heretic
herp *n.* harp
herrial *n.* means of harrying; cause of ruin. *cf.* **harrial**
herrin *n.* herring; **herrin fivver** herring fever, condition caused by poor fishing (B)
herry *v.* plunder; *v.* plunder, rob birds' nests. *cf.* **harry**
hersel *pron.* herself; *pred. adj., adv.* by herself, alone
hert *n.* heart; **hert oot** *v.* build up heart of a stack or cart-load of grain. *cf.* **hairt**

hertnin *n.* encouragement; strengthening

hertsca(u)d *n.* heartburn; a disappointment (B1)

hesp *n.* hasp

het *adj.* hot; *v. pt.* heated (A1); **het fit** hot foot

heth *excl.* faith!

heugh *n.* a crag; rugged steep

heuk, heuck *n.* hook; reaping-hook, scythe. *cf.* **hyeuk**

hey *n.* hay

hey-hoose *n.* hay-shed (S)

hey-makker hay-maker

hey-ruck *n.* haystack

hey-soo *n.* haystack

hi! *imp.* turn left! (instruction for a plough-horse in Buchan) (T)

hicht *n.* height. *cf.* **heicht**

hid *n., v.* hold (S)

hid *v. pt.* had; **hidna** had not

hie *adj.* high (S); **hier** higher. *cf.* **heich**

hielan *adj.* highland

Hielander *n.* Highlander

hielant *adj.* Highland

himpen *adj.* hempen

himsel *pron.* himself; *pred. adj., adv.* by himself, alone

hinch *n.* haunch

hinder-, hinner-en *n.* latter or final part, the extremity; the end; death; the remains of anything; **at the hinder-en** in the end

hindmost *adj.* last. *cf.* **hinmaist**

hine *adv.* far; **hine awa** far off, far away. *cf.* **hyne**

hing *v.* hang *(tr., intr.)*

hing in *v.* get on with something, persevere

hingin *n.* a hanging

hingin-luggit *adj.* having drooping ears; disappointed

hinmaist *adj., n.* last

hinna *v. neg.* have not. *cf.* **haena**

hinner *v.* hinder

hinny *n.* honey

hin-shelvin *n.* movable board on back door of box cart (A2)

hin-slings *n. pl.* part of **britchin**, for attachment to rear of cart shaft (F)

hint *n.* the end; **hint o' hairst** end of harvest

hippen, hippin *n.* baby's nappy

hippen-towie *n.* rope for hanging nappies

hippit, hip-grippit *adj.* having stiff hip-joints and lower back

hire *v.* hire; engage oneself as an employee; season food

hirehoose *n.* farm labour or service; the place or house where servant is engaged to go

hirple *v.* limp; hobble

hirsel *n.* flock of sheep

hirstle *v.* to move with grazing or friction (M). *cf.* **hurschle**

hir't *ppl.* hired; seasoned

his *v.* has; **hisna** has not

hish *v.* drive animals, esp. poultry. *cf.* **heesh**

hist *n.* a great number; *v.* haste; **hist ye back** come back soon

hit *pron.* it

hiv *v.* have; *n.* hoof

hive *v.* swell, cause to swell

hivven *n.* heaven

hiz *pron.* us

hize *See* **hyze**

hizzie *n.* housewife; hussy

hoast *n., v.* cough; **a kirkyaird hoast** severe cough

hobble *n.* predicament; swarm of any kind

hobblet *adj.* perplexed

hoch *n.* lower part of human thigh; hind-leg joint of animal

hod *v.* hide; *pt.* hid; **hodden** *ppl.* hidden

hodden *n.* homespun cloth of wool of the natural colour

hodden-grey *n.* grey homespun

hodge *v.* move or walk awkwardly or jerkily

hoffin *n.* clumsy, awkward person

hog, hogg *n.* young sheep before first shearing

Hogmanay *pr. n.* New Year's Eve

hollach (aboot) *v.* lark (about)

hoo *adv.* how; why. *cf.* **foo**

hooch *n.* dance (S); loud cry esp. when dancing; *v.* shout when dancing

hooer *n.* whore. *cf.* **hure**

hoodie *n.* the hooded crow

hoodie-craw *n.* hooded or carrion crow

hooever *adv., conj.* however. *cf.* **hoosomever**

hooick *n.* small rick of corn or hay (T). *cf.* **scroo**

hooie *v.* barter, exchange (incl. knives between boys)

hoolet *n.* owl. *cf.* **howlet**

hoomble *adj.* humble

hoose *n.* house; **hoosefu** houseful

Hoose, the *n.* the laird's house

hoosebrakker *n.* burglar

hoose-room *n.* house-room

hoosewifeskip *n.* housewifery

hoosomever, hoosomediver *adv.* however

hoot(s) *excl.* of doubt, contempt, irritation; **hoot awa wi** down with; **hoot ty** oh, yes

hooze, the *n.* disease in sheep and cattle

horn-en, -eyn *n.* best room in two-roomed cottage

hornie *in phr.* **fair hornie** fair play

Hornie *pr. n.* the Devil

horny-gollach *n.* beetle; earwig

horrifie *v.* horrify

horseman's wird *n.* code word revealed on joining horsemen's secret society

horse-troch *n.* horse-trough

hose *n.* stocking; **hose an sheen** (*lit.* shoes and stockings) exaggeration (B)

hotch *See* **hodge**

hotchin *adj.* infested, seething, overrun

hotter *v.* simmer, sputter; *n.* a seething mass; the noise or motion of the crowd; jolting movement; the sound this produces; **gie a vrang hotter** make a wrong move

hottle *n.* hotel

hough *n.* thigh

houk *v.* dig. *cf.* **howk**

houp(ie) *n.* mouthful of food or drink. *See* **howp**

hoven *ppl., adj.* swollen, blown out

howder *n.* sudden gust of wind; *v.* bluster

howdie *n.* midwife; **at howdie haste** at high speed

howdie-wifie *n.* midwife (S)
howe *n.* hollow, valley
Howe o the Mearns *pr. n.* valley of the Mearns
howe-backit *adj.* hollow-backed
howff *n.* a place of resort, or evil repute; a haunt
howfin *n.* clumsy, senseless fellow
howk *v.* dig. *cf.* **houk**
howlet *n.* owl (G1). *cf.* **hoolet**
howm *n.* holm (J)
howp *v.* hope; **howpfu** hopeful
hubber *v.* stammer. *cf.* **habber**
hucky-duck *n.* team game for boys (S)
hud *v.* hold; **hud in wi** keep in with. *cf.* **haud**
hudden *ppl.* held
hudd(e)ry *adj.* unkempt, dishevelled
huick *See* **hooick**
hull *n.* hill
hullick, hullock *n.* hillock, heap
hull-run *adj.* uncouth
hult *v.* halt
hummel, hummle *adj.* without horns
hummel-doddie *adj.* hornless
hummel-doddies *n. pl.* woollen mittens without fingers
hummel-thrummy mittens *adj., n.* unknown, perhaps synonym for above
humoursome *adj.* affably disposed
humph *n.* hump, curvature of the back or spine; *v.* carry, lug, lift something heavy
humphie-backit *adj.* hunchbacked
humsh *v.* eat noisily and greedily, munch. *cf.* **hamsh**

hunger *n.* (**ng** pronounced as in singer) hunger; a mean or avaricious person
hungert *adj.* hungry
hungry *adj.* mean; avaricious; **hungry Angus** mean person
hunker *v.* squat down on the haunches; *n. pl.* the haunches resting on the heels; **doon on yer hunkers**
hunker-slidin *n.* evasive behaviour
hunkit *See* **hank**
hunner *adj., n.* hundred
hunnerwecht *n.* hundredweight
hup *adv.* up
hurb *n.* clumsy, awkward fellow; displeasing person; good-for-nothing
hurdies *n. pl.* the buttocks
hure *n.* whore. *cf.* **hooer**
hurl *n.* lift on a vehicle; the sound of laboured breathing due to phlegm in the throat; **hurl in the throat** (when **r** is pronounced gutturally)
hurlie *n.* barrow; handcart
hurlie-bed *n.* low bed on castors, stored under the box-bed
hurschle *v.* move along a seat without rising (A). *cf.* **hirstle**
huz *See* **hiz**
hyaave *adj.* sallow; grey
hyeuk *See* **heuk**
hyne *See* **hine**
hyow(e) *n., v.* hoe
hypal *adj.* crippled (B1)
hypothec, hale *phr.* whole concern
hyse *See* **hyze**
hyste *v.* hoist, lift
hystergowdie *adv.* head over heels

(T). *cf.* **heelster-gowdie**
hyter *v.* walk unsteadily; stumble
hyze *n.* banter; frolic, sport; a

practical joke; **tae hae a hyze wi** to play a trick on

— **I** —

I *pron. (pro.* **aa)** I. *cf.* **A, Aw**
i *prep.* in
ice-tangle *n.* icicle
idder *adj., n., pron.* other
idelty *n.* idleness; *in pl.* idle frolics
idleset, idleseat *n.* idleness
ile *n.* oil
ile-cake *n.* oil cake (for cattle)
ile-skin *adj., n.* oil skin
ilk, ilka, ilky *adj.* each, every
ill *adj.* ill; bad, *e.g.* **ill widder**; wicked; unkind, cruel; hard, difficult; *adv.* badly; **the ill pairt** hell. *cf.* **ull**
ill-aff *adj.* badly off
ill-deen *adj.* unkindly done
ill-eese *v.* ill use, abuse
ill-farrant *adj.* unpleasant in behaviour; bad-mannered
ill-fashence *n.* curiosity
ill-fashioned *adj.* inquisitive
ill-faured, -faurt *adj.* ugly; unbecoming
ill-gatit, ill-gettit *adj.* badly behaved, perverse
ill-gruntit *adj.* ill-natured
ill-guide *v.* maltreat
ill-hung *adj.* (of the tongue) impudent, sharp
ill-naturt *adj.* ill-natured
ill-pairt, the *pr. n.* Hell
ill-pairtit *ppl.* badly shared out
ill-peyt *adj.* extremely sorry

ill-shakken-up *ppl.* disordered, untidy
ill-teen *n.* bad mood
ill-thochtit *adj.* suspicious; ill-disposed
ill-tongue *v.* abuse
ill-trickit *adj.* mischievous
ill-tricks *n.* mischief
ill-willer *n.* adversary; one who wishes you harm
ill-willie *adj.* ungenerous
ill-win *n.* abusive language (A2); scandal, slander
ily-lamp *n.* oil lamp. *cf.* **crusie**
imaagine, imaigin (A1) *v.* imagine
imaiginashun *n.* imagination
immediantly *adv.* immediately
immis *adj.* variable (B1)
impident *adj.* impudent
impreevement *n.* improvement
impruv *v.* improve
in aboot, come *v. with prep.* approach
in-by(e) *adv.* inside; (with verb of motion) from outside to inside
inch, insch *n.* island; stretch of higher ground in the middle of a plain
inchie *n.* small amount
income *n.* ailment of unknown cause
indraacht *n.* suction of air, breath
induck *v.* induct

inflooensie *n.* influenza
ingan, ingin *n.* onion
ingine *n.* engine
ingle *n.* fire; hearth, fireside; chimney-corner
ingle-cheek *n.* fireside
ingle-lowe *n.* blazing fire
ingle-neuk *n.* chimney corner
in-haudin *adj.* currying favour with one, fawning
inklin *n.* inclination
inower *prep.* in and over
inquar *v.* inquire
inquary *n.* inquiry
In'rurie *pr. n.* Inverurie
insnorl *v.* entangle, entrap
interaistin *adj.* interesting
intil, intill *prep.* into; **intill't** into it
intimat *adj.* intimate

intimmers *n. pl.* intestines; inner workings of anything
intoon *n.* land nearest the farm-house
inveet *n.* invitation (A); *v.* (A1)
inveetor *n.* inventory; value of goods inventoried
I'se *pron. with v.* I shall
I'se warn I'll warrant you, I guarantee
isna *v. neg.* is not
isnint *v. interrog.* is it not?
ither *adj.* other
itmost *adj.* utmost
iv(v)er *adv.* ever
iverleevin *in phr.* **at the iverleevin gallop** at high speed (T)
ivnoo *adv.* just now

— **J** —

jaa *n.* jaw; talk, chatter. *cf.* **jaw**
jabb *v.* fatigue, exhaust; **jabbit** *ppl., adj.* exhausted
jaicket etc. *n.* jacket
jalouse *v.* guess; suspect; imagine
jamaica *n.* seizure, as in the *phr.* **he jist aboot hid a jamaica**
Jamie *pr. n.* deriv. of James
jamph *v.* mock, sneer, jeer
jamphin *n.* mockery
jandies, the *n.* jaundice
jannie *n.* school janitor
jant *n., v.* jaunt
Janwar, Janiwar *n.* January
jassamine *n.* jasmine
jaud *n.* a jade
jaup *v.* fatigue, weary; **jaupit** *ppl.*

weary
jaw *n.* chatter; abusive talk; (at sea) wave; *v.* talk; chatter. *cf.* **jaa**
jaw-hole *n.* sink; hole in the wall for dirty water
jee *v.* to move, stir. *cf.* **gee**
jeedge *v.* judge
jeedgement *n.* judgment (B1)
jeel *adj.* cold as ice; *v.* freeze; congeal
jeely *n.* jam; **jeely pigs** jam jars
Jeems *pr. n.* deriv. of James
jeesty *adj.* normally used in the *neg.*; **nae jeesty** no joking matter
jeho(y) *v.* cease, give over
jelly *adj.* jolly
jibble *n.* small quantity of liquid

49

(contemptuous term)

jibble ower *v.* brim or spill over

jile *n.*, *v.* jail

jilp *v. tr.* spill, cause to splash; *intr.* splash about; *n.* a splash of liquid

jimp *adv.* scarcely

jine *n.*, *v.* join. *cf.* **jyne**

jine-on *n.* playground game

jiner *n.* joiner, carpenter. *cf.* **jyner**

jing-bang *in the phr.* **the hale jing-bang** the whole party or affair

jings *excl.* gosh

jink *n.* sudden turn; *v.* elude; dodge; cheat

jinkie *adj.* jaunty (R)

jinnip(e)rous, jinipperous *adj.* trim, spruce; ingenious; natty; finicky, over-particular

Jinse *pr. n.* Janet

jint *n.* joint

jip *n.* pain (sometimes retributive)

jipperty *n.* jeopardy

jist *adv.* just. *See also* **jyst**

jivvle *n.* a gaol; house as uncomfortable as a gaol

jo *n.* sweetheart (J)

job *v.* prick; **jobby** prickly; **jobby nickles** stinging nettles (B)

Jock *pr. n.* John

Jocktober *n.* October (T)

joco *n.* jovial

Johnny Groatie *n.* small cowrie shell (B). *cf.* **kysie**

joog *n.* jug

joogle *v.* joggle, jerk repeatedly

joost *adv.* just (A2). *cf.* **jist**

joostice *n.* justice (A2)

jorum *n.* whisky jug

jot *n.* job; piece of work; **a jot wark** a job of work

jougs *n. pl.* instrument of public punishment, sometimes in church, consisting of iron collar attached to wall and placed around offender's neck

jouk *v.* dodge, duck, swerve; **jouk an lat the jaw gae by** yield to circumstances

joukerie pawkery *n.* trickery, roguery

jow *n.* sound of bell; *v.* move with a rocking motion; ring

jummle *n.*, *v.* jumble

junny *n.* wrench; severe jolt

jyne *v.* join

jyner *n.* joiner, carpenter. *cf.* **jiner**

jyst *n.* joist

— K —

(The initial *k* is usually pronounced before *n*)

kail *n.* colewort; **kail runt** kail stalk; also term of abuse; **caul kail het** *(fig.)* a stale story; **kail throu the reek** severe criticism or scolding

kaim, kame *n.*, *v.* comb

kebbuck *n.* round of cheese

keckle *v.* cackle, chuckle

keeble *See* **kibble**

keech *See* **kich**

keek *n.*, *v.* peep

keek-a-bo *n.* the game of peep-bo

keel *n.* any marking substance *(e.g.* for sheep) (M2)
keeng *n.* king
keengdom *n.* kingdom
keeperin *n.* the work of a game-keeper
keepit *v. pt.* kept
keep tee *v.* keep up
keer *n., v.* cure
keeriosity *n.* curiosity
keerious *adj.* curious, strange; keen, desirous
keest *v. pt.* cast. *cf.* **ceest**
kell *n.* caul; the puckered part of a woman's **mutch** which rises over the back part of the head
ken *v.* know; **kenna** don't know
kenle, kennle *v.* kindle; **kennelt** ablaze with colour
kennlin *n.* kindling
kenspeckle *adj.* easily recognised
kep *n.* cap; *v.* meet, catch, intercept; **kep the win** keep the wind out
kerridge *n.* carriage
keuk *v.* cook. *cf.* **kyeuk**
kibble *adj.* strong, sturdy; well-built; active; agile
kich *n.* excrement; *v.* defecate
kil(l) *n.* wooden tripod round which hay- or cornstack is built
kilt *v.* tuck up (skirts, sleeves etc.)
kiltimmer *n.* term of abuse for a woman of doubtful character; a rough woman; virago
kiltit *adj.* kilted
kimmer *n.* a gossip; married woman; wife
kin' *adj.* kind; *n.* kind, nature, sort; *adv.* rather; **caal kin'** rather cold
kinallie *n.* (Fr. *canaille*) mob

kindlin *adj.* blushing, ruddy (J)
kine *v.* cattle (A)
kinlin *n.* kindling
kinkhoast *n.* whooping cough
kinsh *v.* twist; wind (a rope)
kire *n.* choir. *cf.* **kyre**
kirk *n.* church
kirkit (to be) *ppl.* (to be) at church
kirkton, -toon *n.* village or hamlet with parish church
kirk-yaird *n.* churchyard
kirn *n.* butter churn; mess, state of confusion; *v.* churn butter; stir, mix up; work in slovenly manner
kirsen *v.* christen
kirsenin *n.* christening
kist *n.* chest; coffin; *v.* to put in a coffin
kitchie *n.* kitchen; seasoning, an addition to plain fare; **tak a piece an mak kitchie o yer egg**
kitchie-deem *n.* kitchen-maid
kite *n.* stomach. *cf.* **kyte**
kitlin *See* **kittlin**
kittle *v.* tickle; anger, annoy; upset; *adj.* skilful; (of a person) touchy; (of a task) tricky, difficult, not easily managed; (of an issue) controversial, sensitive
kittlesome *adj. See* **kittle**
kittlet (up) *adj., ppl.* excited
kittlie *adj.* tickly; ticklish
kittlin *n.* kitten. *cf.* **kitlin**
kittly *See* **kittlie**
klyack *See* **clyack**
knablich *n.* small hillock (A2)
knablick *adj.* nobbly
knack *v.* to knock
knag *n.* knob or pin
knap *n.* knoll; *v.* knock; snap with

the teeth; starve (B1); **knap-at-the-win** a mere bite (ref. to stray dog) (M2)

knapdarloch *n.* dung-matted hair or hide on the hind-quarters of cattle or sheep

kneef *adj.* healthy and active

kneevlick *n.* a big lump (of cheese, beef etc). *cf.* **knyte**

kneggum *n.* sharp or disagreeable smell or flavour

kneip on *v.* press on

knibloch *n.* clod of earth; lump (used as mild insult)

knicht *n.* knight

knotty-tams *n.* dish of boiled milk with meal

knowe *n.* knoll, steep field; head

knowe-heid *n.* top of a hillock

knowpert *n.* crowberry

knyte *n.* large piece, lump

korter *n.* quarter; quarter of oatcake. *cf.* **corter**

kowe *See* **cowe**

kowk *v.* retch; vomit

kwintra, kwintry *n.* country

kwite, kwyte *n.* coat; oilskin skirt with bib worn by women in the herring curing yards (B)

kyaaks *n. pl.* cakes (usually oatcakes); **kyaak o breid** round of oatcakes

kyaard *n.* tinker; *v.* abuse; **kyaard-tonguet** given to loose or unwholesome talk

Kyack *pr. n.* nickname for the village of Pitsligo

kyarn *n.* large heap, cairn. *cf.* **carn**

kye *n. pl.* cows

kyeuk *n., v.* cook. *cf.* **keuk**

kyp(i)e *n.* scooped out hollow in ground for use in game of marbles

kyre *n.* choir. *cf.* **kire**

kysie *n.* small cowrie shell (B). *cf.* **Johnny Groatie, calfie's mooie**

kyte *n.* stomach. *cf.* **kite**

kythe *v.* show, display, reveal (B1)

— L —

laad *See* **lad**

lab *v.* lap

lab(b)ach *n.* long story about nothing (R); small quantity to drink (B1)

labster *n.* fisher term for lobster. *cf.* **partan**

lacer *n.* shoe-lace. *cf.* **pint**

lach *n., v.* laugh. *cf.* **lauch**

lachter *n.* laughter; a sitting of eggs. *cf.* **lauchter**

lad *n.* lad; boy-friend; sweetheart;

in phr. **a bit o a lad** rascal; lady's man; **lad o pairts** clever lad from small country school

laddie *n.* small boy

lade *n.* canal carrying water to a mill; load; lead (metal) (S)

ladle *n.* small wooden box with long handle, formerly in use in collecting offerings in church

laft *n.* loft; upper storey; church gallery

lagamachie *See* **lamgamachie**

laich, laigh *adj.* low

laich-in *adv.* in a low voice

laichy-braid *n.* short, stocky person or animal

laid *n.* load

laid *ppl.* (of a crop) flattened

laidle *See* **ladle**

laig *v.* talk idly. *cf.* **lyaag**

laigh *n.* stretch of low-lying ground

laimiter *n.* a cripple

lair *n.* mud, mire; burial place reserved in graveyard; *v.* sink in bog or mud

laird *n.* squire; landowner

lairdskip *n.* lordship; right as proprietor

lairge *adj.* unrestrained in talk

lairn *v.* learn; teach. *cf.* **leern**

lairnin *n.* learning (J). *cf.* **lear**

lair-stane *n.* gravestone

laist *adj., v.* last. *cf.* **lest**

laiteran *See* **lettrin**

lallan *adj.* lowland

lame *n.* crockery, earthenware; shard of earthenware

la(m)gamachie *n.* anything long and loose in movement; rigmarole

lamikie *n.* little lamb

Lammas *n.* beginning of August, a Scottish term

lammie *n.* lamb

lan *n., v.* land

lane *pred. adj., adv.* alone. *cf.* **leen**

lang *adj., v.* long

lang acre *adj., n.* grass verge at roadside (T)

langer *n.* languor, tedium; **haud oot o langer** keep from boredom, amuse

lang-gane *adj.* long-gone

lang-heidit *adj.* intelligent; shrewd

langidge *n.* language; words

lang-leggit *adj.* long-legged

lang-nebbit, -nibbit *adj.* prying; critical; acute in understanding; (of words) difficult to pronounce or understand

langsome *adj.* wearisome

langsyne *adv.* long ago

lanner *n.* land-side horse

lanside *n.* side of the plough next the unploughed land

lanstell *n.* parapet of a bridge

lant *v.* jeer

lanter (wi) *v.* leave in the lurch (with) (B)

lap *v. pt.* leaped

lapper *v.* (of water) lap

larrie, larry *n.* long, flat low wagon, horse-drawn or motorised; lorry

lass(ie), lassock *n.* girl

lassikie, lassockie *n.* young girl

lat *v. pr., pt.* let. *cf.* **leet, loot**

latch *adj.* slow; tardy; lazy (M2)

latten *ppl.* let; **latten be** let alone

latter-oot *n.* the letter-out, the one who feeds in the straw in rope-twisting (F)

lauch *v.* laugh; **lauchen at** laughed at

lauchter *See* **lachter**

lave *n.* the rest; the remainder

lave *v.* leave (S). *cf.* **lea, ley**; *v.* ladle out (B1)

laverock, lavrock *n.* skylark. *cf.* **livrock**

lawbor, lawbour *n.* labour

lawfu *adj.* lawful

lawin *n.* tavern-bill; reckoning

lawlands *n. pl.* lowlands
lawvyer *n.* lawyer
lay *v.* to put more iron on a sock or coulter
lay-aff *n.* harangue; rigmarole; *v.* talk volubly, spout
lay on *v.* work hard; beat severely
lea *v.* to leave (A1). *cf.* **ley, lave**
lead *v.* cart in the corn from the field (A1)
leadin *n.* carting hay, straw (S)
leal *adj., n.* loyal; **leal-loved** well-loved
leam *n.* gleam
lean *in phr.* **lean yersel doon** take a seat
lean-tee *n.* lean-to, shed
lear *n.* learning
leasure *n.* leisure. *cf.* **leesure**
leavie-oh *n.* catching game
ledder *v.* thrash, belabour
lee *n.* lie
leear *n.* liar
leeberary *n.* library
leeberty *n.* liberty
Leebie *pr. n.* deriv. of Elizabeth
leebral *adj., n.* liberal
leed *n.* lead
leeft *v. pt., ppl.* left
leefu-lane *adj.* all alone
leein *ppl., n.* lying
lee-lang (day) *adj.* livelong (day)
leems *n. pl.* implements; apparatus
leen *adj.* alone; **ma leen** by myself; **himleen** by himself; **themleen** by themselves
leenity *n.* lenity, mercy
leepie *n.* measure of oats; wooden box-shaped measure for horse's feed of corn

leerie(-man) *n.* lamp-lighter
leern *v.* learn; teach. *cf.* **lairn**
leernin *n.* learning. *cf.* **lear**
leernt *adj.* learned
leery-bows *in phr.* **tae gang by the leery-bows** (B1) to do mischief
leese-me-on *phr.* expression of pleasure in, or affection for someone/thing; **leese-me-on the Enzie fowk** (C)
leeshens, leeshins *n.* licence
leesome *adj.* pleasant
leesure *n.* leisure. *cf.* **leasure**
leet *n.* list; *v. pt.* let (A1); **leet at him** assailed him. *cf.* **lat, loot**
leeterary *adj.* literary
leethe *n.* a shelter. *cf.* **lythe**; *in phr.* **in the leethe o ye** through your influence (B)
leetiny *n.* litany
leevin *n.* living being; person
lefts-an-richts *n.* soup made from turnip and potato
leg *v.* to walk quickly; *pt.* **leggit**; **draw ma leg** pull my leg
leid *n.* language; dialect
len *n.* loan; *v.* lend; **tak a len o** take advantage of (M2)
lench *v.* launch
lenth *n.* length
lerb *n.* lick, mouthful of fluid (A1); *v.* lap with tongue
lest *adj., n., v.* last. *cf.* **laist**
let off *v.* break wind behind
leuch *v. pt.* laughed
leuk *v.* look
ley *n.* lea, unploughed land; grassland; **ley-corn** oats grown on ploughed-up grassland; *v.* leave (S). *cf.* **lea, lave**

lib *v.* castrate
lichen *n.* fog
licht *adj., n.* light; *v.* light, alight;
  licht on *v.* land on; **let licht that**
  let it be known that
lichthoose *n.* lighthouse
lichtlifie *v.* to make light of; belittle
lichtnin *n.* lightning
lichts *n. pl.* lungs (human/animal)
lichtsome *adj.* pleasant
lick *n.* smack, blow; **at a gweed
  lick** at high speed; *v.* thrash
lickened (wi) *ppl.* likened (to)
lickin *n.* thrashing
lickly *adj., adv.* likely
licky *adj.* lucky
lie-in *n.* the part of an attic room
  lying under slope of roof
lie-money *n.* money retained by
  employer for lie-time
lie-time *n.* the time before pay day
  for making up accounts, in which
  work has been done but payment
  remains or lies over till next pay
  day
lift *n.* sky
lifter *n.* one who gathers grain to
  make sheaves. *cf.* **gaitherer**
liftit *adj., ppl.* elevated; overjoyed
lig *v.* (literary) lie, recline, rest
like, likein *adv.* (used at the end of
  sentences to modify or intensify)
  that's to say; do you mean?
likein *ppl.* as; *adv.* like as; for
  example
liken tae *adj.* apt to
liket, likit *v. pt.* liked
limerin *n.* thrashing
limmer *n.* woman of loose morals;
  playful or *derog.* term applied to

a female; rascal
linder, linner *n.* woollen or flannel
  undershirt
ling *n.* long thin grass (J)
linga *n.* lingo
linglairy *n.* long story, rigmarole
  (B)
link *v.* walk hand-in-hand, arm-in-
  arm; **link at** work vigorously
links *n. pl.* chain by which a pot
  hung over a fire from the **crook**
linn *n.* precipice over which water
  falls; the cascade of water
linth *n.* length. *cf.* **lenth**
lintie *n.* linnet
lip *v.* to be full to the brim; brim
  over
lippen *v.* trust; depend on
lippie *n.* fourth of a peck
lirk *n.* crease, fold. *cf.* **lurk**
list *v.* enlist
lit *v.* let. *cf.* **lat**
litchie *adj.* light-headed
lith *n.* joint; segment
little ane, littlin *n.* small child
liveliheid *n.* livelihood
liver *v.* unload a ship's cargo
livrock *n.* skylark. *cf.* **laverock**
loaf *n.* bread
loan *n.* a small common;
  uncultivated land about a
  homestead
loaning(s) *n.* village common green
lochan *n.* small loch
locker *n.* small compartment in the
  end of a chest
lod *excl.* Lord!
lodesteen *n.* magnet
lodomy *n.* laudanum
loe *v.* love

lood *adj.* loud
loon *n.* lad; boy
loonikie *n.* little boy
loose *n.* louse
loosie *adj.* lousy
loot *v.* bend, bow, make obeisance; let; *v. pt.* permitted, let; **loot ye doon** sit down
loo-warm *adj.* lukewarm
lordlifu *adj.* sumptuous; extravagantly liberal
losh *excl.* euphemism for Lord
loshins *excl. of surprise* (A)
loshtie (be here) *excl. of surprise*
loshtie-goshtie guide's *excl.* good Lord guide us!
loss *v.* lose. *cf.* **tine**
loup *v.* leap. *cf.* **lowp**
Lourenkirk *pr. n.* Laurencekirk (S)
low door *adj., n.* entrance at ground floor level
lowe *n., v.* glow, flame, blaze; **sweer blue lowes** swear vehemently
lown *adj.* sheltered, unfrequented; (of weather) calm, still
lowp *n.* leap; *v.* leap. *cf.* **loup**
lowrie *n.* long, heavy, steel hook used on the market floor
Lowrin *pr. n.* Lawrence
lowse *v.* unyoke, leave off work; loose, loosen; *adj.* loose
lowser *n.* one who cuts bands on sheaves during threshing
lowsin-shooer *n.* heavy shower of rain putting a stop to out-door work on farm (T)
lowsin-time *n.* the end of the day's work; the time for unyoking horses
lowss *adj.* suffering from diarrhoea
lowssen *v.* loosen
lozen *n.* window-pane
luckpenny *n.* sum of money given for luck, *e.g.* returned by the seller to the buyer as discount
lucky daddy *n.* grandfather (A2)
lucky minnie *n.* grandmother (B1)
ludgement *n.* a place to rest
luft *v.* lift
lug *n.* ear; handle
lug-babs *n.* earrings; knot of ribbons over the ears
luggie *n.* small wooden vessel with handles, for table use
lum *n.* chimney
lum-hat *n.* black tile hat
lumbaga *n.* lumbago
lundies, landies *n.* double ropes for skipping
lunt *n., v.* smoke, draw
lurk *n.* fold, crease. *cf.* **lirk**
lut *v.* let; **lutten** *ppl.* let. *cf.* **lat**
luve *n.* love
lyaach *adj.* low. *cf.* **laich, laigh**
lyaag *v.* to talk idly and at length. *cf.* **laig**
lyart *adj.* streaked with grey
lyen *ppl.* lain
lyin-holes *n.* patches of corn or barley flattened by heavy rain and unsuitable for the binder (T)
lyin-shafts *n. pl.* main beams under box cart (F)
lyter *v.* loiter
lythe *n.* shelter; *adj.* sheltered

— M —

ma *pron.* me; my

maa *n.* seagull. *cf.* **maw, myaave**

maasie *n.* knitted jersey

mackerels' backs an meers' tails *phr.* high cirrus clouds (B)

mad *adj.* angry

madden-dreem *n.* madness; folly; mad pranks (B1)

maet *n.* food; **aff o's maet** off his food; *v.* feed; **maetit** fed

maet-haill *adj.* able to take one's food

mager *prep.* in spite of; *v.* act in spite of; master (B1). *cf.* **mauger**

Maggie Rennie *in phr.* **a different Maggie Rennie** a different kettle of fish (B)

maggot *n.* whim, caprice, fancy

maggotive *adj.* full of whims, moody

maiden *n.* designation once given to farmer's eldest daughter

maik *n.* halfpenny

maikst *n.* a halfpennyworth

maillyer *n.* the quantity of oatmeal received from the mill at one time

main *n., v.* moan

mainners *n.* manners. *cf.* **menners**

Mains o Backchines *pr. n.* fictitious farm representing an inferior fee (T)

mair *adj.* more

Mairch *n.* month of March

mairch *n.* boundary; *n., v.* march

mairch-dyke *n.* boundary wall

mairket *n.* market. *cf.* **mercat**

mairrage *n.* marriage; wedding. *cf.* **mairritch**

mairritch *n.* marriage; wedding. *cf.* **mairrage**

mairry, mairry on (to) *v.* marry; *ppl.* **mairret, mairrit**

mairt *n.* ox killed at Martinmas for winter use (A). *cf.* **mart**

mairt *See* **mart**

maist *adj.* most; *adv.* **maistly**

maister *n.* master; stale urine used as detergent; **maister-pig** jar containing such urine; *v.* master

mait *See* **maet**

maitter *n.* matter

mak *v.* make. **mak nae odds** make no difference; **maksna, disna mak** does not matter; **mak yer feet yer freen** it's best to go

maker, makker *n.* poet

makins (o) *n.* makings (of)

mak on *n.* pretence; *v.* pretend

malagruze *v.* bruise

mallie *n.* fulmar

mammy *n.* mother

man *n.* husband; man

mang *v.* long for eagerly; **mangin tae** dying to

mannie *n.* man; *pl.* **mannies**. *cf.* **mennies**

mannikie *n.* little man; term of endearment for small boy

mant *n., v.* stammer

mappie *n.* rabbit (used on board ship to avoid taboo word, *rabbit*)

mardle *n.* crowd

Marget *pr. n.* Margaret
markness *n.* darkness (A2)
marless *adj.* not matching
maroonjus *adj.* harsh; outrageous (A)
marra-been *n.* marrowbone
marra, marrow *n.* match, equal
marrowless *adj.* unmarried
mart *n.* ox killed at Martinmas; market; building used for agricultural auctions; such a sale. *cf.* **mairt**
Martimas *n.* Martinmas
masel(lie) *pron.* myself; *pred. adj., adv.* by myself, alone
mashlie *n.* mixed grain, peas and oats
mask *v.* infuse (tea)
mason's mear *n.* trestle
mauger *prep.* in spite of (M). *cf.* **mager**
maumie *adj.* mellow
maun *v.* must; **mauna** *v. neg.* must not
maut *n.* malt; **the maut was abeen the meal** (leading to intoxication)
mavis *n.* thrush (M)
maw *n.* mouth; seagull (M1); *v.* mow, cut with a scythe
mawkin *n.* hare (A, M). *cf.* **myaakin**
mawmie *See* **maumie**
maxie *n.* a maximus, the gravest error in Latin prose composition
maze *n.* state of amazement
meal *n.* oatmeal; **meal-an-ale** mixture of oatmeal, ale, sugar and whisky, traditional fare at harvest-home celebrations; the celebration itself
meal-bowie *n.* barrel for oatmeal
meal-bunk (S) *See* **meal-kist**
mealer (S) *See* **meal-kist**
mealie puddin *n.* oatmeal pudding
meal-kist *n.* meal-chest in which farm servant stored meal and other eatables
mealock *n.* crumb of oatcakes etc.
mealy-mou't *adj.* mealy-mouthed
meangie *adj.* tight with money, mingy
mear *n.* mare. *cf.* **meer**
meat *n.* food (J). *cf.* **maet**
mebbe *adv.* perhaps
meelyin *n.* million
meelyinaire *n.* millionaire
meen *n.* moon. *cf.* **mune**
meen *v.* pity
meeninit *n.* mignonette
meenister *n.* minister. *cf.* **minaister**
meenit *n.* minute
meenlicht *n.* moonlight. *cf.* **munelicht**
meent *ppl.* meant
meer *n.* moor. *cf.* **muir;** *n.* mare. *cf.* **mear**
meesic *n.* music
meesic-fan *n.* musical instrument
meet *in phr.* **meet the cat** have a spell of bad luck (B)
meeve *v.* move
meggie-monyfeet *n.* centipede
meggins alive *excl. of surprise* (M1)
megreem, megrim *n.* migraine
megstie me *excl. of surprise* (M1)
meikle *adj.* big, large, great. *cf.* **muckle**
mell *n.* mallet, heavy hammer; *v.*

mix; meddle

melt *n.* the spleen

mengyie *n.* crowd, huddled mass (A)

menner *n.* manner; *pl.* **menners** manners; **weel-mennert** well-mannered

mennies *n. pl.* men (A1). *cf.* **mannies**

mense *n.* common-sense

mensefu *adj.* courteous, respectful; well-bred

menseless *adj.* rough, unmannerly

mercat *n.* market. *cf.* **mairket**

merch *v.* march. *cf.* **mairch**

merchan *n.* shopkeeper, retailer

merciment *n.* mercy; tolerance

merdle *n.* confused crowd of people or animals. *cf.* **mardle**

Merry Dancers *pr. n.* aurora borealis. *cf.* **Northern Lights**

mertyreese *v.* torture as a martyr

mervel *n.* marvel

messages *n. pl. in phr.* **go the messages** do the shopping

Mey *n.* month of May

micht *n.* might

michty me *excl. of surprise*

midden *n.* dunghill

midden-bree *n.* moisture from dunghill

midden-plunk *n.* wooden plank up which barrowload of dung could be wheeled up midden

midden-tap *n.* top of the dunghill

midder *n.* mother. *cf.* **mither**

middle *v.* meddle

middlin *adj., adv.* middling; fair(ly), moderate(ly), semi-

midgeck *n.* midge

midgie *n.* midge

midrig *n.* mid ridge

mids *n.* middle, midst; the open furrow between two ridges; a halfway point; *adv.* halfway

mildyow *n.* mildew

milk-broth *n.* dish made with milk and barley

milker *n.* milk cow

milkness *n.* the business of preparing milk (A2)

mill *See* **mull**

millert *See* **mullart**

milt *n.* spleen of an ox

mim, mim-like *adj.* prim

mim-mou'd *adj.* prim

min *n.* man (used as form of address); **hey, min!**

minaister *n.* minister (A2)

mind, min' *n.* mind; *v.* remember; remind

mink *n.* noose

minna *v. neg.* might not. *cf.* **mithna**

min(n)eer, mineerum *n.* great noise; fuss

minnie *n.* mother; pet name for a mother

minnon *n.* minnow; any small fresh-water fish

minse *See* **mense**

mint *n.* aim, intention; *v.* attempt, endeavour; *ppl.* **mintit** (C)

mirk *n.* darkness

mirky *adj.* smiling; merry

mirles, the *n. pl.* measles

mirra-hine, merry hyne *int.* off you go and good riddance

misca *v.* speak ill of; abuse; slander

mischeef *n.* mischief

miscomfit *v.* displease, offend;

59

disappoint (B1)

misdoot *v.* doubt, disbelieve

misfortnat *adj.* unfortunate

mishachlt *adj., ppl.* deformed; misshapen (B)

mishanter *n.* accident

mislippen *v.* neglect (A); mismanage; deceive (M); distrust (A2)

missaucre *v.* destroy, hurt severely

missie *n.* teacher

missionar *n.* missionary

mistaen *ppl.* mistaken

mistak *n.* mistake

misthrive *v.* fare badly; *ppl.* misthriven

mith *v.* might; **mithna, mithnin** might not. *cf.* **minna**

mither *n.* mother (A); **mither wit** native wit. *cf.* **midder**

Mither Tap *pr. n.* a peak of the hill, Bennachie

mitten *v.* grab hold of, seize

mixter *n.* mixture

mixter-maxter *adv.* in a state of confusion; *n.* mixture

mizzer, mizzor *n., v.* measure

mizzerment *n.* measurement

moch *n.* moth

moch-aeten *adj.* moth-eaten

moch-baas *n. pl.* moth balls

mochie *adj.* muggy, misty, damp; moth-eaten

moderate *v.* to preside at a Presbyterian Church court or at the election, calling or ordination of a minister

moderator *n.* one who presides at a Presbyterian Church court

modren *adj.* modern

moggan, moggin *n.* stocking (sometimes used as purse); footless stocking

moleskins *n. pl.* trousers of thick cotton

molie *n.* molecatcher

'mon *prep.* among

Monanday *n.* Monday (A)

moniment *n.* a spectacle

mony *adj.* many; **mony een** many a one

monyfaulds *n. pl.* entrails (consisting of many folds), intestines

moo *n.* large rick of hay or corn; **moo-bag** feeding-bag for horses; **moofae** mouthful; **moo o hairst** opening of harvest. *cf.* **mou**

moo-ban *v.* utter, articulate; mention (B1)

moocher *n.* scrounger

moold *n., v.* mould

mools *n. pl.* moulds; earth of a grave

moose *n.* mouse

moosewob *n.* cobweb

morn, the *adv.* tomorrow; **the morn's nicht** tomorrow night

mornin *n.* morning dram

mortifiet *adj., ppl.* humiliated

moss *n.* moor where peats are dug

mossin *n.* peat-cutting

mou *n.* mouth; **moufu** *n.* mouthful

moulter, mouter *n.* multure, miller's fee for grinding corn

mowdie(warp), mowdiewart *n.* mole

mowse *adj. used in neg.* **nae mowse, nae a mowse concairn** no joking matter; not safe; **nae**

mowse job no easy job
mowser *n.* moustache
moyen *n.* influence, means; *v.* accomplish by means; allure
muck *n.* dung; dirt; refuse; *v.* to clean a byre or stable; **muck the line** clear putrid bait from fishing line
muck-barra *n.* manure barrow
muckit *adj.* dirty
muckle *adj.* large; *adj., n., adv.* much
muckle-boukit pregnant (B1); burly; bulky
muddim *n.* madam
mudgeon *n.* facial expression; **he gied nae mudgeons he heard** (M2)
muggy, muggly *adj.* (of weather) drizzly and foggy
muir *n.* moor. *cf.* **meer**
muir-cock *n.* moorcock
muirlan *n.* moorland
muldoan, muldoon *n.* the basking shark
mulfa *n.* tinful *(deriv.* from **mill** a tin) (R)
mull *n.* meal- or threshing-mill; *n.* snuff-box; tin box with a lid; **snuff mull** snuff box. *cf.* **mill**
mullart, muller(t) *n.* miller

mullart's wird *n.* supposed secret password among millers
multiteed *n.* multitude
mum, mummle *v.* mumble
mump *v.* grumble
mune *n.* moon. *cf.* **meen**
munelicht *n.* moonlight
munsie *n.* the knave in cards; someone in a fix (B1); contemptible figure (A2)
munt *v.* mount
murgeon, murjin *n.* grimace. *cf.* **mudgeon**
murky *adj.* dark
murle *v.* crumble; **murly tuck** oatcakes crumbled into milk
murlin *n.* basket fitting into top of the fish-wife's creel
murn *v.* mourn
murnins *n. pl.* mourning clothes
musaeum *n.* museum
mutch *n.* woman's cap
mutchkin *n.* liquid measure equal to English pint
muther *n., v.* murder
muv *v.* move (B1). *cf.* **meeve**
myaakin *n.* hare. *cf.* **mawkin**
myaave *n.* seagull (Fraserburgh) (B)
myowte *n.* sound; whisper; murmur

—— N ——

na *adj., adv.* no. Also used to turn verb *neg. e.g.* **cudna, camna**
naarhan *adv.* nearly. *cf.* **nearhan**
nab *v.* seize; steal; take into custody
nabal *See* **nabble**

nabble *n.* churlish person; *adj.* ill-natured, churlish; grasping
nace *adj.* destitute
nackety *adj.* neat; *n.* a neat person
nacky *adj.* dexterous, adroit, skilful

61

nae *adj.* no, not; **nae een** no one; **nae weel** not well, ill

naehandy *pred. adj., adv.* a lot of; of great size; **there wis cyaaks naehandy, a queue naehandy**

naet *adj.* neat

naether *conj., pron., adj.* neither. *cf.* **nether, naither**

naething *n.* nothing

naewye *adv.* nowhere; on no account (S)

naftie, naphtie *n.* liquor (from Eng. naphtha)

nain, nown *adj.* own; **haud yer nain** hold your own; **yer nainsel** one's own self

nairra *adj.* narrow

nairra-myn(d)it *adj.* narrow-minded

naisty *adj.* nasty

naither *conj., pron., adj.* neither. *cf.* **nether, naether**

naithmost *adj.* undermost; **naithmost wynin** lower part of field (F)

naitional *adj.* national

naitral *adj.* natural

naitur *n.* nature

naitur-girss *n.* natural herbage

nakit *adj.* naked. *cf.* **nyaukit**

nammle *adj.* enamel (B)

nane *adv., pron.* none

napkin, naipkin *n.* pocket handkerchief

napper *n.* head

napron *n.* apron (B1)

nar *adj., adv.* near(ly); mean (B1)

na-say *n.* denial; refusal; *v.* deny, refuse

natheless *adv.* nevertheless

natur, Natur *n.* Nature. *cf.* **naitur**

navus-bore *n.* knot-hole in wood

near-beg(y)aun *adj.* miserly

near-beg(y)aunness *n.* niggardliness

nearhan *adv.* nearly; close by. *cf.* **naarhan**

neb *n.* beak; nose

necessar *adj.* necessary

nedder, nedderin *pron., conj.* neither

neebour *See* **neiper**

Neebra *pr. n.* village of Newburgh near Ellon

needcessity *n.* necessity, need

needsna *v. neg.* does not need

neen *pron.* none; *adv.* at all; **nae neen pleased**

neep *n.* turnip; *v.* to feed turnips

neep-click *n.* tool for pulling turnips (F)

neeper *See* **neiper**

neep-hasher *n.* implement for slicing turnips for fodder

neep-heid *n.* fool

neep(ie)-lantrin *n.* turnip-lantern

neep-pluck *n.* tool for pulling turnips (F). *cf.* **neep-click**

neep-reet *n.* land cleared of turnips for grain crop to follow (F)

neep-rinner *n.* old fashioned imple-ment for hoeing turnips

neep-rinnin *n.* turnip-hoeing

neep waatch *n.* turnip watch

neer-dee-weel *n.* ne'er-do-well

ne'er *adv.* never

neest, neesht *adj.* next. *cf.* **neist**

neffy *n.* nephew

negleat *v.* neglect (B1)

negleck *v.* neglect

neibour *See* **neiper**

neibourheid *n.* friendly relations between neighbours

neiper, neipor *n., v.* neighbour. *cf.* **neebour, neibour, neeper**

neiper-like *adj.* neighbourly

neist *adj.* next. *cf.* **neest**

neive *n.* fist; **neivefu** fistful; **steekit neives** clenched fists. *cf.* **nieve, niv**

nep *adj.* hairy (B)

nepkin *n.* napkin

nerra *adj. See* **nairra**

nervish *adj.* nervous

nether *conj., pron., adj.* neither. *cf.* **naither**

nettercap *n.* spider. *cf.* **ettercap**

neuk *n.* corner

neukit *adj.* having corners, crooked

new *adv.* newly

new-fangelt *adj.* newly invented; innovatory

newlins *adv.* newly, recently

news-gizzent *adj.* news-starved

news(e) *n., v.* chat

newsy *adj.* chatty; full of news

nib *n.* nose, beak. *cf.* **neb, niz, nob**

nibawa *adj.* snappy, crusty

nicher *n.* (of horses) neigh, whinny

nicht *n.* night

nicht-boun *adj.* overtaken by night

nick *n.* notch; *v.* make pregnant (B). *cf.* **bairn**

Nick, Aul *pr. n.* the Devil

nicket *adj.* disappointed

nickum *n.* mischievous boy

Nicky Cloots *pr. n.* the Devil

nicky-tams *n. pl.* buckled leather straps worn below the knee by farmworkers. *cf.* **waal-tams**

niev(e) *n.* fist. *cf.* **neive**

niffer *v.* to barter, bargain; exchange

nimp *n.* a very small part

nip *n.* advantage; speed; **deil a nip** not a bit (M2)

nippit *adj.* tight-fitting; curt in manner

nippock(ie) *n.* very small piece

nirl *v.* cause to shrink or shrivel; **nirlt** *ppl.* shrivelled

niv *See* **neive**

niver, nivver *adv.* never; **nivver een!** *excl.* certainly not!

niz *n.* nose (A). *cf.* **nib, nob**

nizzin *n.* drubbing; sharp reception

no *adv.* not (C1, G1, S). *cf.* **nae**; (used as interrogative after positive statement) isn't he, hasn't it etc. (A2)

nob *n.* nose (A). *cf.* **nib, niz**

nocht *n.* nought, nothing

nochtie *n.* puny in size. *cf.* **noughtie**

nominat *ppl.* nominated

non *n.* name given in mid 18th century to non-intrusion section of the Church of Scotland

noo *adv.* now; **noo an than** now and then; *also* **noo an aan, noos an aans**

nooadays *adv.* nowadays

nor *conj., quasi-prep.* than

norlan *adj.* northland

Noroway *pr. n.* Norway

noshun *n.* notion, idea; **noshun o** romantic fancy for; liking for

nosy-wax *n.* simpleton (B1)

not, nott *v. pt., ppls.* needing, needed; had to; **notna** did not need

notice *v.* take care of (A1)

notionate *adj.* opinionative

noughtie *adj.* puny, trifling. *cf.*
   nochtie

nown *adj.* own

nowt *n.* (collective) neat, cattle;
   (sing.) an ox, steer (A1)

nummer *n.* number

nyaakit *adj.* naked. *cf.* **nyaukit**

nyatter *v.* speak fretfully, angrily;
   grumble (A, M1)

nyattery *adj.* peevish, grumbling,
   ill-tempered

nyaukit *adj.* naked. *cf.* **nyaakit**

nyod *excl.* euphemism for God

—— **O** ——

o, o' *prep.* of; on; **o' the tae han, o'**
   the tither on the one hand, on
   the other

obaidient *adj.* obedient

objeck *n., v.* object

obleege *v.* oblige

occupee *v.* occupy

och *excl.* oh

ocht *n.* aught, anything; *v.* **ought**;
   ochtna ought not

od *excl.* God

odder *adj., n., pron.* other. *cf.* **ither**

odds *n.* difference

o'ercome *n.* burden of a discourse

o'erleuk *v.* overlook

oes *n. pl.* grand-children (M)

o'ertak *v.* overtake

offeeshyat *v.* officiate

offen *v.* offend

offisher *n.* officer

oilie *n.* fisherman's oilskin frock
   (B); oil lamp

'oman *n.* woman. *cf.* **umman**

on *conj.* (used with *pt. ppl.*)
   without; **on-been** without being;
   on-hed without having; **on-deen**
   without doing

on *prep.* **on aboot** talking about;

on for keen on; in the mood for;
   far on, weel on tipsy

on- *prefix.* un- (C). *See* **oon-**

on-cairry *n.* carry-on

ondeemas *adj.* extraordinary

onding *n.* a heavy fall of rain or
   snow

ongaun *n.* activity; *in pl.*
   proceedings

ongauns *n.* goings-on

ongrutten *adj.* without shedding
   tears

onleet *adv.* without a word of a lie

onless *conj.* unless

onmynit (o) *adj.* unmindful (of)

ontill, oontill *conj.* till; *prep.* on to

ontirin *adj.* untiring

onwal *adj.* annual

onwuttin *adj.* unaware, abstracted

ony *adv., pron.* any; *adv.* at all; **gin**
   it's ony weet if it's wet at all

onybody *n., pron.* anybody

onyeen *n., pron.* anyone

onyroad *adv.* anyway

onything *n., pron.* anything

onywye *adv.* anyway; anywhere;
   anyhow

oo *n.* wool

oof *n.* Moray Firth name for the monkfish. *cf.* **caithick**
ook, ouk *n.* week
ool *v.* treat harshly; *ppl.* **oolt**
oolet *n.* owl (A)
oonbapteest *adj.* unbaptised
ooncanny *adj.* uncanny; dangerous
ooncarin *adj.* uncaring
oonchancie *adj.* uncanny; risky, not safe to meddle with
ooncommon *adj.* uncommon
oonder *prep.* under. *cf.* **ooner**
oondergrun *adj., adv.* underground
oondevallin *adj.* unceasing
oondisjeestit *adj.* undigested
oondootitly *adv.* undoubtedly
oonendin *adj.* unending
ooner *prep.* under. *cf.* **oonder**
oonerstan *v.* understand
oonertakin *n.* undertaking
oonexpeckit *adj.* unexpected
oonfashed *adj.* untroubled
oonfeelin *adj.* unfeeling
oonfersell *adj.* lacking energy
oongrutten *adj.* not wept over
oonhandy *adj.* unhandy
oonhappy *adj.* unhappy
oonheedin *adj.* unheeding
oonhonesty *n.* dishonesty
oonjustice *n.* injustice
oonkent *adj.* unknown
oonlawfu *adj.* unlawful
oonless *conj.* unless
oonmynit o *adj.* unmindful of
oonnaitral *adj.* unnatural; supernatural
oonprenciplt *adj.* unprincipled
oonrichteous *adj.* unrighteous
oonslockened *adj.* unquenched
oonstable *adj.* unstable

oontill *conj.* till
oontirin *adj.* untiring
oonwaashen *ppl., adj.* unwashed
oonweel *adj.* unwell
oonwullin *adj.* unwilling
oonwuttin *adj.* unaware, abstracted
oor *n.* hour; *adj.* our
oorie *adj.* eerie; dismal
oorlich *adj.* (of people) miserable-looking from cold, hunger etc; (of weather) dull and cold; melancholy; *n.* starved-looking, stunted person
oorly *adv.* hourly
oors *pron.* ours
oorsels *pron.* ourselves; *pred. adj., adv.* by ourselves, alone
oot *adv., prep.* out; **oot amint** out of things; **oot amon** *prep.* out of; **oot the door** facing ruin; **oot o han** beyond control; **oot wi** out of favour with; **oot-win** wind off the sea; **oot o yer box** out on the tiles
ootbrak *n.* outbreak
oot-by *adv.* outside; out in the fields; out and a little way off; *adj.* out of the way; distant
oot-cry *v.* protest
ootfeedle *n.* outfield
ootgang *n.* outgoing, departure *e.g.* from a tenancy at end of season
oothoose *n.* outhouse
ootlat *n.* outlet; expression
ootlay, ootlie *n.* outlay
ootlin *n.* stranger; outcast
ootmaist *adj.* outmost
ootower, -owre *prep.* out and over; out of; **ootower the cairt**
oots-an-ins *n. pl.* hairpins

oots wi *v.* take(s) out
ootwith, -wuth *adj.*, *adv.* outward; *adv.* outwardly, fully
opeenion *n.* opinion
opingan *n.* opinion
or *conj., prep.* before; until
ordeen *v.* ordain
ordinar *adj.* ordinary
orpiet *adj.* peevish, querulous (A2)
orra *adj.* odd; idle, worthless; shabby
orra-beaster *n.* the man who worked the odd horse on a farm (T)
orra loon *adj., n.* boy who did odd jobs on farm
orrals *n.* anything left over, refuse
orra man *adj., n.* man who did odd jobs on farm; wire-tightening lever (F)
orra wark *adj., n.* odd jobs
ou *excl.* oh
ouk *n.* week; **this day ouk** a week today. *cf.* **ook**
ousel *n.* blackbird (M)
overly *adj.* incidental

ow awa *excl. of sympathy*
owdience *n.* audience
ower, owre *adv., prep.* over; **ower the heids o** because of
owercassen *adj.* (of the weather) overcast
owercome *n.* a frequently repeated phrase or theme; burden or message
owergaan *n.* severe reproof; close examination
owergae *v.* go over; pass (through or over)
owergeen *adv.* (of time) past
owerlay *v.* overlay, cover over
owernicht *adv.* overnight
owersman *n.* person with authority over others
own *v.* admit
owse *n.* ox; *pl.* **owsen**
owthereese *v.* authorise
oxter *n.* armpit; bosom; *v.* embrace; **oxterfu, oxterlift** *n.* armful
oxter-pooch *n.* inside pocket
oxter-staff, -stav *n.* crutch

—— **P** ——

paal *n.* mooring post or bollard
Pace *See* **Pase**
pack-merchants *n. pl.* small scudding clouds
paewae *adj.* sickly, unwell (T)
pailace *n.* palace
pair, pairie *n.* pair of horse
pairis *n.* parish
pairl *n.* pearl
pairt *n.* part; *v.* part; divide; **pairt**

oot *v.* share-out (S)
pairtin *n.* share-out; parting; *ppl.* parting
pairtner *n.* partner
pairtrick *n.* partridge (M, C). *cf.* **paitrick**
pairty *n.* party
paitrick *n.* partridge (S, M1). *cf.* **pairtrick**
palaiver *n.* (of a person) show-off

palin *n.* paling, stake fence

pammer *v.* walk about aimlessly, saunter; stamp around noisily. *cf.* **paumer**

pang *v.* cram

pan loaf *adj.* loaf with hard crust; *fig.* affected way of speaking

pap *n.* teat; sea anemone

Pape *n.* the Pope

park *n.* field (A). *cf.* **fiedle**

parley *n.* period of truce in games, after the cry **parleys-on**

parritch *n.* porridge (J)

partan *n.* the common crab

parteeclar *adj.* particular

Pase *n.* Easter. *cf.* **Pess, Pesch**

pass *n.* passage

passin *prep.* more than

pat *n.* pot; small ball of butter; *v. pt.* put; **pat tee** put by, put aside

patcher *n.* turnip-seed sowing device (F)

Patie *n.* deriv. from Peter

pattren *n.* pattern

pawky *adj.* shrewd; sly

pawmie *n.* a stroke on the palm with a **tawse** or cane (J)

pawrent *n.* parent

pawtron *n.* patron

pawtronage *n.* patronage

pawtronise *v.* patronise

peanny *n.* piano

pech *v.* pant

peek *v.* cheep; complain; **peekin-eevie** discontented girl

peel *n.* pill; pool

peel-an-aet tatties *n. pl.* potatoes boiled in their skins and peeled just before eating

peelie-wally *adj.* sickly

peelin *n.* skin; thrashing

peen *n.* pane of glass

peenge *v.* complain, whine

peenie *n.* pinafore

peer *adj.* poor. *cf.* **puir**

peerie *n.* spinning top

peer(s)-hoose *n.* work-house

peerman *n.* holder for fir candle

peer-man *n.* wire-tightening lever in fencing (F)

peer wi *v.* match, equal

peesie(weep) *n.* lapwing (S). *cf.* **pee-weet**

peetifu *adj.* pitiful

peetrol *n.* petrol

peety *n., v.* pity

pee-weet *n.* lapwing (M, R). *cf.* **peesie**

pelt *n.* trash, rubbish

peltin-pyock *n.* worthless rag

pend, pen(n) *n.* arch; arched passageway or entry, esp. one leading from the street into a back court

penner *n.* penholder

pensy *adj.* (would be) stately

pent (rhymes with hint) *n., v.* paint

perjink *adj.* precise; neat in appearance; prim; fussy

perlyaag *n.* rubbish; mixture of odds and ends, esp. rubbishy food; goodies (B1)

pernickety *adj.* very particular; over-fastidious

perswaad *v.* persuade

perteen *v.* pertain

Pesch (A1) *See* **Pase, Pess**

peshifie *v.* pacify (B1)

Pess *n.* Easter (M1). *cf.* **Pase**

peter *in phr.* **pit the peter on** bring

to a sudden stop, bring up short

pey *n., v.* pay

peyed-thankless *adj.* ungrateful (B)

peymen *n.* payment

phizog *n.* face

physeeshun *n.* physician, doctor

picher *n.* nervous excitement (B1)

picht *n.* Pict; small person

pick *n.* small quantity

picker *n.* lever for removing staples

pickiesae *n.* hat similar to deerstalker (T)

pick-mirk *adj., n.* pitch-dark

pickthank *adj.* ungrateful. *cf.* **pykethank**

picter, pictur *n.* picture

piece *n.* portable snack

pig(gie) *n.* pitcher; earthenware jar; stone hot-water bottle

pike *n.* frost-nail. *See* **pyke**

pilget *n.* fight, struggle, plight; **in a pilget wi pain** (B1)

pilk *v.* pilfer

pilla *n.* pillow

pilpert *n.* cold, badly fed child (B1)

pin *n.* clothes peg

pine *n.* pain. *cf.* **pyne**

pint *n., v.* (near rhyme with hint); paint; *v.* (rhyming with Eng. pint) point; *n.* (rhyming with Eng. pint) shoe-lace. *cf.* **pynt**

pint stoup *n.* drinking vessel with a handle containing a Scots pint

pirl *v.* poke, stir; trifle; *intr.* ripple

pirn *n.* reel on which yarn or thread is wound

pirn-taed *adj.* pigeon-toed

pirr *n.* sudden burst of activity; **on the pirr**

pirr-winnie *n.* breeze

pish *v.* urinate

pit *v.* put; *ppl.* **pitten**; **tae pit past** put away; **pit, pitten oot** put out, discomfitted, worried (A1); **tae pit aboot** to inconvenience

pitawtie *n.* potato (B1)

piz *n. pl.* peas

piz-meal, pizzers *n.* pease-meal

place *n.* laird's residence

plack *n.* small coin (J)

plaid *n.* long piece of woollen cloth with chequered or tartan pattern, outer article of Highland dress, worn over the shoulder; as above, used as a blanket

plaik *n.* plaything (M1)

plaise *v.* please (S)

plaised *adj.* pleased (C1, G1, S)

plaister *n.* plaster

planesteens *n.* pavement

plank *v.* place, lay

plantin *n.* plantation

plashie, plash fluke *n.* plaice

playgreen *n.* playground

playgrun *n.* playground

pleast *adj.* pleased. *cf.* **plaised**

pleece *n.* police

pleege *v.* plague (B1)

pleesint *adj.* pleasant

pleesur, pleesure *n.* pleasure

pleiter *See* **plowter**

plenish *v.* furnish a house; stock a farm

pleuch *n.* plough (A, M1). *cf.* **ploo**

pleura *n.* pleuro-pneumonia

plicht *n.* plight

plisky *n.* mischievous trick; plight (B1)

plivver *n.* plover (A1)

plizzant *adj.* pleasant

ploiter *n., v. See* **plowter**

ploitery *adj.* wet; muddy

ploo *n.* plough; **ploo-feathers** projecting wing on the share of a plough, which cuts out the furrow; **ploo-sock** ploughshare; **ploo-stilts** plough handles, sock of plough which cuts out the furrow

plook *n.* pimple

plooky *adj.* pimply

plooman *n.* ploughman

plot *v.* scald; burn, scorch

plottin *adj.* very hot

plowt *n.* blow, punch

plowter *n.* act of working or walking in mud or water; *v.* splash in mud or water, squelch; work messily; potter. *cf.* **pleiter, ploiter**

ploy *n.* frolic, escapade

pluff *v.* shoot (peas) through a tube

plump-churn *n.* plunge churn (F)

plunk *n.* plank of wood

plunkie *n.* homemade sweetmeat made with treacle or syrup and flour (A2)

plyaak *n.* toy (A1, A2)

plype *v.* fall *plump* into water

plyper *v.* walk in mud or water

pock, poke *n.* bag. *cf.* **powk, pyock** pocket (J). *cf.* **pooch**

poddick *n.* frog (G). *cf.* **puddock**

points *n. pl.* shoe-laces. *cf.* **pints**

poleetics *n.* politics

politeeshun *n.* politician

pollis *n.* police (J)

pom-pom *n.* the Field Marshall diesel tractor, the nickname deriv. from sound of engine

pooch *n., v.* pocket

poochle *See* **puchal**

pooder *n.* powder; **lattin oot the pooder** divulging the secret

pooer *n.* power; **pooer o pot an gallows** the old feudal power to hang or drown (A2)

poond *n.* pound sterling (J). *cf.* **pund**

poopit *n.* pulpit

poor *v.* pour

poortith *n.* poverty

pooshan, pooshin *n., v.* poison. *cf.* **pushion**

pooshinous *adj.* poisonous

poother-deevil *n.* primitive home-made firework

porritch *n. pl.* porridge *(takes pl. v.). cf.* **pottich**

port *n.* lively tune on the bagpipes

poseetion *n.* position

postie *n.* postman

potestatur *n.* prime

pot fit *n.* one of the feet of a cauldron; **stick oot like a pot fit** stick out like a sore thumb

potterlow *n.* ruined condition; unsightly mess; **geen tae potter-low** gone to pot, completely spoiled

pottich *n. pl.* porridge (A1); **he made his pottich an suppit them.** *cf.* **porritch**

pottiestattur *etc. See* **potestatur**

pottit-heid *n.* dish made from head of ox or pig, boiled to a jelly

poun *n.* pound sterling

pow *n.* poll; head

powk *n.* bag. *cf.* **pock, poke;** *v.* poke

powster *n.* posture; position, situation

practeese *v.* practise

praisent *n.* present

pran *v.* crush; hurt severely or fatally

preceese(ly) *adj., adv.* precisely

precent *v.* lead the psalmody in a Presbyterian church

precunnance *n.* condition; footing

pree *v.* taste; experience

preef *n.* proof. *cf.* **pruif**

preen *n., v.* pin

preen-heidit *adj.* pin-headed; unintelligent

preevilege *n.* privilege

prefairrance *n.* preference

prefar *v.* prefer

prejudeece *n.* prejudice

prence *n.* prince

prenciple *n.* principle

prent *n., v.* print

press *n.* wall-cupboard

prick *v. intr.* (of cattle) to stampede, to escape insect bites

pridefu *adj.* proud (J). *cf.* **prood**

prig *v.* plead

'Prile *n.* April; **'Prile eeran** April (fool's) errand

prile *n.* three cards of equal value, *e.g.* **a prile o queens** (B)

primpit *adj.* prim (R)

prob *v.* to pierce, prod; release gas from stomach of cattle by piercing

prodeegious *adj.* prodigious

projeck *n.* project

pron *n.* residue of oat husks and oatmeal left over after the milling process, bran

prood *adj.* proud

prop *n.* ploughing marker (F); landmark or memorial

prophesiet *v. pt.* prophesied

proteck *v.* protect

protick *n.* rash or idle adventure; bit of mischief

protty *adj.* pretty; **a protty penny**

proveesions *n. pl.* provisions

pruif *n.* proof. *cf.* **preef**

pruv, pruve *v.* prove

pu *v.* to pull

puchal, puchil *adj.* reserved, proud; self-important (A2). *cf.* **poochle**

puckle *n.* a small quantity, some

puddle *v.* play with hands or feet in water

puddick, puddock *n.* frog; flat wooden platform for transporting heavy loads on farms

puddock's eggs *n. pl.* nickname for sago or tapioca pudding

puddock-steel *n.* toadstool

puggled *ppl.* worn out

puir *adj., n.* poor

pule *n.* seagull (Gardenstown) (B)

pul-throwe *n.* cord with which cleaning rag is pulled through rifle

pultice *n.* poultice

pump *v.* break wind behind

pumphel *n.* pen for cattle; square church pew

pun, pund *n.* pound (in weight)

punctwal *adj.* punctual

purchase *n.* a hold or grip

purpie *adj.* purple

pushion *See* **pooshan**

putt *v.* push, shove; **ae putt an row**

a hard struggle
putten *ppl.* put; sent
pye *n.* a counting-out rhyme in children's games and the serving of food; **say a pye**
pyke *v.* pick; steal; **pyke their pooch** cost them a lot; *n.* spike (of a railing etc). *cf.* **pike**
pykethank *See* **pickthank**
pykit *ppl.* spiked
pykit weer *n., ppl.* barbed wire (F).

cf. **barbit-weer**
pyne *n.* pain. *cf.* **pine**
pyner *n.* animal suffering pain (M2)
pyocher *n.* troublesome cough; *v.* to clear the throat
pyock *See* **poke** *etc.*
pyooch *v.* cough
pyot *n.* magpie
pyshon *See* **pooshan**

— Q —

quaet *adj.* quiet. *cf.* **quait**
quaetness *n.* quietness, peace
quaich *n.* drinking cup with two handles
quaikin-aish *n.* aspen
quait *adj.* quiet. *cf.* **quaet**
quake, quaik *n.* heifer
quarterer *n.* tramp with quarters on the farm in exchange for farm work (F)
quat *v.* quit; stop what one is doing
queed *n.* cud
queeger *n.* mess, muddle; mixture
queel *adj., v.* cool
Queenie arabs *n. pl.* inhabitants of the Queenie (Keith Inch) in

Peterhead (B)
queet *n.* ankle
queetikins *n.* gaiters. *cf.* **cuitikins**
quern *n.* stone hand-mill
queyn, quine *n.* girl
quig *n.* mix up
quigger *n.* mess, muddle; mixture
quile *n.* coal; burning coal
quine *n.* girl
quinkins *n. pl.* something of no value
quirky *adj.* tricky
quisson *n.* question
quite *See* **quyte**
quo *v.* quoth
quyte *n.* coat; petticoat. *cf.* **kwite**

— R —

raa *adj.* raw
raan *n.* fish roe
rackle *n.* chain of tin pipe-lid
rackon *v.* reckon
rade *v. pt.* rode. *See also* **redd**
rael *adj., adv.* real; really

raelly *adv.* really
raeper *n.* reaper; **tiltin-raeper** reaping-machine, requiring a man to knock off the sheaves with a rake
raff *n.* riff-raff

71

raffy *adj.* plentiful (M); *n.* a rank growth (A1)

ragie *adj.* raging; scolding

raggit *adj.* ragged

raggit-robin *n.* (flower) *lychnis flos-cuculi* (S)

raiffle *See* **reffle**

raik *v.* to rake; roam about; reck, care; **fat raiks?** what does it signify? (A2). *cf.* **rake**

raikins *See* **rakins**

raip *n.* rope. *cf.* **rape**

raise *v.* excite, infuriate, madden; **raise din** make trouble; **raise him wull** drive him crazy

raise *v. pt.* got up

raise-o-the-win *n.* a stroke of good luck (T)

raist *adj.* excited, angry

raith *n.* quarter of a year; term at school

raither *adv.* rather. *cf.* **redder**

raivel *v.* entangle; wander in speech

raivelt *adj.* tangled; mentally confused

raiverie *n.* rumour (M2)

rake *n.* great energy; **cam mair rake** worked faster, with more energy; *v.* search; range, stray; roam, wander

rakins *n.* gathering of loose hay or strands of corn which escape the reaping-machine

rally (on) *v.* scold; speak angrily to

rammack *n.* rough piece of wood; worthless article

rammy *n.* uproar

rampauge *n.* fury, rage; *v.* to rage

ramsh *adj.* hasty, rash

ramshackle *adj.* disorderly; un-

methodical; thoughtless; headstrong

ranagant *n.* wild, loose-living person (B1); good-for-nothing

ran-dan *n.* carouse; rumpus (A); **oot on the ran-dan**

randy *n.* virago; loose-tongued woman

ranegill *adj.* renegade; rough character; criminal

rank *v.* get ready, esp. dress to go out

rank oot *v.* bring out, look out in preparation

rant *n.* lively tune

ranter *v.* mend, stitch; put together

rantletree *n.* the beam across the chimney from which the **crook** is suspended

rantree *n.* rowan tree, mountain ash

rape *n.* rope, esp. of straw. *cf.* **raip**

rare *adj.* excellent

rase *v. pt.* rose

rash *n.* rush

rauchle *adj.* noisy, clamorous

rave *v. pt.* tore. *cf.* **rive**

raw *n.* row

rawn-tree *n.* mountain ash. *cf.* **rowan, rodden, raantree**

rax *v.* stretch; hand

readin-sweetie *n.* conversation lozenge

ream *n.* cream; *v.* foam; buzz (of thoughts); overflow; **reamin fu** brimming

rebat *v.* retort; speak again

recaipt *n.* recipe

reck *v.* to take heed of

recreet *v.* recuperate

redd *v.* clear out, to rid; **redd yer**

throat clear your throat; **redd yer crap** get something off your chest

redd up *v.* clear up; (a person) criticise

redd *ppl., adj.* rid; **wun redd o** get rid of

redd *adj., adv.* read(il)y, willing(ly); **as redd wark as nae**

reddance *n.* riddance

redder *adv.* rather. *cf.* **raither**

rede *v.* advise (J)

red-lan *n.* ploughed land

ree *n.* enclosure; hen run

reed *adj.* red. *cf.* **reid**; *n.* rood by measurement

reed-het *adj.* red-hot

reef *n.* roof; **reef a ditch** roof a ditch, vacate your home with no other to go to (T)

reek *n., v.* smoke. *cf.* **rik; reek-bouk** belch of smoke (R)

reek-hen *n.* a hen exacted for every reeking chimney or inhabited house

reem *n.* cream

reemis(h) *n.* resounding crash, din, clatter; *v.* rummage

reemishin *v. n.* uproar; clatter

reenge *v.* range, roam

reerie *n.* row; **kick up a reerie**

reesle, reeshsle *v.* rustle; hustle noisily

reest *n.* roost; *v. intr.* roost; sit; refuse to move; *v. tr.* arrest; bring to a halt; **reest the fire** bank up the fire. *cf.* **reist**

reet *n.* root; **the reet an the rise o't** beginning and end of it (M2); the whole story, affair

reeve *v. pt.* tore. *cf.* **rive**

reevin *adj.* (of wind) high, strong; (of fire) burning brightly

reeze *n.* high praise; *v.* praise

refar *v.* refer

refeese *v.* refuse

reffle *v.* ransack

regaird *n., v.* regard

reglar *adj.* regular

reid *adj.* red; **a reid een** a new net (B); **reid fish** the salmon (this being a taboo word at sea). *cf.* **reed**

reid-biddy *n.* mixture of cheap red wine and methylated spirit or other alcohol

reid-cheekit *adj.* red-cheeked

reid-heidit *adj.* red-headed

reid-kaimed *adj.* red-combed

reist *v.* roost; sit; bank up a fire. *cf.* **reest**

reistin *adj.* restive

reive *v.* to plunder

releegion *n.* religion

releegious *adj.* religious

remeid *n.* remedy

remis *See* **reemis**

remorse *v.* express regret about; repent (A2)

repoort *n., v.* report

repree *v.* reprove

requar, requair *v.* require

respeck *n., v.* respect

retour *n.* a renewal, replacement

reuch *adj.* rough (J). *cf.* **roch**

revarse *n.* reverse

reverie (B1) *See* **raiverie**

reyn *n.* rain. *cf.* **ryne**

ribbet *n.* rabbit (S). *cf.* **rubbit**

richt *adj., n., v.* right; **richtit**

righted

richteous *adj.* righteous

rickle *n.* loose heap or stack (*e.g.* of peats set up to dry)

rickmatick *n.* concern, affair; collection

riddel *n.* sieve

rideeclous *adj.* ridiculous

riever *n.* thief

rift *n., v.* belch

rig *n.* ridge; section of a field; practical joke; **play a rig** play a trick; *v.* to dress

riggin *n.* ridge, roof; head, skull; **riggin o the nicht** middle of the night

riggit-oot *adj.* all set; equipped (S)

rig-lamb *n.* male lamb with only one descended testicle (T)

riglin *n.* animal with testicle undescended

rig oot *n.* outfit; *v.* prepare (a ship for the fishing season) (B)

rik *n.* smoke. *cf.* **reek**

rime *n.* hoar-frost

rim-rax *n.* a good feed (B1)

rin *v.* run; (of a cow) be in heat (F)

rine *n.* rein. *cf.* **ryne**

ringel-een *n.* wall-eyes

rink *v.* clamber; range about noisily

rinnins *n.* main outlines

rin oot *n.* urination

rint *n.* rent

rin-the-wuddie *n.* fugitive from the gallows

rin-watter *n.* natural flow of water, esp. one which will drive a mill-wheel without a dam; *fig.* just enough money to pay one's way

ripp *n.* a handful of unthreshed corn or hay

ripper *n.* hand-line for catching cod

ripper-yole *n.* yawl used for ripper-fishing

rippit *n.* uproar (M, B1)

rise *n.* joke at someone's expense; **hae a rise oot o, tak the rise o** play a trick on

risp *v.* rasp

rist *n.* rest

rive *n.* tear; bite, large mouthful; *v.* pull forcibly; burst asunder; tear; **rivven** *ppl.* pulled apart

rizzar *n.* redcurrant

rizzon *n.* reason

rizzonable *adj.* reasonable

roadit *adv.* on the road, on one's way; **get roadit** set off

roasen, roassen *ppl.* roasted; *adj.* roasting hot

Rob(bie) *pr. n.* dim. of Robert

robsorby *n.* a make of scythe, synonymous with the implement (T)

roch *adj.* rough

roch an richt *phr.* rough in manners

rock *n.* distaff

rockin *n.* evening gathering of neighbours with **rock** and spindles; a spinning-bee (M)

rocky-on *n.* sea-shore game involving a stone cairn (B)

rodden *n.* mountain-ash (berry)

rodden-, roddin-tree *n.* mountain ash or rowan

rogie *n.* little rogue, term of endearment for a child

rone *n.* a slide

Room *pr. n.* Rome (A2)

room, the *n.* the best room in a small house

roon *adv., prep.* round

roon-shoodert *adj.* round-shouldered

roose *v.* rouse (to anger); salt herring

rooser *n.* watering-can

Roosian *n.* rabbit (Russian)

roosin-tub *n.* tub in which herring were salted

roost *n., v.* rust

roosty *adj.* rusty. *cf.* **rousty**

rosit *n.* resin; **rositie** resinous; **rositie eyn** resined thread used for sewing leather

rottack *n.* useless, discarded object; *pl.* lumber, junk

rottan *n.* rat

rounder *n.* an ungutted fish

roup *n., v.* auction

roup oot *v.* sell up by auction

roupy *adj.* hoarse

roust *v.* roar, bellow (also of animals)

roust *v.* rust. *cf.* **roost**

roustin *adj.* rusting;

rousty *adj.* rusty. *cf.* **roosty**

routh (o) *n.* plenty (of); *adj.* abundant. *cf.* **rowth**

rowe *v.* roll; wheel (a barrow)

rowie *n.* a morning roll

rowle *n., v.* rule

rowler *n.* ruler

rowt *v.* (of cattle) bellow, roar (G1)

rowth (o) *n.* plenty (of). *cf.* **routh**

royd, royt *adj.* (of children) wild, unruly, capering

rozet *n.* resin; cobbler's wax. *cf.* **rosit**

rubbit *n.* rabbit

ruck *n.* rick, stack; **het ruck** steaming stack built before crop has dried out; **thackit ruck** stack thatched for the winter; **wattert ruck** badly built and porous (T)

ruck-foon *n.* stack foundation

ruck-ledder *n.* stack ladder

ruck-post *n.* wooden support for off-centre stack

rug *n.* high profit, bargain perhaps to the seller's disadvantage (A1); tug; *v.* pull sharply, tug

rumigumshun (A1) *See below*

rum(mil)-gumption *n.* common sense (M1)

rummle *v.* rumble; *ppl.* rummlin

runch *n.* wild radish (F)

rung *n.* heavy staff

runk *n.* old, outworn animal; contemptuous term for a woman of ill repute

runklt *ppl., adj.* wrinkled. *cf.* **wrunklt**

runt *n.* withered hag, m. or f.

runtit (o) *ppl., adj.* having lost all (as in the game of marbles); completely deprived of

ryne *n.* rein. *cf.* **rine**

rype *v.* ransack, rifle; steal

— S —

's *pron.* his; **aff o's maet** off his food
sa, saa *v. pt.* saw
saabre *n.* sabre
saach *n.* willow. *cf.* **sauch**
saadist *n.* sawdust
saan *n.* sand
saar *n.* savour
saarless *adj.* tasteless, insipid. *cf.* **saurless**
sab *v.* sob
sae *adv., conj.* so
saeven *adj.* seven. *cf.* **seyven**
saeventy *adj.* seventy
saff *adj.* safe
saft *adj.* soft; weak; simple
saftie *n.* weak(-minded) person; slipper (G). *cf.* **softie**
saftness *n.* softness
saick *n.* sack; **a saickfu o sair beens** a hiding
saicret *n.* secret
saiddle *n.* saddle
saiddler *n.* saddler
sailary *n.* salary
sair *adj., n.* sore; *adv.* sorely, badly; very much, greatly; **sair aff** badly off, hard up; **sair awa wi't** worn out; in a bad state; **sair come at** far gone, worn out; **sair dung** hard-pressed; **sair fecht** hard struggle; **sair heid** headache; **sair hert** sad heart; **sair made** hard pressed; **sair on** hard on (clothes etc.)
sair *v.* serve; satisfy (esp. with food/drink) (M1); satiate, sate; **sair maetit** well-fed (A1); **weel-sairt** well satisfied with food or drink; **ill-sairt** not having had enough; **sick sairt** satiated. *cf.* **ser**
sairgint *n.* sergeant
sair-heidie *n.* sponge-cake in paper cup
sairin *n.* serving, helping; deserts; fill; **she got her sairin o't**
sairious *adj.* serious. *cf.* **sarious**
sairly *adv.* badly
sairs *n.* ailments
Saiterday, Setturday *n.* Saturday
saitisfie *v.* satisfy, *ppl.* **saitisfiet**
saiven *adj.* seven
sal *See* **saul**
sall *v.* shall. *cf.* **saul**
salvenda (B1) *See* **solvendo**
sang *excl.* blood!
sang *n.* song
san-gless *n.* hour-glass
sanna *v. neg.* shall not
sanshach *adj.* saucy; disdainful; irritable
sant *n.* saint
santifie *v.* sanctify
santly *adj.* saintly
sappy *adj.* moist, full of juice; heavy in the water, laden with fish (B); **sappy sodjers** ball game
saps *n.* bread with milk and sugar
sarious *adj.* serious. *cf.* **sairious**
sark *n.* shirt; chemise

sarket, sarkit *n.* undershirt; shirt or jersey

sate *n.* seat

satteral *adj.* stiff; tart

sattle *v.* settle

sauchen *adj.* unsociable

saugh *n.* willow; **saugh-wans** willow wands. *cf.* **saach**

saughy *adj.* abounding in willows

saul *n.* soul; also used as *excl.*; *ppl.* sold

Sauners *pr. n.* Alexander

saurless *adj.* tasteless; spiritless

saut *n.* salt; **wirth saut till his kail** worth his salt

saut-backet *n.* salt-box

sauter *n.* salter; one who can do severe things

sautie *adj.* tasting of salt

sautie-bannocks *n.* oatmeal pancakes

saut-lick *n.* salt brick for cattle (T)

saw *n.* salve, ointment; *v.* sow (S)

Sawboth *n.* Sabbath

sawer *n.* sower

sawna *v. pt. neg.* did not see

Sawney *pr. n.* deriv. of Alexander

Sawtan *pr. n.* Satan

sax *adj.* six; **sax-pair toon** farm with six pairs of horses

saxpence *n.* sixpence

saxteen *adj.* sixteen

saxty *adj.* sixty

say-awa *n.* discourse, narrative, monologue

scaa *n.* barnacle. *cf.* **scaw**

scaad *v.* scald

scabbie *adj.* scabbed

scabbit *adj.* scabby; shabby

scadden *n.* person of spare figure; contemptuous term for person or thing

scaffy *n.* street-sweeper

scaith *n.* injury; damage

scalder *n.* stinging jellyfish

scam *n.* singe, scorch; scald slightly. *cf.* **scaum**

scance *v.* scan; *n.* a look

scarecraw *n.* scarecrow

scart *n., v.* scratch (A). *cf.* **scrat**

scashle *n., v.* quarrel

scaul *v.* scold; *n.* a scold; scolding

scaum *v.* singe, scorch, scald slightly. *cf.* **scam**

scaup *n.* thin, poor soil; bank of mud or soil exposed at low tide

scaur *n.* bare place on side of hill; cliff

scavie *n.* mishap (B1)

scaw *See* **scaa**

schaim *n.* scheme

scholar *n.* school pupil

schule *n.* school (J)

scienteefic *adj.* scientific

sclaff *n., v.* stroke

sclaffert *n.* a stroke with the palm of the hand; slap

sclait *n.* slate. *cf.* **sklate**

sclaive *See* **sclave**

sclap *v.* walk in flat-footed or shuffling way. *cf.* **sclaup**

sclarry *v.* daub, smear (J)

sclaup *See* **sclap**

sclave *n.* gossip, scandal-monger; *v.* spread a story by gossip

sclaver (M2) *See* **sclave** *v.*

sclim *v.* climb. *cf.* **clim**

scob *v.* put in splints

scomfish *v.* suffocate (A1)

scoof *n.* quick swig; *v.* swallow

food or drink quickly. *cf.* **scowf**

scool *v.* scowl

scoon(e)ral *n.* scoundrel

scoor *v.* scour

scoorin-buird *n.* scrubbing-board

scooshle *v.* shuffle

scoot *n.* term of contempt applied to man or woman

scooth *n.* scope. *cf.* **scowth**

score, over the *phr.* beyond what is reasonable

scorie-hornt *adj.* calloused (G)

scouf *See* **scoof**

scoug *n.* shelter; pretence; ruse

scouk *n.* evil look; *v.* skulk. *cf.* **skook**

scouth *n.* freedom of movement, elbow-room, scope

scouth-an-routh *phr.* freedom to range and plenty of food

scowff *v.* scoff at, mock (R)

scowth *n.* freedom to move; scope. *cf.* **scouth, scooth**

scraich *n., v.* shreik

scrat *n.* shallow furrow; scratch; *v.* scratch (M). *cf.* **scart**

scrauch *n.* screech

scran *v.* scavenge for

scrath *n.* cormorant

screed *n.* long piece of writing

screef *n.* surface of water

screeve, screive, scrive *v.* write

screeve *n.* a large scratch; *v.* scratch, scrape

screid *See* **screed**

scrie *v.* cry; proclaim

scries-buird *n.* announcement board (at church)

scriffan *n.* membrane, film, thin cover. *cf.* **striffin**

scrog *n.* stunted bush

scronach *n.* shrill cry; fuss, outcry (A2)

scroo *n.* small rick of corn or hay. *cf.* **hooick**

scruff *n.* raff-raff

scrunt *n.* anything stunted in growth

scry *v.* cry; proclaim, advertise

scud, the *n.* slap with a **tawse** on the open hand

scuddle *v.* mess about at domestic work; **scuddlin claes** second-best clothes

scuddy *adj.* niggardly

scudge *v.* do rough, menial work. *cf.* **skudge**

scuff *v.* touch lightly in passing

scuff o rain *n.* sudden, passing shower

scull, skull *n.* shallow wicker basket. *cf.* **skull**

scunner *n., v.* disgust; **scunnert o** or **wi** *ppl. adj.* disgusted; bored, fed up, sick of; **tae tak a scunner till** to go off something

scunnerashun *excl., n.* offensive sight or thing

scunnerfu *adj.* disgusting, loathsome

scurry *n.* seagull (Peterhead) (B)

scurry-waster *n.* seagull (M1)

scushle *v.* shuffle

scutter *n.* messy or difficult work; nuisance; *v.* potter, work messily, awkwardly; **scutter aboot** mess about

scutterie jobbie *adj., n.* messy or trifling job

scypal *n.* rascal, rogue. *cf.* **skypal**

scythe-brod *n.* sharpening board for scythe

seagoo *n.* seagull (A1, R)

seama(w) *n.* seagull (M1)

search *n.* milk strainer (F)

seck *n.* sack. *cf.* **saick**

seck-apron *n.* sackcloth apron. *cf.* **harn-apron**

seck-lifter *n.* hand-barrow (F)

sedarin *n.* scolding, dressing-down

seddle *See* **saiddle**

seek *adj.* sick (S)

seek *v.* look for; ask for; invite; desire; **fit are ye seekin?** what do you want, what are you looking for?

seekener *n.* sickener, something which upsets

seelence *n.* silence

seelent *adj.* silent

seely *adj.* blessed; happy

seelyhoo *n.* the caul rarely found on the head of a new-born child and thought a good omen

seen *prep.* since; *adv.* soon; ago

seenit *n.* Synod

seer(ly) *adj.* sure(ly) (A, B1)

seerup *n.* syrup

seet *n.* site; building-ground

seetivation *n.* situation

seg *v.* sag; **seggit** *ppl., adj.* sagged, sunk down

seg(g)s *n.* sedge; the yellow iris

seiven *adj.* seven

seiventeen *adj.* seventeen

seiventy *adj.* seventy

sel *n.* self

seleck *v.* select

sell *n.* chain to bind cattle (F)

sellfitness *n.* selfishness

selt *v. pt., ppl.* sold

semmit *n.* undershirt

sen *n.* messenger sent ahead of a bridegroom to summon the bride; *v.* send

ser *v.* serve. *cf.* **sair**

ser'in *See* **sairin**

serve's *excl.* preserve us!

set *v.* lease, let

set tee *v.* begin

settin *n.* clutch of eggs a hen sits on to hatch

settril *adj.* slightly stunted in growth

sey *n.* sieve; *v.* strain through a sieve, strain milk. *cf.* **sye**

seyven *adj.* seven (A1). *cf.* **saeven, saiven**

shaave *v.* sow. *cf.* **shauv**

shacklebane, -been *n.* wrist-bone

shadda, shaeda *n.* shadow

shaef, shafe *n.* sheaf. *cf.* **shaif; the croonin shafe** the last straw, the tin lid

shafter, shaftit weskit *n.* sleeved waistcoat (F)

shaif *n.* sheaf. *cf.* **shaef, shafe, shave**

shair *adj.* sure (S)

shak *n., v.* shake; **the Big Shak** the near-ruinous shaking of barley by high winds one night in the 1960s

shakker *n.* part of a threshing mill which shakes out the straw

Shakkin Briggie *pr. n.* bridge across the River Dee at Cults near Aberdeen

shakkin-spoot *n.* wooden chute conveying corn to the elevator lifting it to the corn loft

shakky *adj.* shaky

shakky-doon *n.* make-shift bed

shall *n.* shell; **shall san** shell sand, used as grit for hens (T)

shallie o tay old term for a cup of tea (B)

shally *adj.* abounding in shells

shalt(ie) *n.* pony

shalt-loon *n.* farm-boy looking after the shalt (F); groom

shammelt *adj.* uneven, irregular

shan-dre-dan *n.* any old rickety vehicle

shangie *n.* fight; scrimmage

shank *v.* to knit; *n.* stocking being knitted; the leg; **to shank it** to walk; **shanks' meer** shanks' pony

shankless *adj.* having no leg(s)

shapit *ppl.* shaped

shargart *ppl.* stunted

sharger *n.* a stunted person or animal; lean, scraggy person

sharn *n.* cow-dung; **sharn-bree** liquid cow-dung

sharny *adj.* dung-covered; dirty

sharp *n.* frost-nail; *v.* sharpen

sharrie *n.* quarrel; fight

shauchle *v.* shuffle in walking

shauv *v.* sow (S). *cf.* **saw**

shauven *ppl.* sown

shave *n.* sheaf. *cf.* **shaif**

shaven *ppl.* shaved

shaw *n.* green leaf; small wood (J); *v.* sow; show

shear *v.* reap

sheath *n.* holder for needles during knitting

sheave *n.* slice of bread

shed *v.* part the hair or sheep's wool

shee(n) *n.* shoe(s). *cf.* **shoon, shune** *v.* to shoe

sheel *n., v.* shovel; *v.* to shell

sheelock *n.* corn husk; unfilled ear of corn

sheelter *n.* shelled mussel (B)

sheemich *n.* person or thing of no value

sheen *n., v.* shine; *pl.* of **shee**

sheers *n.* scissors

sheet *v.* shoot

sheet-iron *n.* corrugated iron

sheilin *n.* temporary dwelling for shepherds

shelt, sheltie *n.* pony. *cf.* **shult**

shelvin *n.* movable board on box cart, to increase capacity

sheugh *n.* ditch; furrow; hollow, trench

shew *v.* sew. *cf.* **shoo**

shewin-machine *n.* sewing-machine

shiel *n.* shovel; scoop for fish

shillans *n.* grain freed from husks

shilpit *adj.* feeble

shim *n.* horse-hoe, small plough for weeding

shine *n.* party. *cf.* **henshine**

shippie *n.* steam drifter (B)

shirra *n.* sheriff

shirrameer, shirramineer (B1) *n.* tumult, uproar

shirry *n.* sherry

shiv, shive *v.* shove, push

shochle *v.* waddle

shog, shoggle *n., v.* shake. *cf.* **shoogle**

shoggly, shoogly *adj.* shaky

shoggly-wullie *n.* a table jelly

shoo *v.* sew. *cf.* **shew; shooin**

sewing; *v. pt.* sowed. *cf.* **shaw**

shooder *n., v.* shoulder; **shoodrin** *ppl.* shouldering. *cf.* **shouder**

shooderheid *n.* shoulder joint

shooer *n.* shower

shoogle *v.* to shake. *cf.* **shoggle**

shoogly *adj.* unsteady (of a table etc.)

shoon *n.* shoes. *cf.* **sheen, shune**

shoorie *n.* light shower

shoot *n., v.* suit

shoppie *n.* small shop

short *adj., in the phr.* **short i the trot** quick-tempered; irritable

shortcomes *n.* shortcomings

shortsome *adj.* amusing, making the time seem short

shot *n.* the shooting of a fishing net; the catch

shottie *n.* turn

shoud, showd *n., v. tr., intr.* swing

shouden-boats *n.* swing-boats at carnival

shouder *n., v.* shoulder. *cf.* **shooder**

shouther *See* **shouder**

shouther-the-win *(adj.), n.* (having) one shoulder higher than the other

shrood *n.* shroud

shud *v.* should

shue *v.* sew. *cf.* **shoo**

shuit *v.* suit. *cf.* **shoot**

shullin *n.* shilling

shult *See* **shelt**

shune *n. pl.* shoes. *cf.* **sheen, shoon**

shuner *adv.* sooner (S)

shunner *n.* cinder; **harn bags an shunners** sackcloth and ashes

shyve *n., v.* throw (of rope or fishing line only) (B)

sib *adj.* closely related, akin

sibness *n.* relationship

sic, siccan *adj.* such; **sic-an-sic** such-and-such

siccar *adj.* secure, certain; dependable, reliable

sich *n.* sigh

sicht *n.* sight; **a sicht for sair een** a welcome sight

sick lamb *n.* pet lamb brought up on the bottle, drawn by the call 'sick'

siclike *adj.* such-like

siclikes *n.* things like that; *prep.* just like

sid *n.* seed; *v.* should. *cf.* **sud; sidna** shouldn't

sidelins *adv.* sideways

siderig *n.* side ridge

side-shelvin *n.* movable board on side of box-cart

sidiewyes *adv.* sideways

sids *n. pl.* oat husks, used for **sowans**

siftin riddle *adj., n.* riddle for small seed

signaatur *n.* signature

sik *v.* seek; desire; **nae sikken't** don't want it. *cf.* **seek**

sile *n.* sand-eel (B). *cf.* **sunnel**

siller *n.* silver; money

silly-made-up *adj.* (of a child) mischievous

simmer *n.* summer

simmer-hoose *n.* summer-house

sin *n.* son; sun; *prep.* since; **sin, seen, sinsyne** since then

sinacle *n.* vestige, trace (B1)

sin-brunt *adj.* sun-burned

sinder, sin'er, sinner *v.* separate, sunder

sindoon *n.* sundown, sunset
single *v.* hoe turnips
sing-sang *n.* singsong speech
sinker *n.* weight for fastening horse in stall (F)
sinny *n.* senna
sinry *adj.* sundry
sinsyne *adv.* since then
sipper *n.* supper
siree *n.* soirée
sitiwat *ppl.* situated
sit saft *v., adv.* enjoy an easy life (B)
sitt *n.* soot
siven *adj.* seven
sivven *n.* raspberry
size *n.* chives
sizzon *n., v.* season
skaalie *n.* slate pencil. *cf.* **skeily**
ska(i)ken *v.* feel disgust at, be nauseated by (food); **ska(i)kent wi't.** *cf.* **skechan**
skaikit *ppl.* bedaubed; besmeared
skail *v. tr.* spill; *intr.* disperse (school pupils etc); *v. tr.* dismiss. *cf.* **skale**
skaillie *n.* slate-pencil. *cf.* **skaalie**
skaillies *n. pl.* something spilt or scattered
skaim *v.* scheme. *cf.* **skem**
skaith *n.* harm
skale *n.* school (S). *cf.* **skweel**
skale *v. tr.* dismiss; spill; *intr.* scatter. *cf.* **skail, skel**
skalie, skallie *n.* slate pencil. *cf.* **skaalie, skeily**
skance *n.* glance
skate *n.* jade (term of contempt)
skech *v.* go about in a silly, vain way

skechan *See* **skaiken**
skeel *n.* skill; **skeely** skilful
skeily *n.* slate pencil. *cf.* **skaalie**
skel *v.* spill. *cf.* **skale**
skelb *n.* splinter
skelf *n.* shelf; thin flat fragment or slice; splinter esp. lodged in skin
skellach *n.* wild mustard, charlock
skelp *n.* smack, whack; chunk, slab, sizable area; *v.* dash, run
skelve *n.* shelf (B1); *v.* laminate (B1). *cf.* **skelf**
skem *v.* scheme. *cf.* **skaim**
skep *n.* beehive; *v.* handle bee-hives
skew *adv.* askew
skew-fittit *adj.* splay-footed. *cf.* **skyow-fittit**
skice *v.* to run off quickly. *cf.* **skyce**
skichent *adj.* showing contempt. *cf.* **skech**
skicy *adj.* mean, unfair
skiff *v.* rain, snow, hail lightly
skiffin *n.* light fall (of rain, snow)
skiffie *n.* scivvy (S)
skiken *See* **skaiken**
skink *n.* shin or knuckle of beef from which soup may be made
skinnymalink *n.* a thin person
skip *v.* slide on ice
skirl *n., v.* scream
skirl(ie) *n.* squall of wind with rain or snow
skirlie *n.* oatmeal cooked with onions, dripping and seasoning; a very small quantity (A1)
skirp *n., v.* splash; *n.* fragment
skirt *v.* hurry off (A)
skiry *adj.* gaudy. *cf.* **skyrie**
Skite *pr. n.* nickname of Drumlithie
skite *v.* slip or slide suddenly; run

off quickly; rebound, ricochet;
squirt, splash; *n.* slip or skid; a
squirt of liquid; small amount of
liquor, a dram

skitie *adj.* slippery

skitter(s) *n.* diarrhoea

sklaik *n., v.* lick, smear with the
tongue. *cf.* **slaik**

sklate *n.* slate

sklater *n.* slater

sklent, sklint *v.* slope, slant; glance

sklype *n.* derog. term for someone
of dirty habits

sklyte, sklyter *v.* slip awkwardly,
fall heavily; *n.* a heavy fall;
expanse (G)

skook *v.* skulk. *cf.* **scouk**

skowf *v.* quaff; drink off. *cf.* **scoof**

skraich *v.* screech

skreefer *n.* skimmer for surface soil
and weeds (F)

skreek o day *n.* dawn

skrie *v.* shriek, cry; proclaim

skudge *v.* do rough menial work. *cf.*
scudge

skull *n.* shallow wicker basket. *cf.*
scull

skum *v.* skim

skurken *v.* dry out; shrink, shrivel

skwaal *v.* squall, scream

skweel *n.* school. *cf.* **squeel**

skweenge *v.* scrounge (of dogs and
people)

skwyle *v.* squeal. *cf.* **squile**

skyce *v.* scurry. *cf.* **skice**

skycie *adj.* unsporting, ungenerous

skyow *v.* to go askew; **skyow-fittit**
splay-footed. *cf.* **skew-fittit**

skypal *n. (var. of* **skybald**) rascal,
rogue. *cf.* **scypal**

skyre *v.* shine or glitter gaudily. *cf.*
skire

skyrie *adj.* gaudy; showy

skyte *See* **skite**

slabber *n.* mud; slush; slop

slack *v.* slake or quench thirst

slaik *v.* lick, smear with the tongue.
cf. **sklaik**

slammach *n.* gossamer, webs of
small spiders

slap *n.* opening, gap in wall or
fence

slater *n.* woodlouse

slauchter *n., v.* slaughter

slauchter-hoose *n.* slaughter-house

slaw *adj., adv.* slow

slee *adj.* sly; **sleely** *adv.* slyly

sleed *v. pt.* slid (S)

sleek *n.* alluvial deposit of mud left
in tidal rivers. *cf.* **slich**

sleekit *adj.* smooth, glossy; sly,
sneaky

sleepit *v. pt.* slept; **sleepit in**
overslept

sleicht *n.* sleight

sleumin *n.* hint; surmise

slewie *v.* walk with heavy, swinging
gait (B1)

slich *See* **sleek**

slicht *adj., n.* slight

sliddery *adj.* slippery

slider *n.* retaining rod for cattle-
binding; harness fitment on cart
shaft; ice-cream between two
wafers

slip *n.* loose frock or pinafore

slip the timmers *v.* die (M)

sliv(v)er *n., v.* slaver

slivvery-doctor *n.* harmless
jellyfish (B)

Sloch, the *pr. n.* village of Portessie
slocher *v.* (of a pig) wallow in mud
slock, slocken *v.* slake thirst
slorach *n.* wet or dirty, disgusting mess (B1)
slubber *v.* sip noisily
slung *n.* a low fellow
slype *n.* worthless fellow
sma *adj.* small; **sing sma** say little (as matter of discretion); **sma drink** of no consequence; **sma lins** small fishing lines; **sma watter** calm waters (B); **sma weet** a soft drizzle
smad *n.* blemish, smudge
smachrie *n.* hotch-potch of foods, esp. sweets
smarrach *n.* confused crowd. *cf.* **swarrach**
smatchet *n.* pert, impudent person
smeddum *n.* intelligence; shrewdness
smeeky *adj.* smoky (G1)
smeerich *n.* a kiss. *cf.* **smoorich**
smeerless *adj.* lacking spirit, energy, sluggish; handless (B1)
smeeth *adj.* smooth
smeirless *See* **smeerless**
smert *adj.* smart
smiddy *n.* blacksmith's shop
smiler *n.* small rake
smird *n.* smut, smudge. *cf.* **smad**
smirr *n.* drizzle, fine rain
smit *v.* infect; **smittin** infectious
smith *n.* blacksmith
smoocherin *n.* fine rain
smoor *v.* smother (J). *cf.* **smore**
smoorich *n.* kiss. *cf.* **smeerich**
smore *v.* smother
smout *n.* term of endearment for a young animal or child
smucht *v.* choke
smuchter *v.* smoulder
smyteral *n.* collection of small objects
sna, snaave, snaw *n.* snow. *cf.* **snyaave**
snap-an-rattle *n.* dish of oatcakes crumbled into milk (F). *cf.* **murly-tuck**
snapper *n., v.* (of a horse) stumble
snappus *adj.* testy, snappy (A2)
snavie *adj.* snowy (S)
snaw *n.* snow. *cf.* **sna**
snaw-bree *n.* melted snow; slush
snaw-fite *adj.* snow-white
sneck *n.* latch; *v.* sneak
sneck-drawin *adj.* crafty, sly (A2)
sneck-harl *v.* rough-cast a wall with mortar
sned *n.* scythe handle; *v.* cut, prune
sneeshin *n.* snuff
sneevil *v.* snivel
snell *adj.* (of the wind) cold, sharp
snicher *v.* snigger, laugh up one's sleeve
snifter *v.* sniff, draw air through the nose
snipe *See* **snype**
snippet *adj.* having a white streak down the face
snocher *v.* sniff; breathe noisily; snore
snod *adj.* tidy; neat; *v.* tidy up (C)
snod-in-aboot *n.* haircut (T)
snoot *n.* snout, nose; peak of a cap
snootit *adj.* (of a cap) peaked
snoove *v.* move smoothly, glide
snorl *n.* tangle, difficulty
snotter *n.* nasal mucus; *v.* let mucus

run from nose; snuffle; blubber

snowk *v.* (of an animal) smell about

snype *n.* rebuff; reverse of fortune; setback, let-down, loss by cheating; *v.* cheat, defraud; **snypit o** cheated by

snyte *v.* blowing the nose with finger and thumb

sober *adj.* weakly; of spare figure

socht *ppl.* sought. *cf.* **seek**

sock *n.* ploughshare

sodger *n.* soldier

softie, soft biscuit *n.* a kind of plain floury bun

some *adv.* rather, to some extent; **some caul** rather cold

some-ane, -een *n., pron.* someone

son-afore-the-father *n.* flowering currant (the blossom appearing before the leaves)

sonsy *adj.* plump and pleasant

soo *n.* sow; rectangular stack of hay or straw; **soo-moo't** having projecting upper-jaw

sooch *See* **souch**

sooder *n., v.* solder

sooie *n.* dough trimmed off edges of oatcake before baking

sook *v.* suck

sooker *n.* tree sucker; cow suckling calves

sookin caafie *adj., n.* suckling calf

soom *n.* sum; *v.* swim (C)

soon(d) *n., v.* sound. *cf.* **soun**

sooperaniwat *ppl.* superannuated

soople *adj.* supple. *cf.* **souple**

soor *adj.* sour

soord *n.* sword. *cf.* **soward**

soorness *n.* sullenness; surliness

soorocks *n.* sorrel

soosh *v.* beat severely, flog

sooter *n.* cobbler. *cf.* **souter**

sooth *adj., n.* south

sooth-kwintra *adj.* southern; English

sorn *v.* sponge upon; loaf

sorra *n.* sorrow; the Devil, used in impatient questions, *e.g.* **fat sorra idder** what other?; **she hisna her sorras tae seek** she has plenty trouble on her hands

sorrafu *adj.* sorrowful

sort *v.* mend; see to, attend to, deal with (sometimes harshly)

sortin *n.* scolding

soss *n.* mess

sotter *n.* disgusting mess

souch *n.* sigh, whistling or rushing sound; *v.* sigh, make rushing sound. *cf.* **sough**

souder *n.* solder

souff, sowf(f) *v.* whistle in a low tone; *n.* fool, simpleton

sough *n.* sigh, low whistling sound; *v.* sigh etc. *cf.* **souch**

soun *adj., n.* sound; *adv.* soundly

souple *adj.* supple

souter *n.* shoemaker; **souter's deevil** shoemaker's last. *cf.* **sooter**

southron *adj.* southern

sowans, sowens *n.* dish made by steeping and fermenting the husks or siftings of oats in water, then boiling

soward *n.* sword. *cf.* **soord**

sowd *n.* a large sum; a quantity

sowff *See* **souff**

sowl *n.* soul

spaad, spad *n.* spade. *cf.* **spaud**

spae *v.* to tell fortunes
spae-wife *n.* female fortune-teller
spaingie, spainyie *n.* W. Indian
    cane, sometimes smoked by boys;
    osiers for basket-making among
    fishermen (B)
spairge *v.* bespatter
spak *v. pt.* spoke
span *n.* span of life
spang *n., v.* spring, stride; span,
    outstretched width of hand
spark *v.* splash, mark with drops of
    water. *cf.* **sperk, spirk**
sparry *n.* sparrow (J)
sparty tow *n.* coir yarn
spate *n.* flood
spaud *See* **spaad**
spaul *n.* shoulder or forequarter of
    an animal
spaver *n.* trouser fly
spawcious *adj.* spacious
spean *v.* wean
speecial *adj.* special
speel *v.* climb
speen *n., v.* spoon; **speen aboot**
    spoon about as farmworkers
    shared the same broth bowl
speer, speir, spier *v.* ask
speerit *n.* spirit
speeshal(ly) *adj., adv.* special(ly)
speet, speeth *n.* spate, flood (B1)
speldin *n.* fresh haddock, split
    open, salted and dried in the sun
spell *n.* wood shaving
spell-beuk *n.* spelling-book
spen *v.* spend; wean (F); spawn. *cf.*
    spean
spence *n.* spare room
sperk *v.* splash
spew *v.* vomit

spiel *v.* climb. *cf.* **speel**
spik *n.* speech; conversation;
    subject of talk or gossip; *v.* speak
spile *v.* spoil
spinner, at a *phr.* at a smart rate of
    speed, at a dash
spinnle *n., v.* spindle; **spinnle-**
    shanks spindly legs
spiritool *adj.* spiritual
spirk *n.* spark; drop of rain; splash
    or spot; *v.* splash; rain slightly. *cf.*
    sperk, spark
spit *v.* to rain slightly
splatch *n.* splash
splay *v.* to mend a tear in cloth by
    sewing edges together without
    patching
spleet-new *adj.* quite new
spleeter o weet *n.* heavy shower of
    rain
spleeters *n. pl.* spillings, splashings
spleuchan *n.* tobacco-pouch. *cf.*
    splochan
splew *v.* spit out, spue
splewin *n.* vomit; term of abuse,
    e.g. **ye lazy splewin**
split *n.* quarrel; *v.* separate
split-the-win *adj., n.* Y-junction
splochan *n.* tobacco pouch. *cf.*
    spleuchan
sploiter *v.* splash, spill
splore *n.* frolic; revel
splouter *v.* splutter
spluen (B1) *See* **splewin**
splutrich *n.* a scattered mess (B1)
splyter *See* **sploiter**
spoot *n.* spout; rone pipe
sprachle *v.* sprawl. *cf.* **sprauchle**
sprag *n.* piece of wood or iron used
    to block a wheel; medium-size cod

spraikle *v.* speckle
spraing *n.* streak, usually glittering
sprauchle *See* **sprachle**
spreeth *n.* a large number (B1)
sprent *n.* spring or elastic force of anything (B1)
spring *n.* lively tune
spring-cairt *n.* cart mounted on springs
sprod *n.* an implement for dislodging limpets from a rock
sproot *n.* Brussels sprout; *v.* grow, sprout
sprot *n.* reed, rush; a coarse grass
spull *v.* spill; **spullins** spillings. *cf.* **skale**
spunk *n.* a match; mettle, energy; courage
spur-bauk *n.* cross-beam in the roof of a building (B1)
spurdie *n.* house-sparrow
spurgie *n.* house-sparrow (O)
spurk (J) *See* **spirk** *etc.*
spurkle, spurtle *n.* wooden rod for stirring porridge etc. *cf.* **theevil**
spurtle-shanks *n. pl.* thin legs
spyauck *n.* example, guide; **a gryte spyauck** a good example
squaar, squarr *adj., n., v.* square
squallach *v.* squeal
squeeb *n.* firework
squeel *n.* school. *cf.* **skweel**
squile *v.* squeal. *cf.* **skwyle**
sta(a) *n.* stall
staamer *v.* stagger
stacher *v.* stagger
stack *n.* a pile of peats; *v. pt., ppl.* stuck
stackit *ppl.* (e.g. of hay) built into a stack

stackyaird *n.* rick-yard
staffy-nevel *adj.* staff-in-hand; **staffy-nevel job** a fight with cudgels
stag-moss *n.* alpine club moss
staig *n.* stallion
stail *v.* steal (S)
stainch *adj.* staunch. *cf.* **stanch**
stairch *n., v.* starch
stairt *n., v.* start, begin
stairvation *n.* starvation. *See* **sterve**
stairve *v.* to starve. *cf.* **sterve**
staito *n.* statue (A2)
stale *v.* steal
stamach, stam(m)ack *n.* stomach; *v.* stomach; endure
stame *n.* steam
stame-mull *n.* steam-driven threshing-machine. *cf.* **stem-mull; stame-mull breid** thick, poorly-made oatcakes (F)
stammack *See* **stamach**
stammygaster *n.* shock; *v.* flabbergast
stan *v.* stand; **stannin** *ppl.* standing
stance *n.* site; station
stanch *adj., v.* staunch. *cf.* **stainch**
stane *n.* stone. *cf.* **steen**
stane-cast *n.* stone's throw
stang *n.* sting; pole; steering-rod; tongue of a Jew's harp; **stang o the trump** the best of all, best of a family
stank *n.* pond; ditch; marshy ground; *(fig.)* **help a chiel ower a stank**
stap *n.* step; *v.* stop; block up; stuff
starkly *adv.* strongly, bravely
starn, starnie *n.* star; small quantity

sta(r)shie *n.* row, uproar. *cf.*
  stushie
staucher *v.* to stagger
steadin *n.* steading, farmstead
stech *v.* cram; satiate, gorge; create
  a stifling atmosphere; **stecht** *ppl.*
  overheated (G)
steed *v. pt.* stood. *See* **stan**
steek *v.* shut; clench; stitch; *n.* stitch
steel *n.* stool; fellow (B1)
steelbow *n.* system under which
  farm stock, implements etc. could
  be held by the tenant under
  contract to the landlord
steen *n., v.* stone. *cf.* **stane**
steen-chackert *n.* stone-chat (M)
Steenhive *pr. n.* nickname for
  Stonehaven, Kincardineshire
steeny *adj.* stony
steepin *n.* a wetting, drenching;
  stipend, minister's salary
steepit loaf *phr.* bread poultice (B)
steer *n., v.* stir, bustle
steigh *v.* fill with bad air or fumes
steil *See* **steel**
steilert *n.* steelyard, weighing
  machine (F)
stem *v.* (nautical) keep a certain
  course
stem-mull *n.* steam-driven
  threshing-machine. *cf.* **stame-
  mull**
stench *v.* staunch
sten(d) *v.* stride (A2)
stent *n.* extent of task, stint; *v.* stint
sterve *v.* starve. *cf.* **stairve; sterve
  o, wi the caul** feel chilled;
  stervation bitter cold
stey *adj.* steep; *n.* stay, support; *in
  pl.* corsets; *v.* stay

stibble *n.* stubble; **stibble ruckie**
  mini-cornstack built by cottar
  loons from stubble roots (T)
stick *v.* stick; come to a premature
  halt in a job etc.; **stickit minister**
  student of the ministry who has
  failed to be licensed as a preacher
stick in *v.* to persevere
stickly *adj.* (of peat) fibrous, woody
stiffen *n.* stiffening, starch
still an on *adv.* nevertheless
stilp *v.* stalk
stilpert *n.* stilt; long-legged, lanky
  person or animal
stilt *n.* handle of plough (F)
stime, styme *n.* a tiny amount
stinch *adj.* staunch; strict
stirk *n.* young bullock; a stupid
  fellow
stirkie's sta *n.* the place in the cowshed reserved for the stirk; the
  place of a child, *(e.g.* father's lap)
  when the mother has a younger
  baby
stirlin *n.* starling
stite *n.* nonsense; stumble. *cf.* **stoit,
  styte**
stiter *v.* stumble. *cf.* **stoiter**
stob *n.* thorn; stake; **stobbit**
  thatched by means of a stake; *v.*
  stub (the toe etc.)
stock *n.* chap, fellow
stockit *adj.* obstinate
stodge *v.* walk slowly, stomp
stoit, stoiter *v.* stagger, totter. *cf.*
  stite, styter, stotter
stoker *n.* odd job-lot of fish, sold
  by a ship's crew for cash (B)
stoo *v.* cut (off) (animal's tail,
  shoots of tree, a fishing net)

stook *n.* a shock of sheaves; *v.* to put into shocks

stookie *n.* stucco, plaster of Paris

stookin *n.* the arrangement of corn in shocks, usually ten/twelve sheaves per shock

stoon(d) *n., v.* ache; throb. *cf.* **stound**

stoor *n.* flying dust. *cf.* **stour**; *v.* pour (can be used of rain); gush

stoorie *adj.* dusty

stoorum *n.* gruel

stoot *adj.* stout; strong (A, A2)

stop *v.* live or stay at an address

store the kin *phr.* to keep the human race in existence by living on. *fig.* to survive, to keep going, last out in general (M)

stot *n.* castrated bullock older than a stirk; **stot** *n., v.* bounce; walk with a spring; stagger

stots-and-bangs *adj., adv.* intermittent(ly); *n.* occasional work

stotter *v.* stumble. *cf.* **stoiter**

stound *See* **stoond**

stoup *n.* deep, narrow vessel for holding liquids: flagon; jug; *in pl.* props, supports; the two pieces of a cart which project beyond the body

stoupie *n.* small liquid measure; cream pot (B1)

stour *n.* dust; a downpour. *cf.* **stoor**

stourie *adj.* dusty

stovies *n.* stoved potatoes cooked in stew-pan with onion, fat and meat scraps

stow *v.* steal; **stowen** stolen; **stown-wyes** by stealth, secretly

stowff *n.* slow, measured gait; *v.* stump; plod

stra *v.* straw; *in phr.* **stra his beets** put straw (as soles) into his boots (formerly a custom of farm servants) (R). *cf.* **strae**

straaberry *n.* strawberry

strab *n.* stalk of loose straw lying on the field after harvesting or sticking out from a sheaf or stack; anything adhering loosely to one's clothes

strachen *v.* straighten. *cf.* **straichen**

stracht *adj., adv.* straight; **stracht-edge** strip of iron used to align the **couter** and **sock** with the body of the horse plough (T). *cf.* **straucht**

stracht-oot-the-gate *adj.* straightforward

strack *v. pt.* struck

strade *v. pt.* strode

strae *n.* straw; *v.* to give straw to animals; **strae his beets** put straw into his boots for warmth (T). *cf.* **stra**

strae-soo *n.* long stack of straw

straichen *v.* straighten. *cf.* **strachen**

straik *n., v.* stroke. *See* **strake**

straik *n.* sharpening board or stone for scythe; wooden cylinder for levelling a bushel measure (F)

strainer, strainin post *n.* post taking the strain of the wire in fencing (F)

strait *adj.* rigid

strak *v. pt.* stroked. *See* **strake**

strake *v.* stroke. *cf.* **straik**

stramash *n.* uproar, commotion

strang *adj.* strong; *n.* urine

strapper *n.* young farm servant looking after the **shalt** (F). *cf.* **shalt-loon**

strappin *adj.* tall, handsome and agile

strathspey *n.* Highland dance

strauchen *v.* to straighten

straucht *adj.* straight. *cf.* **stracht** *v.* straighten (A1). *cf.* **strauchen**

strauchtwye *adv.* straightaway

stravaig *v.* wander

streck *adj.* strict. *cf.* **strick**

streek *v.* stretch. *cf.* **streetch, rax**

streen, the *n., adv.* yesterday evening; last night; yesterday. *cf.* **yestreen**

streetch *v.* stretch (A2). *cf.* **streek, rax**

streeve *v. pt.* strove; struggled; fell out, quarrelled

strenth *n.* strength

strick *adj.* strict; *v.* strike

stridelins *prep.* astride

strik *See* **strick**

strin *n.* jet of milk from a cow's teat

stripe *n.* small open drain

strive *v.* quarrel; **striven** *ppl.* having quarrelled, fallen out

stroop(ie) *n.* spout (of teapot etc); spout; water tap; outlet at spring

stroud *n.* silly song

strucken *ppl.* struck

strunge *adj.* surly, gruff, morose

strush, strushie *n.* quarrel; disturbance

strushel *adj.* untidy, slovenly

strushlach *n.* untidy woman

struve *v. pt.* strove

strype *n.* small stream

stucken *ppl.* stuck

studdy *n.* anvil

stue *n.* dust. *cf.* **styoo, stoor**

stumpart, stumper *v.* walk clumsily in a stumping way

stur *n., v.* stir. *cf.* **steer**

sturken *adj.* sulky, sour

sturt *n.* strife (C)

styoo *n.* dust. *cf.* **styoo, stoor**

styoomer *n.* foolish person

styter *v.* stumble, totter; **styterin fou** incapably drunk. *cf.* **stoiter**

sub *n., v.* advance wages

subjeck *n.* subject

succar *n.* sugar

sucken *n.* the district thirled to a mill; generally, the district in which anyone carries on business (A2)

suddent *adj.* sudden (C)

suddenty *n.* suddenness; **in (on) a suddenty** suddenly

sudderinwid *n.* southernwood

sug *n.* easy-going individual

sumph *n.* fool, simpleton

sung *ppl., adj.* singed

sunnel *n.* sand-eel (B)

sunsheen *n.* sunshine

sup *v.* take food or liquid, esp. with a spoon

sup(pie) *n.* sip, small quantity

superannuat *ppl.* superannuated

suppersteetion *n.* superstition

supplicant *n.* a beggar

surtoo, surtout *n.* old-fashioned coat

suspeck *v.* suspect

swack, swak *adj.* supple, nimble

swacken *v.* make supple, pliant

swad *n.* swede, Swedish turnip

Swaddish neep *n.* swede
swaleheidit (S) *See* **swall-heidit**
swall *v.* swell
swall-heidit *adj.* swollen-headed
swally *v.* swallow
swap *v.* to rope thatch with a **cloo**
swarf *n., v.* faint, swoon
swarrach *n.* crowd, swarm. *cf.*
  smarrach
swashy *adj.* grand, dashing
swat *n., v.* sweat, *pt.* **swat; swattit**
  sweated (M). *cf.* **swate, swyte**
swatch *n.* sample
swate *v.* sweat (A2). *cf.* **swat,**
  swyte
sweel *v.* swill, rinse; swirl
sweem *v.* swim
sweemer *n.* swimmer; **twinty-**
  minute sweemer doughball (B)
sweeng *n., v.* swing
sweengletree *See* **swingle-tree**
sweer, sweir *adj.* lazy; unwilling; *v.*
  swear
sweer-tree, puin the *phr.* a game in
  which two people sitting on the
  ground, hold a stick between
  them and try to pull each other up
sweer(-wird) *n.* swear(-word)
sweesh *v.* swish, brush
sweety-wife *n.* female sweet-seller
sweir *See* **sweer**
sweirty *n.* laziness
sweetie-boolie *n.* round sweet
sweeties, readin *n. pl.* conversation
  lozenges
sweevle *v.* swivel

swey *v.* sway, swing
swick *n.* cheat; blame; *v.* swindle
swidder *See* **swither**
swig *v.* sway, move from side to
  side (J)
swine's hoose *n.* pigsty
swingletree *n.* as in Eng., bar in a
  plough-draught to which the
  theats are attached
swipe *v.* sweep. *cf.* **swype**
swippert *adj.* nimble. *cf.* **swyppirt**
swite *n., v.* sweat. *cf.* **swyte**
swith *adv.* swiftly
swithe *v.* hasten, get away
swither *n.* quandary; *v.* to be
  undecided; hesitate. *cf.* **swidder**
swourd *n.* sword. *cf.* **soord,**
  soward
swult *v.* sob deeply (B)
swuppert, swyppirt *adj.* nimble,
  agile; swift
swye *n.* pivoted rod in chimney for
  hanging pots over the fire-place;
  sway, influence; *v.* sway
swype *v.* sweep. *cf.* **swipe**
swyte *n., v.* sweat. *cf.* **swat, swate**
sye *v.* strain liquid; pour milk
  through a sieve. *cf.* **sey**
syer *n.* milk strainer. *cf.* **syre**
syne *adv.* since, ago; then
sype *v.* seep, drip; **sypit** *ppl.*
  soaked
syre *n.* drain in street gutter,
  including the covering grating. *cf.*
  syer

— T —

tablin *n.* top stones on a gable

tack *n.* lease of a farm; leased farm; **tack o life** lease of life

tacket *n.* stud, hobnail; **tackety beets** hobnailed boots

tackie, takie *n.* the game of tag

tae *n.* toe; *prep.* to; for; by; **tae masel** by myself. *cf.* **tay**

tae, the *adj.* the one, contrasted with the other. *cf.* **the taen**

tae-ee *n.* a pet

taen *ppl.* taken (S). *cf.* **tane, teen**

tag *n.* leather strap, tawse; **i the tag** hard at work

taik *n.* stroll; **tak taik** take stock (T)

taikle *n.* harness; tackle

tailer *n.* tool for taking roots off turnips (F)

tail-eyn *n.* the tail end

taings *n. pl.* tongs, hinged wire-tightener in fencing

tait *n.* lock of hair, wool etc.; small portion

tak *v.* take; **tak aboot** take care of, look after, see to; **tak aff** copy down; **tak in han** undertake; **tak throwe-han** discuss; **tak sheet** take flight (*orig. naut.* B, T)

Tam *pr. n.* deriv. of Thomas

Tamintoul *pr. n.* Tomintoul village

tamteen *n.* a tontine

tane *adj.* the one. *cf.* **taen**

tangles *n. pl.* kind of seaweed

tansy *n.* ragwort; tansy

tantaleeze *v.* tantalise

tap *n., v.* top

tapdress *n.* manure on the surface

tapner *n.* tool for removing turnip-tops (F)

tappit *adj.* crested

tappit-hen *n.* crested hen; Scottish quart measure of ale or claret, with a knob on its lid

tapsalteerie *adv.* topsy-turvy

tapster *n.* the person at the top

tare *n., v.* tear

tares *n. pl.* beans and peas grown among oats for cattle feed (T)

tarick *n.* Arctic tern (B)

tarlich *n.* any puny, worthless creature

tarraneese *n., v. (lit.* **tyrannise**) tease, torment

tarry-fingert *adj.* light-fingered

tase oot *v.* tease out (S)

tashed, tasht *adj.* fatigued; well worn

tasment, tastement *n.* will, testament. *cf.* **tesment**

tassie *n.* drinking cup; glass; goblet

tatterwallop *n.* ragged person

tatterwallops *n. pl.* rags and tatters

tattie, tatie *n.* potato

tattie-boodie *n.* scarecrow (A)

tattie-bootie *n.* scarecrow (C)

tattie-chapper *n.* potato masher

tattie-clamp *n.* earth pit for storing potatoes

tattie-doodle *n.* scarecrow (S)

tattie-dulie *n.* scarecrow (J)

tattie-howker *n.* potato-digger

tattie-howkin *n.* potato harvest
tattie-liftin *n.* potato harvest (J)
tattie-shaws *n.* potato foliage
taucht *ppl.* taught
taul *v. pt.* told. *cf.* **telt**
tawpie *n.* stupid fellow, blockhead
tawse *n.* leather strap for punishment
tay *n.* tea
tayspeen *n.* teaspoon; **tayspenfae** teaspoonful
tchach *excl. of disgust, contempt, impatience etc.*
tchoot *int.* tush!
ted *n.* toad, applied to men as term of contempt, to children or young women as term of endearment
tee *adv.* too; also
tee, keep her *naut. phr.* alter course to windward (B)
teel *n.* tool
teem *adj., v.* empty; **teem yer crap** get it off your chest
teen *n.* tune; humour, temper; **ill teen** bad mood; *ppl.* taken; **teen wi** charmed by, pleased with; **the teen** the one, *(in contrast with* **the tither** the other). *cf.* **tak, taen**
teep *n.* type
teer *n.* tare; tear
teet *v.* peep
teeth *in phr.* **a teeth in the sky** a broken rainbow (T)
teethache *n.* toothache
teetle *n.* title
teind *n., v.* tithe. *cf.* **tiend**
telt *v. pt., ppl.* told
tent *n.* care; **tak tent** give heed to
tentily *adv.* carefully, attentively

tenty *adj.* careful, attentive
term-time *n.* end of working contract: Whitsunday; Martinmas
terrible *adv.* exceedingly
terrifee *v.* terrify; **terrifeet** *ppl.* terrified
tesment *n.* will, testament. *cf.* **tasment**
teuch *adj.* tough. *cf.* **tyeuch**
teuchat, teuchit *n.* lapwing; **teuchat's storm** wintry weather in March, when the lapwings arrive
teuchter *n.* (sometimes disparaging) *ref.* to anyone from the North, to a Highlander or Gaelic-speaker
teuk *v. pt.* took
thack *n., v.* thatch; **thackit** *ppl.* thatched
thae *adj.* those (S, J, C)
thaese *See* **thase**
than *adv.* then; **than-an-awaa** long ago
thase *adj.* these
that *adv.* so, *e.g.* **it wis that caul**
theat *n.* trace by which horses draw plough etc.; **kick owre the theats** kick over the traces, become reckless; **lat the theats slack** take it easy; **oot o theat** unreasonable
theek *v.* thatch (J). *cf.* **thack**
theet *See* **theat**
theevil *n.* wooden rod for stirring porridge. *cf.* **spurtle**
thegidder, thegither *adv.* together
theirsels *pron.* themselves; *pred. adj., adv.* by themselves, alone; **theirsels twa** just the two of them

thenk *v.* thank (S)

thereoot *adv.* outside; in the open air

thewless *adj.* feeble

thiefie *adj.* thief-like, sneaky

thig *v.* beg, borrow, be a genteel beggar; generally applied to the practice of begging seed oats to sow first crop on entering a farm

thigger *n.* genteel beggar

thingumboob, thingumenderry *n.* thingummybob

thin-skint *adj.* sensitive, easily upset

thirl *v.* to thrill; tingle; to bring under legal obligation; **thirlt** *ppl.* bound, enthralled

thirlage *n.* bondage

thocht *n., v. pt., ppl.* thought

thocht-been *n.* wish-bone

thochtie *n.* a little bit

thole *v.* bear; endure; tolerate

thon *pron.* that; *adj.* that, yonder; those. *cf.* **yon**

thoom, thoomb *n., v.* thumb; **thoom-piece** *n.* oatcakes buttered with thumb; **thoom-raip** *n.* thumb rope

thoosan(d) *n.* thousand

thorther, thorter *v.* cross harrow (F)

thow *n.* thaw

thowless *adj.* lacking energy or mettle

thraan *adj.* stubborn. *cf.* **thrawn**

thrammle *n.* chain on cattle-binding, for attaching **sell** to a stake

thrang *n.* throng; *adj.* crowded; thick, intimate; busy

thrapple *v.* throttle; *n.* throat

thrash *n.* threshed grain

thrashin-mull *n.* threshing-mill

thraten *v.* threaten

thrave *n.* two **stooks** or 20/24 **shaifs**; *v. pt.* thrived

thraw *v.* throw, twist

thrawcruik, thrawheuk *n.* implement for twisting straw ropes

thrawn *adj.* stubborn; twisted

thraws, in the *phr.* in the grip of (fig.)

threep *n.* a vehemently held opinion; *v.* argue, quarrel; insist

threeple *adj.* triple, threefold; *v.* treble

threeplet *n.* triplet

threet *n., v.* threat; **threet'nin** *ppl.* threatening

three-threids-an-a-thrum *phr.* cat's purr (G)

threeve *v. pt.* thrived

threip *See* **threep**

thrissle, thristle *n.* thistle

thrist *n.* thirst

thristy *adj.* thirsty

thro(u) *prep.* through. *cf.* **throw**

throu-beerin *n.* livelihood, means of sustenance (A1)

throu-han *adv.* under consideration; **tak throu-han** discuss

throu-idder, -ither *See* **throwder**

throu-the-muir *n.* quarrel

throw(e) *prep.* through; **throwe the bows (of behaviour)** beyond all bounds; *adj.* finished. *cf.* **throu**

throw-come *n.* ordeal

throwder *adj.* untidy; muddled; in

a confused state

throw-gang *n.* passage

thrums *n.* ends of yarn; purring of a cat; **span her thrums** purred

thummle *n.* thimble

thunner *n.* thunder

tice (wi) *v.* coax

tichen *v.* tighten

ticht *adj.* tight

tick an tack *n.* the game of tag. *cf.* **tackie**

ticket *n.* someone of untidy appearance

tidder *adj., n.* the other. *cf.* **tither**

tiend *n., v.* tithe. *cf.* **teind**

Tiesday *n.* Tuesday. *cf.* **Tyesday**

tig *n.* fit of ill-humour; a sudden whim; **tae tak a tig** (R) to take a notion; *v.* touch lightly, tap; **tig wi** dally; have to do with; **tig-tire** a state of suspense

tike *n.* dog; unpleasant man

till *prep.* to; compared to

tillie-pan *n.* metal pan used as a scoop (F)

tillygraph *n., v.* telegraph

tillyphone *n., v.* telephone

tilter *n.* used for tilting loose sheaves off an old-fashioned mower or reaper

time-sairin *adj.* time-serving

timmer *n.* timber; **wun-timmer** seasoned timber (T); **Timmer-mairket** ancient fair held in Aberdeen in August; *adj.* wooden

timmer on, up *v.* work vigorously

tin *n.* money (A)

tin-can *n.* corrugated iron

tine *v.* lose; **tint** *pt., ppl.* lost

tink *n.* (term of contempt) foul-mouthed, quarrelsome, vulgar person

tinkie *n.* tinker, one of the travelling people; **tinkie's maskin** tea made in the cup

tinkler *n.* tinker; **tinkler's curse** something of no value

tint *ppl., adj.* lost; *n.* tent

tippen *n.* the hair that binds a hook to a fishing line

tipperteen *n.* bit of card with pin passed through it resembling a teetotum, a top

tire *n.* tiredness

tirl *n.* vibration; short bout of anything; *v.* vibrate

tirl the sneck *phr.* twirl the handle of the latch

tirr *v.* strip off; uncover, undress; unroof, tear off slates/thatch

tirran *n.* tyrant; awkward or exasperating person

tirravee *n.* commotion

tit *n.* teat; *v.* jerk, twitch, pull

tither, the *adj.* the other. *cf.* **tidder**

tittersome *adj.* (of weather) unsettled; (of a horse) restless

titty *n.* (child's word) sister

tobacca *n.* tobacco

tocher *n.* dowry

tod *n.* fox

toit *v.* trot; totter from age

tolerat *v.* tolerate

tongue *v.* scold, abuse

tongue-betroosht *adj.* outspoken

tongue-tackit *ppl., adj.* tongue-tied

tool *n.* towel

toom *adj.* empty (G1, M, J). *cf.* **teem**

toon *n.* a town; farmstead. *cf.* **toun**

toondie, toondy *See* **toonkeeper**

toonkeeper *n.* the person left in charge of a farmstead on Sunday. *cf.* **catcher, toondie**

toonser *n.* town-dweller

toopachin, toopican *n.* pinnacle, summit; steeple, turret

toor *n., v.* tower; **toorin** *ppl.* towering. *cf.* **tour**

toorie *n.* topknot (on bonnet)

toosht *v.* handle carelessly

tooshtie *n.* small quantity

toosle, toozle *v.* dishevel; tussle

toosy *adj.* tousled. *cf.* **tousy**

tooter *v.* work ineffectually

tooteroo *n.* wind instrument

tootie *n.* dram

toot-moot *n.* low muttered conversation; whispering (B1)

topper *n.* first class person or thing

toppers *n. pl.* rubber knee boots worn by fishworkers (B)

tory *n.* grub of cranefly, which consumes germinating grain

tossel, toshil *n.* tassle

tossle *v.* tousle. *cf.* **toosle, touzle**

tottum, totum *n.* a teetotum, four-sided top spun in games of chance; the game itself

toun *n.* farm. *cf.* **toon**

tour *n.* tower; **tourin** *ppl.* towering

tousy *adj.* tousled, dishevelled. *cf.* **toosy**

touzle *v.* ruffle, dishevel. *cf.* **toosle, tossle**

tow *n.* rope; strong twine; **claes tow** washing line

tow-heidit *adj.* fair-haired (G)

towmond, towmon *n.* twelve-months

trachel, trachle *n.* burden, hindrance, struggle; *v.* draggle; trudge; overwork. *cf.* **trauchle**

trachelt *adj.* overburdened, draggled. *cf.* **trauchlet**

track *n.* an oddity (used of untidy person); *v.* to train an animal to go in traces or harness

trackie *n.* earthenware teapot

traecle *n.* treacle

traet *v.* treat

trag *n.* trash

traik *n.* long, tiring walk, trudge; *v.* trudge

trail *n.* dirty, untidy woman; part, portion; *v.* tramp, trudge

trail the rape old Hallowe'en spell consisting in dragging a straw rope round the house (M)

traivel *n.* journey; walk (S); *v. tr., intr.* travel; walk

traleel *n.* something long and trailing; a tall person (B1)

tram *n.* shaft of barrow or cart

trammle *n.* chain on cattle-binding. *cf.* **thrammle**

tramp-cole *n.* large haycock, made up of smaller ones (F)

trampit *v. pt.* tramped

trams *n.* shafts as of a cart

trance *n.* passage in a house; entrance-hall

transack *n.* transaction; deal; dealings

trauchle *See* **trachle**

trauchelt *See* **trachelt**

travise, trevis *n.* division between stalls in cowshed

trebble *n.* trouble (B1). *cf.* **tribble**

treesh *v.* curry favour; treat in a

friendly, flattering way; call to
cattle

treetle *v.* trickle; trot (G)

treid *v.* tread (J)

tribble *n., v.* trouble. *cf.* **trebble**

tribbler *n.* a troublesome thing (A)

trickit *adj.* tricky; wicked; delighted (S); **fair trickit wi masel**

trickit (up) *ppl.* dressed (up)

triffle, trifflie *n.* trifle; small sum

trig *adj.* tidy; *v.* to tidy up, dress
smartly; *ppl.* **triggit (oot)**

trink, trinkie *n.* narrow channel;
rut

trinkle *n., v.* trickle

trippin *in phr.* **his face wis trippin
im** he looked glum, displeased

troch *n.* watering trough for cattle
and horses

trock *n.* goods of no value; trash; *v.*
exchange, barter. *cf.* **troke**

trogs *excl.* troth! (as an oath)

troke *See* **trock**

troo *v.* trust; believe

trool *n.* trowel

troonk *n.* lobster pot (term used in
St Combs)

troosers *n. pl.* trousers

troot *n.* trout

trowth *n., int.* truth

trowthfu *adj.* truthful

true, true the squeel *v.* play truant

truff *n.* turf

trump(e) *n.* Jew's harp

truncher *n.* trencher, wooden
platter

trykle *n.* treacle

trypal *n.* tall, lanky, ill-shaped
person

tryst *v.* appoint a meeting; entice; *n.*

an appointed meeting

trytle *v.* lag (A1)

tull *prep.* to; till

tulzie *n.* quarrel

tummle *n., v.* tumble

tummle-doon *adj.* tumbledown

tummler *n.* glass tumbler

tummle the cat *phr.* do a
somersault (O)

tummlin-tam *n.* hay-gatherer (F)

turk *adj.* angry, annoyed (A1)

turkis *n.* a pair of pincers

turned gyang *ppl., n.* row of
sheaves on a stack, with the shear
underneath (F)

turnkwite *n.* turncoat; backslider

turn-oot *n.* attendance

turn ower *v.* fare moderately well

Turra *pr. n.* nickname for Turriff

Turra Coo *pr. n.* dairy cow confis-
cated from a Turriff farmer who
refused to stamp the insurance
cards of his workers, when the
Health Insurance Act was intro-
duced in 1913. A riot ensued
when the cow was put up for sale

turse *v.* dress; adjust one's clothes

twa *adj.* two

twa-han *adj.* two-handed

twal *adj.* twelve

twalmont(h) *n.* a twelve-month
period

twa-three *adj., n.* two or three, a
few, several

tweetle *v.* tootle on a wind
instrument

tweezlock, tweezlick *See*
thawcruick

twig *n.* glance; *v.* glance; catch
sight of; see through a dodge

twine *n.* string; *v.* turn, twist
twiner *n.* rope-twister
twinty *adj.* twenty
twise *adv.* twice (A1)
tyangs *n. pl.* tongs
tyaave, tyauve *v.* work strenuously, struggle; *n.* struggle
tyce *v.* entice
tye *excl.* giving assent. *cf.* **ay**
Tyesday *n.* Tuesday (A). *cf.* **Tiesday**

tyeuch *See* **teuch**
tyeuk *v. pt.* took
tyke *n.* dog; ticking for beds. *cf.* **tike**
tyler *n.* tailor
tylie *n.* tailor
tyne *See* **tine**
type *v.* labour hard; **a typin job** physically exhausting job (A1)
typit *adj., ppl.* worn out by hard work

— **U** —

ug *v.* to feel disgust; **uggit** disgusted
ugsome *adj.* disgusting, ghastly, horrible
ulkie *adj.* each, every. *cf.* **ilka**
ull, ull- *See* **ill, ill-**
ulless-guidless *adj.* harmless
ull-wull *n.* ill will
umberella *n.* umbrella
umman *n.* woman. *cf.* **'oman**
umrage *n.* umbrage
un- *for most words beginning with* **un**, *see* **oon**
unbehauden *adj.* not obliged
unca, unco *adj.* strange; unknown; odd; peculiar; extraordinary; **unca man** stranger; *adv.* extremely; very
uncanny *adj.* dangerous, threatening (supernaturally); unearthly, ghostly; weird
unce *n.* ounce
unceevil *adj.* uncivil
unco *See* **unca**
unco-gweed *n.* self-righteous

uncolies *adv.* strangely; very much, extremely
unctioneer *n.* auctioneer. *cf.* **ungshineer**
unedicat *adj.* uneducated
ungshin *n.* auction
ungshineer *n.* auctioneer
unlade *v.* unload
unnersteed *v. pt.* understood
unsocht *ppl., adj.* unsought
unvrocht *adj.* unworked (land)
up-castin *n.* rising of clouds above horizon threatening rain
upcome *n.* quick-witted remark
upfessin, upfeshin *n.* upbringing
uphaud *v.* uphold
upo *prep.* upon
upple *v.* (of weather) clear
upsettin *adj.* pretentious
upsides wi *adv.* even with
up-tail *v.* depart in a hurry; run off
uptak *n.* apprehension
up-through *n.* upper part of the country
upwuth *adv.* up the way, upwards

— V —

vailyable *adj.* valuable
vailye *n., v.* value
vainish *v.* vanish
valinteen *n.* valentine
vauntie *adj.* vain; exultant;
ostentatious
vawcant *adj.* vacant
vawpour *n.* vapour
veelent *adj.* violent
veeperate *adj.* venomous, vicious;
bitterly abusive
veesion *n.* vision
veeshus *adj.* vicious
veesit *n.* visit
veesitor *n.* visitor
vennel *n.* alley, narrow lane
vera, verra *adj., adv.* very
verlies *adv.* actually
veshel *n.* vessel
vex *v.* distress, upset; **vexed** *ppl.*
distressed; sorry
viackle *n.* vehicle
vice *n.* voice. *cf.* **vyce**
virr *n.* force, vigour, 'go'
vizzy *n.* look; view; **vizzy backart**
backward look
vokie *adj.* jocular (A2). *cf.* **vyokie**

voo *v.* vow
vooch *v.* vouch
vrack *n.* wreck, ruin
vran *n.* wren
vrang *adj., n.* wrong. *cf.* **wrang**
vrap *v.* wrap
vrapper *n.* working smock, overall;
woman's loose jacket, blouse
vrastle *v.* wrestle (B1). *cf.* **warsle**
vrat *v. pt.* wrote
vratch *n.* wretch
vreath *n.* a wreath of snow
vreet *v.* write; *n.* handwriting
vreeter *n.* writer
vreetin *n.* handwriting
vreetin-dask *n.* writing-desk
vreetin-paper *n.* writing paper
vricht *n.* wright, joiner, carpenter
vring *v.* wring
vrocht *v. pt.* wrought, worked
vrote *v. pt.* wrote
vrung *ppl.* wrung
vrutten *ppl.* written. *See* **vreet**
vyaig *n.* loose woman
vyce *n.* voice. *cf.* **vice**
vyokie *adj.* jocular. *cf.* **vokie**

— W —

wa *adv.* away; *n.* wall; way; **come
yer was ben** come away in or
through. *cf.* **awa**
waal *n.* well
waal-tams *n. pl.* Buchan name for
nicky-tams

waan *n.* wand
waar *adj.* worse; **waar o the weer**
the worse for wear. *cf.* **waur**
waares *n.* wares
waav *n.* wave
wab *n.* web, woven fabric

wabbit *adj.* exhausted
wabster *n.* weaver
wa-cast *adj., n.* (anything) worthless
wacht *See* **weicht**
wachy *adj.* stale (B)
wad *v.* wed, marry; would. *cf.* **wid**
waddin *n.* wedding
waddit *v. pt.* wedded, married
wadge *v.* brandish threateningly
wadna *v. neg.* would not
wadset *v.* mortgage
wae *n.* woe; *adj.* sad, sorrowful; sorry; **wae for** sorry for; **wae's me** woe is me!
waefu *adj.* woeful
waesome *adj.* sorrowful, sad
waff *n.* puff of wind; whiff, odour
waffle *adj.* limp from weakness; shaky
wag *v.* wave, shake
wag-at-the-wa *n.* wall clock with pendulum
wa-gawn *adj.* departing; *n.* departure
waik *adj.* weak. *cf.* **wyke**
waikness *n.* weakness. *cf.* **wykeness**
wainished-like *adj.* (vanished-like), thin, pinched
wair *v.* spend. *cf.* **ware**
waister *n.* something, someone of no further use, due to infirmity, disease etc.
waistry *n.* waste. *cf.* **wastrie**
wale *v.* choose; *n.* choice, selection
wale *int.* well (S). *cf.* **weel**
walgin *n.* something large and roomy (incl. an article of dress)
wall *n.* well. *cf.* **waal**

wallant *adj.* (of flowers) withered
wallet *n.* bag for carrying personal necessaries on journey
walloch *n.* Highland dance; *v.* cry, shriek, wail
wally-draggle,-draigle *n.* sloven; good-for-nothing; insignificant, untidy person. *cf.* **warridrag**
walthy *adj.* wealthy
wame *n.* belly; stomach. *cf.* **wime**
wamfle *adj.* flexible
wammle *v.* roll, undulate, writhe
wan *adv.* way; **Kintore wan** in the direction of Kintore; *n.* wand, fishing-rod; *v. pt.* won; **wan aff** got off
wan'er, wanner *v.* wander
wanworth, wanwurth *n.* a mere nothing, something of little value (A1)
wap *n.* sharp stroke; *v.* strike sharply; flap
war *v.* were; **warna** were not
wardle *n.* world. *cf.* **warl**
wardly *adj.* worldly
ware *n.* cash (S); wire (S). *cf.* **weer** *v.* spend. *cf.* **wair**
wark *n.* work; **a wark** a job; fuss; **sic a wark** what a fuss
warl, warld *n.* world. *cf.* **wardle**
warly-wise *adj.* worldly-wise
warn *v.* warrant
warna *v. neg.* were not
warridrag *n.* good-for-nothing; undersized person or animal; slow-coach; **warriedrags, towrags an swypins o the pier** riff-raff (B)
warsh *adj.* insipid. *cf.* **wersh**
warsle, warstle *v.* wrestle, struggle

warst *adj., n.* worst

was *in phr.* **was-a-year** a year ago

washen *ppl.* washed

waskit *n.* waistcoat. *cf.* **weskit**

wast *adj.* west; **waster** western; **wastward** *adv.* westward

wastrie *n.* waste. *cf.* **waistry**

wat *adj.* wet

watna *v. neg.* wot not, did not know

watrence *n.* an entry cut through hedge or bank to give stock access to drinking water

watter *n.* water; **wattery** water closet, lavatory

watter-brash *n.* heartburn (with watery acid eructations)

watter-gless *n.* water-glass, a solution used for preserving eggs

wauble *adj.* of a weak watery flavour; wobbly; *v.* wobble

wauch *n.* swig

wauchle *v.* struggle; waddle; wade

waucht *n.* large draught; weight. *cf.* **wecht**

wauchty *adj.* weighty, heavy

wauger *n., v.* wager

wauges *n. pl.* wages

wauk *n., v.* walk

wauken *v.* waken

wauker *n.* walker; **by wauker's bus** on Shanks' pony, on foot

waukie *n.* walk; walkway, path

waukrife *adj.* wakeful

waur *adj.* worse; **waurst** worst; *v.* spend (money); **waur i the weer** the worse for wear

wean *n.* child (A, M)

wear awa *v.* to take one's leave; to fade away; die

weariet *adj.* wearied

wecht *n.* weight. *cf.* **wacht, waucht** sieve with solid base

wedder *n.* wether, castrated ram

wee *adj.* small; *n.* a little bit; a little while; **bide-a-wee** stay a while

weeda *n.* widow

weel *adj., excl.* well

weel-a-wat *excl.* assuredly

weel-a-wins *See* **weel-a-wuns**

weel-a-wite *excl.* assuredly

weel-a-wuns *excl.* of soothing and endearment

weel-faured, -faurt *adj.* well-favoured, handsome

weel-geddert *adj.* well off

weelins *v., n.* full use of one's limbs or faculties, *e.g.* **tae hae the weelins o yer airms** (B1)

weel-kent *adj.* well-known

Weelum *pr. n.* William

weemen, weemin *n.* women

weemple an wample *phr.* turn and twist

weeng *n.* wing

weepies *n.* ragweed (J)

weer *n.* wear; wire; knitting-needle; *v.* wear; **weerin geylies throu** nearly finished; **weer on** (of time) approach; **weer tee** come to, recover

weers o, on the just about (to), on the point of. *cf.* **aweers**

weesh(t) *v. pt.* washed

weesht *imp.* hush

weet *adj., v.* wet; **weety** rainy

weffle *adj.* pliable

weichen (doon) *ppl.* weighed down

weird *n.* fate, destiny

weirdless *adj.* ill-fated; worthless

weit *See* **weet**
welkin *n.* sky (M1)
went *n.* glance; glimpse; blink
wersh *adj.* tasteless. *cf.* **warsh**
we's *pr. with v.* we'll; we're
weskit *n.* waistcoat. *cf.* **waskit**
wha *pron.* who (G1). *cf.* **fa**
whaal *n.* whale
wham *pron.* whom
whang *n.* blow; lash
whapper *n.* lie
whaup *n.* curlew; empty peapod (T)
whaur *adv.* where (G1). *cf.* **far**
whause *pron.* whose
whazzle, wheezle *v.* wheeze
wheel *n.* spinning wheel
wheeber *n.* whistling sound
wheeble *See* **wheeple**
wheech, wheek *v.* move through the air with a whizzing sound; whisk away; flick
wheelie-birr *n.* child's imaginary toy car (T)
wheen *n.* number; quantity
wheep *n.* whip. *cf.* **whup, fup**
wheeper-in *n.* school attendance officer
wheep-han *n.* whip-hand, upper-hand
wheeple *n.* shrill, intermittent note with little variation of tone; *v.* whistle; call (of birds)
wheeriorums *n. pl.* intricate pieces of machinery
wheetie *adj.* mean, shabby
whigmaleerie *n.* a fantastic, useless ornament; foolish fancy; contraption
whilie *n.* a little while

whilk *rel. pron.* which
whip-the-cat *n.* tailor with no fixed place of business, who goes from house to house (M)
whirligig *n.* any rapidly revolving object
whitet-, whitie-broons *n. pl.* unbleached thread
whittle *n.* long knife
whummle *v. tr., intr.* overturn (J)
whundyke *n.* fence consisting of furze bushes
whup *n., v.* whip. *cf.* **wheep, fup**
whusky *n.* whisky
whylock *n.* little while
wi *prep.* with
wice *adj.* wise. *cf.* **wyce**
wice-like *n.* seemly, respectable
wicht *n.* wight; person
wick *n.* corner; corner of the eye or mouth
wicket *adj.* wicked
wid *adj.* mad (A1); *n.* wood. *v.* would; *cf.* **wud**
widda *n.* widow. *cf.* **widdie**
widden *adj.* wooden
widder *n.* weather. *cf.* **wither**
widder-gaw trick (**gaw**) of the weather (T); *v.* wither
widdie *n.* small wood; gallows; widow (J). *cf.* **weeda; as dry as a widdie** haddock dried without being split
widdiefu *n.* rogue; scamp
widdie-waan *n.* willow wand
wide *n.* weed; *v.* wade. *cf.* **wyde**
widna *v. neg.* would not
wife, wifie *n.* woman, married or not
wik *n.* week**

wik-en *n.* week-end
wil *adj., adv.* wild, wildly
wile *v.* choose, select; **wile warst** the worst of the selection. *cf.* **wale**, **wyle**
wilipen *v.* (vilipend), vilify, defame
willieway *v.* (wellaway! alas!) bewail, lament
wime *n.* belly; stomach
wimple *v.* wind; meander
win *n.* wind; *v.* dry (the stooks); harvest; go, reach a place; get; **win awa** go away; **win oot** get out, escape; **win tee wi** get even with; catch up with; **win up wi** catch up with
win-casten *adj.* cast aside by the wind
winceys *n.* petticoats made of wincey
windae *n.* window. *cf.* **winnock**
windae-sneck *n.* window catch
windlestrae *n.* tall, thin, withered stalk of grass of various kinds; crested dogstail grass
windlin *See* **winlin**
windy *n.* window (J)
wink *v.* brim
winker *n.* eyelash
winlin *n.* bundle (of straw)
winna *v. neg.* will not
winner *n., v.* wonder
winnerfu *adj.* wonderful
winnister *n.* fan for winnowing corn
winnock *n.* window (A1)
winny *adj.* windy; boastful; *v.* winnow (S)
winraa *n.* gathered row of hay (F)
winrin *ppl.* wondering

wint *v.* want, be without; desire
winter, to get *phr.* to clear the fields of harvested grain
wi'oot *prep.* without. *cf.* **withoot, athoot**
wip *v.* wrap, bind tightly. *cf.* **wup**
wir *pron.* our
wird *n.* word
wire intae *v.* set to work on
wirker *n.* worker
wirm *n.* worm
wirsels *pron.* ourselves. *cf.* **oorsels**
wirsit *adj., n.* worsted
wirth *n.* worth
wis *v. pt.* was
wise *v. tr.* advise
wish! *imper.* turn right! (command to Buchan plough-horse) (T)
wisna *v. neg.* was not
wiss *n., v.* wish. *cf.* **wuss**
wissen *v.* wither, shrivel
wistna *v.* did not know (M)
wite *n., v.* blame. *cf.* **wyte**
wither *n.* weather. *cf.* **widder**
withoot *prep.* without. *cf.* **athoot**
witril, wittrel, witterel *n.* peevish, waspish person
witter *n.* barb of a dart or hook; *in pl.* the throat
wivven *ppl.* woven
wizzen *n.* gullet; *v.* wither, shrivel
wob *n.* web
wobby *adj.* covered with cobwebs
womble-brees *n.* soup made with offal
womle *v.* be squeamish; (of the stomach) rumble queasily
won *v. pt. See* **win**
wonner *n.* wonder
woo *n.* wool

woorlich (B1) *See* **oorlich**
woorthy *n.* worthy
wordle *n.* world. *cf.* **wardle**
wordy *adj.* worthy, deserving
wormit *n.* wormwood
worn awa *ppl.* deceased
worry *v.* choke; strangle
worsit *n.* worsted; woollen yarn, knitting wool; **worsit-bag** *n.* wool-bag
worth *in phr.* **gaed worth** went to pot
wrack *n.* wreck; destruction
wraith *n.* drift; wrath
wrang *adj., n.* wrong; **wrang spy** mistaken identity
wrapper *n.* working apron, overall. *cf.* **vrapper**
wreth (B1) *See* **raith**
wreith *n.* wraith, ghost
wricht *n.* carpenter. *cf.* **vricht**
wrocht *v. pt.* worked (S). *cf.* **vrocht**
wrocht-up *adj.* overwrought
wrunkelt *adj.* wrinkled
wud *adj.* mad; *n.* wood; *v.* would; **wudna** would not. *cf.* **wid**
wudden *adj.* wild; mad
wudden-dream *n.* sudden frantic motion or effort
wuddie, wuddy *n.* gallows. *cf.* **widdie**
wulk *n.* whelk; periwinkle
Wull, Wullie *pr. n.* William
wull *adj.* wild; bewildered; *adv.* astray; *n., v.* will; **o wull** of one's own accord
wull-like *adj.* wild-like

wullin *adj.* willing
wully-goo *n.* grotesque person
wumman *n.* woman
wummle *v.* turn over and over. *cf.* **whummle**
wumple *n.* tangle of objects; *v.* (of a river) twist, turn
wun *v. pt.* wound; harvested; *see* **win**
wunna *v. neg.* will not
wunt *v.* want
wup *v.* bind, bandage, wrap. *cf.* **wip**
wur *v. pt.* were
wusp *n.* wisp
wuss *n., v.* wish. *cf.* **wiss**
wut *n.* wit; *in pl.* wits
wutness *n.* witness
Wutsunday *n.* Whitsunday
wutter *n.* barb on a fish hook
wyce *adj.* wise. *cf.* **wice**
wyde *n.* weed; *v.* wade. *cf.* **wide**
wye *n.* way; **there's nae twa wyes aboot it** there's only one possibility
wye *v.* weigh; **wyed, wyet** *ppl.* weighed
wyke *adj.* weak
wykeness *n.* weakness
wylin *n.* selection
wyme *n.* belly; womb
wynd *n.* narrow lane or street
wynin *n.* division of a field (F)
wyte *n.* blame; *v.* wait
wyve *v.* weave; knit
wyver *n.* spider
wyvin *n.* weaving; knitting

— Y —

(yab-)yabber *v.* talk excitedly
yab-yabble *n.* gabble
yacht *v. pr., pt.* own, owned; owe
yafa *adj.* awful (M). *cf.* **aafa**
yaird *n.* yard (unit of measurement)
Yakkie *pr. n.* Peterhead name for the Eskimo, deriv. from Yaqui (B)
yaldie *n.* yellow-hammer (C)
yalla *adj.* yellow; *n.* yellow turnip
yammer *v.* chatter, whine
yamph *adj.* hungry, ravenous (A1)
yap *adj.* hungry; **yappy** hungry-looking
yard *n.* farm garden
yark *v.* jerk, tug; work hard; **yark in** drive in
yarlins *n.* device for winding yarn into skeins
yarp *v.* carp, complain
yarr *n.* corn spurrey
yaucht *See* **yacht**
yaum *n.* foolish talk (R)
yaummer *v.* cry out. *cf.* **yammer**
yauws *n. pl.* arms *e.g.* of a windmill
yavil *n.* second year crop
yavil-broth *n.* second day's broth
yavin *n.* awn, the beard of oats or barley
yawfu *adj.* awful. *cf.* **yafa**
ye *pron.* you
yea *adv.* yes
yearock *n.* hen not exceeding a year old, pullet. *cf.* **earock**
Yeel *n.* Christmas. *cf.* **Yule, Eel**
yeld *adj.* (of an animal) barren; not yielding milk for any reason. *cf.* **eel**
yeldrin *n.* yellow-hammer
yer *pron.* your
yerd *n.* yard (unit of measurement)
yerl *n.* earl
yersel *pron.* yourself; *pred. adj., adv. phr.* by yourself, alone
ye's *pron. with v.* you'll
yestreen *adv., n.* yesterday evening. *cf.* **the streen**
yett *n.* gate
yill *n.* ale
yim *n.* thin film or coating on a surface
yird *n.* earth, soil; the earth
yird (doon) *v.* bury; **yirdit** *ppl.* buried; covered in earth, dirty
yirlin *n.* yellow-hammer
yirn *v. tr., intr.* curdle; **yirnt milk** curds and whey
yirnin *n.* rennet; the stomach of a calf; the human stomach (A2)
yist *v.* hiccup
yivvery *adj.* eager, hungry for
yoam *v.* to blow with warm air; belch
yock *n., v.* itch
yockie *adj.* itchy
yoke *n.* yoke, wooden spar for pulling a plough; *v.* to attach horse to plough, harness, etc; to start work; begin; **yoke intae** begin
yokin *n.* working period during which horses are in harness

yokin-time *n.* the time to begin or resume farm-work

yole *n.* yawl, small two-masted sailing-boat

yon *adj.* that, those

yonner *adv.* yonder

yont *adv.* yonder, farther away or along

you eens *pron. pl.* you

youkie *adj.* itchy. *cf.* **yockie**

youthheid *n.* youth

yowden-drift *n.* wind-driven snow

yowder *n.* bad smell of fumes from burning

yowe, yowie *n.* ewe; fir cone

Yule *pr. n.* Christmas; Christmas Day; the Christmas season till after New Year, now mainly lit. *cf.* **Yeel, Eel**

PART TWO

English~Doric

— A —

Aberchirder *pr. n.* (nicknamed)
Foggieloan
Aberdeen *pr. n.* Aiberdeen
Aberdeen football team the Dons
Aberdour *pr. n.* Aiberdour
ability *n.* can; capawcity
ablaze *adv.* alow(e); alunt
about *prep.* aboot
above *adv., prep.* abeen; atheen
abreast *adv.* abreist
abundance *n.* rowth; (to have) to
be biggit oot; **in abundance**
galore
abundant *adj.* rowth, routh
abuse *v.* ill-eese; (verbally) tongue;
ill-tongue; kyaard; misca
abusive language ill-win (A2)
abusive *adj.* (bitterly) veeperate
accept *v.* accep; *ppl.* acceppit
accident *n.* amshach; mishanter
accommodate *v.* accommodat
accomplish *v.* (by means) moyen
accord, of one's own *phr.* o wull
account *n., v.* accoont; **on no
account** naewye (S)
accountable *adj.* accoontable
accoutrements *n. pl.* graith
accumulate wealth *v.* fog
ache *n., v.* stoond, stound
acquaint *v.* (intimate) forquant
acquaintance *n.* acquantance
acquainted *ppl.* acquant (G);
acquaint (B); acquint (S)
acre *n.* aacre; awcre
across *prep.* athort
act *v.* ack

action *n.* ack
active *adj.* forcie; kibble
actor *n.* ackir
actually *adv.* verlies
acute *adj.* (in understanding) lang-
nebbit, -nibbit
adapt *v.* adap; **adapted** adappit
add (on or to) *v.* eek, eik, eke
addition *n.* eek, eik
addition to, in *prep. phr.* forbye
admit *v.* own
adorn *v.* busk
adornment *n.* (vain or fanciful)
flumgummery
adroit *adj.* nacky
advance *n., v.* (wages) sub
advancement *n.* fordal, fordle
advantage *n.* nip
advantage of, take *phr.* tak the
gweed o; tak a len o
advertise *v.* scry
advise *v.* rede (J); wise
adze *n.* each
aerated drink *n.* ale
affable *adj.* humoursome
affair *n.* rickmatick; **the whole
affair** the hail rickmatick
afflicted *adj.* afflickit
afford *v.* affoord
afraid *adj.* feart; **don't be afraid**
fearna
after *prep., conj.* aifter, efter; **after
all** efter-an-aa
afternoon *n.* aifterneen (A); aifternin (S)
afterwards *adv.* aifter, efter;

108

efterhin, aifterhin
against *prep.* agin
aged *adj.* eildit
agent *n.* aagent; deester
agile *adj.* keeble; kibble; swuppert
agitate *v.* flucht; **agitated** fluchtit
ago *adv.* syne; seen; **a year ago** a
  year syne; was-a-year
agree *v.* gree
ahead *adv., prep.* aheid; **get ahead
  with** get fordalt wi
ailment *n. (in pl.)* sairs; (of
  unknown cause) income
aim *n.* mint; *v.* ettle; mint
ajar *adv.* ajee, agee
akin *adj.* sib
alarm *n.* alairm
alas *excl.* alis(s)
alder *n.* arn-tree (J)
ale *n.* ale; yill. *cf.* **aerated drink**
alehouse *n.* chynge-hoose
Alexander *pr. n.* Ackie; Ake; Akie;
  Saaners, Sauners; Saaney,
  Sawney; Sandy
alight *v.* licht
all *adj.* aa; **all over** *adv.* athort; **not
  at all** deil the bit
alley *n.* vennel
allure *v.* goy
alms *n.* awmous
alone *pred. adj., adv.* aleen, alane;
  masel etc.; (ma leen, yer leen, oor
  leen, him leen, her leen; their,
  them leen); **all alone** aa ma leen
  etc.; **quite alone** bird-aleen;
  leeful-leen, -lane
along *prep.* alang
aloud *adv.* heich
allow *v.* alloo; *v. pt.* alloot
Almighty *adj.* Almichty

alms *n.* amous
aloof *adj.* abeech, abeich
already *adv.* aready
also *adv.* an aa; tee; tae (S)
always *adv.* aye
amazement *n.* (state of) maze
ammunition *n.* ammuneetion
am not *v. neg.* amnin; **am I not**
  amnin aw?
among *prep.* amang; amo; amon;
  amin (S); 'mon
amount *n.* amunt; (small) inchie
amusement *n.* ameesement
amusing *adj.* shortsome
ancient *adj.* aancient, auncient
and *conj.* an
Andrew *pr. n.* Andra; Andro
Andrewmas *pr. n.* Anersmas
anger *v.* kittle
angry *adj.* mad; raist; turk
animal *n.* (old, outworn) runk
ankle *n.* queet
announce *v.* lat licht that
announcement board *n.* (at
  church) scries-boord
annoy *v.* kittle
annoyance *n.* bucker
annoyed *adj.* turk
annoying *adj.* angersome
annual *adj.* annwal; onwal
another *adj., pron.* anidder;
  anither; anodder (A2)
ant *n.* emmerteen
anvil *n.* studdy
anxious *adj.* airch (A2); arch (**ch**
  gutteral)
any *adj., adv., pron.* ony
anybody *n., pron.* onybody
anyhow *adv.* onywye
anyone *n., pron.* onyeen

anything *n.* aacht, ocht; onything
anyway *adv.* onyroad; onywye; onygate
anywhere *adv.* onywye
apart *adv.* apairt
apparatus *n.* leems
apparently *adv.* appearandly
appeal *n., v.* appale
apple *n.* aipple
appoint *v.* appynt; (a meeting) tryst
appointed meeting *n.* tryst
apprehension *n.* uptak
approach *v.* come in aboot; (of time) weer on
approve *v.* appruv
April *n.* Awprile; Prile
apron *n.* aapron; naapron; (working) wrapper; (of sackcloth) seck-aapron
apt to *adj.* liken tae
arch *n.* airch; (also arched passage-way) pend, pen(n)
Archie *pr. n.* Airchie
Arctic tern *n.* tarick
argue *v.* argie; argie-bargie; argle-bargle; threep, threip; **argue the matter** delve the bank (B1)
argument *n.* argie-bargie; argle-bargle; argiement
arithmetic *n.* coontin
arm *n.* airm; gaidy (A)
armchair *n.* airm-cheer; bow-cheer
armful *n.* oxterfu; oxterlift
armpit *n.* oxter
arms *n. pl.* (e.g. of a windmill) yaaws, yauws
army *n.* airmy
around *adv.* aroon; roond an aboot; *prep.* aroon
arrange *v.* arreenge

arrest *v.* nab; reest
arrow *n.* barbet
arse *n.* erse; doke
art *n.* airt
articulate *v.* moo-ban
ash, ashes *n.* aiss; ess; (on top of a pipe) dirry
ash-can *n.* aiss-backet
ash-heap *n.* aiss-midden
ask *v.* (request) bid; (for) sik, seek; (a question) speer, speir
askance *adv.* asklent
askew *adv.* skew
asp *n.* aisp
aspen *n.* quaikin-aish
assail *v.* lat at
assistant *n.* (minister's) helpender
associate *v.* (with) colleague (wi)
assure *v.* asseer; asser
assuredly *adv.* awyte; *excl.* weel-a-wat; weel-a-wite
astir *adv.* asteer
astonish *v.* dammer (R)
astray *adv.* wull
astride *adv.* stridelins
as well *adv.* an aa
at all *adv.* ava; neen (nae neen pleast); ony (gin it's ony weet)
atom *n.* (particle) hait
attach *v.* (horse to plough) yoke
attempt *v.* mint
attendance *n.* turn-oot
attendance officer *n.* (school) wheeper-in
attend to *v.* sort
attentive *adj.* tenty
attentively *adv.* tentily
attracted to, to be *v.* tae hae a lang ee at
attractive *adj.* bonnie, bonny

auction *n.* rowp, roup; ungshin; **sell up by auction** rowp oot
auctioneer *n.* ungshineer
audience *n.* owdience
aught *n.* ocht
August *n.* Aagist
aurora borealis *pr. n.* the Merry Dancers
austere *adj.* door, dour
Australia *pr. n.* Australya

authorise *v.* owthereese
aware *adj.* awaar
away *adv.* awa; wa; furth; **away abroad** awa foreign; **far away** hine awa
awful *adj.* aafa, affa, aafu; yafa
awl *n.* (shoemaker's) ellieson; elshin
awry *adj.* agee; ajee
axle *n.* aixle

—— **B** ——

babbler *n.* gab
baby *n.* bairn; bairnikie; babbity
baby's flannel coat *n.* barrie
back band *n.* (of harness) backbin
back-bone *n.* back-been
back-garden *n.* backie
backslider *n.* turnkwite
backwards *adv.* backlins
bad *adj.* coorse; ill; ull; *adv.* ill; ull; **in a bad state** sair awa wi't
badly *adv.* ill; sairly
badly off *adj.* ull-aff; sair-aff
badly behaved *adv., adj.* ill-gatit, ill-gettit
bade *v.* bad
bad-mannered *adj.* ill-farrant
bad-tempered *adj.* crabbit; cankert
bag *n.* pock, poke; powk; pyock; (farmworker's) chackie; (for personal necessities on journey) wallet
baggage *n.* (loose woman) limmer
baker *n.* baxter
baking *n.* byaakin
bald *adj.* beld; baaldie-heidit
ball *n.* (bouncing) ba; ballie; (of

rope, cord, wool) clew, cloo; (of butter) pat
ball *n.* (dance) baal
ballad *n.* ballant
bamboozled *ppl., adj.* boggit; bumbazed
bandage *v.* wup
bang about *v.* breenge
bankrupt, became *v. pt.* broke
bank up *v.* (a fire) reest, reist
banns *n. pl.* (giving notice of impending marriage) cries
bantam *n.* bantin
banter *n.* hyze
baptise *v.* bapteese
baptism *n.* bapteesement
barb *n.* (of a hook) witter; wutter
Barbara *pr. n.* Baabie, Baubie
barbed-wire *n.* barbit-weer; pykit-weer
bare *n.* nakit; nyakit; **bare patch in field** blain
barefooted *adj.* barfit
bargain *v.* cowp; niffer
bark *v.* (of a dog) bowff; bouch
barley *n.* (when four or six-rowed)

bear, bere

barnacle *n.* scaa, scaw

barrel *n.* bowie; (for oatmeal) meal-bowie

barren *n.* (of an animal) eel; yeld

barrow *n.* barra; hurlie; seck-lifter

barter *v.* hooie; niffer

base *n.* (in children's games) dell

bashful *adj.* blate; bauch

basin *n.* (wooden for brose) bicker

basket *n.* (for fish) creel; (fitted into top of fish-wife's creel) murlin; (shallow, wicker) scull, skull; (esp. for sowing seed) happer

bass *n.* bess; **to sing bass** bess

bat *n.* baakie; baukie

bathe *v.* baathe; dook

bather *n.* dooker

bayonet *n.* baignet

be *v.* be; **be not** *v. neg.* (don't be) binna; **be without** *v.* wint

beak *n.* neb, nib

beam *n.* (of sun) blink; (across chimney from which the crook is suspended) rantletree

bear *v.* thole

beard *n.* baird; birse; (of oats or barley) aan, awn

beat *v.* (surpass) baet; bleck; cow; ding; (strike) clowt; dird; (severely) soosh; **beaten** *ppl.* baet; **that beats everything** yon cows aa

beaten track, off the *prep. phr.* at the back o beyond; oot o kent boons

beautiful *adj.* byowtifu; bewotifie

beauty *n.* byowty

because *conj.* cause; **because of** *prep.* ower the heids o

bed *n.* (small) beddie; (wooden, shut in with doors) bun-bed; (~ doors) bed-lids; (~ in semi-parlour end of but-an-ben) but-bed; (low, on castors) hurlie-bed; (makeshift) shakky-doon; **in bed, put to bed** beddit

bedaub *v.* skaik

bed-clothes *n. pl.* bed-claes

bedraggle *v.* bedraigle

bedridden person *n.* beddal

beehive *n.* (simple type) bee-ruskie; skep

beetle *n.* gollach, goloch; horny-gollach

befall *v.* befa; come ower; fa

before *adv., prep.* afore; ere; or; *conj.* ere, or; **before long** belyve

beforehand *adv.* aforehan

beg *v.* thig

began *v. pt.* begood

beggar *n.* gaberlunzie; supplicant; (threatening) sorner; (genteel) thigger

begin *v.* fa tee; set tee; stairt, stert; yoke

beginning *n.* aff-go

behaved, badly *adj.* ill-gatit, -gettit

beheld *v. pt.* beheeld

behind *adv., prep.* ahin(t)

beholden *adj.* behudden, behauden

behoof *n.* beheef

behove *v.* beheeve

belabour *v.* belaabour

belch *n., v.* rift; (of vapour etc.) yoam

believe *v.* troo

belittle *v.* lichtlify

bell *n.* (sound of) jow

bellow *v.* (of cattle) rowst; rowt (G1)

bellows *n. pl.* bellas
belly *n.* wame; wime, wyme
belly-band *n.* (of harness) belly-ban
belong *v.* belang; **he belongs to Buckie** he belangs Buckie
below *prep.* aneth; ablo(w), alow (S); in alow
bench *n.* binch
bend *n.* bennin
bend *v.* boo; loot; (with age) creep doon; *ppl.* boo't; **bend double** boo't twa-faal
beneath *See* **below**
benighted *ppl., adj.* nicht-boon, -boun
benumb *v.* daver; dozen
beside *prep.* aside
besides *adv.* forby(e); forbyes; *prep.* (apart from) byes
besmear *v.* drabble
bespatter *v.* spairge
best *n.* (of the lot) stang o the trump; (~ room) the room; (~ room in two-roomed cottage) horn-en, -eyn
bet *v.* beet
between *prep.* atween; atweesh; **between times** atween hans
bewail *v.* willieway
bewildered *adj.* wull
beyond *adv.* ayon; ayont
bid *n.* (at sale) bode
big *adj.* muckle; meikle
bilberry *n.* blaeberry
bill *n.* bull; lawin
bin *n.* (for corn, turnips) bing
bind *v.* bin'; bin (rhyme with tin); (tightly) wip; wup
binding *n.* (for cattle) binnin

birch *n.* birk; birken (C)
bird *n.* (unfledged) gorbel; gorblin; gog (S); (state of egg with young bird partially formed) gorbellt
birth, give *v.* (of rabbits) cleck
bit *n.* (small) bittock; thochtie; wee
bitch *n.* bick
bite *n.* gnap; rive; (a mere) knap-at-the-win
black *adj.* bleck; blaik
blackberry *n.* bramble; brammle
blackbird *n.* blackie; ouzel (M)
blacken *v.* blaik; blaiken, blecken
blackguard *v.* blackguaird; *joc.* bleck
blacking *n.* bleck; bleckin
blacksmith *n.* smith; brookie
blacksmith's shop *n.* smiddy
bladder *n.* bledder
blame *n.* wyte
blanket *n.* (fisher term) plaid
blast *n.* (of wind) blaffert; bluffert; bloiter; blouter
blaze *n.* bleeze; lowe
bleak *adj.* (of weather) oorlich
bleary-eyed *adj.* bleart; bleery
bleed *v.* blood (S)
blessed *adj.* seely
blight *n.* blicht
blind *adj.* blin
blink *n.* went; *v.* (weakly) blinter
blockhead *n.* gomeril; tawpie
block up *v.* stap
blonde *n.* blon
blood *n.* bleed
blood-curdling *adj.* bleed-jeelin
blood-red *adj.* bleed-reid
blossom *n.* floorish
blow *n.* clowt, cloot; daad; lick; plowt; whang; (of a sounding

kind) binner; (resounding) clink;
v. blaa; blaave; blyaav; (the nose
with finger and thumb) snyte;
(with warm air) yoam

blown out *ppl.* (of cattle, having
over-eaten) hoven

blubber *v.* bubble; snotter

blue *adj.* blae; **black and blue** blae

bluebell *n.* blewart

bluish *adj.* blae

blunt *adj.* (of speech) aff-han

blushing *ppl., adj.* kindlin (J)

bluster *v.* howder

board *n.* brod; boord; (moveable on
front of boxcart) front shelvin; (at
rear) hin shelvin; (for sharpening
scythe) scythe-brod; straik

boarding-school *n.* buirdin-squeel

boast *v.* blaw; braig; blyaav; craa,
craw

boastful *adj.* winny

boat *n.* (built with planks edge to
edge) carvel-biggit; (built with
planks overlapping) clinker-
biggit; **in the same boat** i the
same box (A1)

Boddam *pr. n.* (nickname) Dowp

bogie-roll *n.* (tobacco) bogie-rowe

boil *n.* beil; beilin; blin lump; *v.*
bile, byle

boiling *n.* (e.g. of rhubarb) bilin,
bylin

boistrous *adj.* bowsterous;
hallyrackit

bold *adj.* baul; bauld; croose; deft

boll *n.* (old Sc. measure) bow

bollard *n.* paal

bolster *n.* bowster

bolt *v.* tak sheet

bondage *n.* thirlage

bone *adj.* been; **a bone to pick** a
craa to pluck

boney *adj.* beeny

bonfire *n.* bale-fire; bondy (O)

book *n.* beuk, byeuk

boot *n.* beet; buit (S); (rubber knee
boot worn by fish-workers)
topper

bored (with) *ppl., adj.* scunnert (o,
wi)

borrow *v.* borra; thig

bosom *n.* bosie; oxter. *cf.* **armpit**

botch *v.* bucker

both *adj., pron.* baith

bother *v.* badder; bather

bottle *n.* (earthenware) pig; (hot
water) pig; (with handle(s) for
holding liquor) grey-beard

bottom *n.* boddom; (buttocks) doke

bought *v. pt.* bocht; coft (G1)

bounce *v.* stot; daad, daud (aboot);
(up and down) dyst

bound *v. pt., ppl.* bun; bunt; thirlt

boundary *n.* boon, boun; mairch;
boundary wall mairch-dyke

bow *n.* (tied) doss; *v.* boo; loot

bow and arrow *phr.* bow an barbet

bowl *n.* (for bowling) bool; (large
wooden for baking) bossie;
(wooden dish for oatmeal) brose
caup

bow-legged *adj.* bow-hoched

boy *n.* loon; laddie; (small)
laddikie; (fisher term) bokie;
(coddled) Grunnie's John; (term
of endearment) mannikie

boyfriend *n.* laad

braces *n. pl.* (for trousers) galluses

brag *v.* blaa, blaw; blyaav; braig

brain(s) *n.* harns

brainless *adj.* glaikit
bran *n.* pron
branch *n.* brench, brinch
brandish *v.* (threateningly) wadge
brass *n.* bress
bravely *adv.* starkly
brawl *n.* brulzie
bread *n.* loaf; breed, breid
breadth *n.* breid
break *v.* brak
breakfast *n.* brakfast
break down *v.* (from drink, exhaustion, illness) fooner
break wind *v., n.* pump; let off
breast *n.* breest, breist
breath *n.* braith (G); breith (J); in-draacht; (of wind) funk; **out of breath** birsin
breeching *n.* (part of harness round hind-part of shaft horse to allow backward movement) britchin
breeze *n.* pirr-winnie
brew *n.* browst
bridegroom *n.* bridegreem
bridge *n.* brig
bridle *n.* (with blinkers) blin bridle
bright *adj.* bright; croose; (gaudy) galliart (B1)
brighten *v.* brichen; (of person) *intr.* cantle up
brim *v.* (be full to the brim, brim over) lip; ream; wink; **brimming** *ppl., adj.* reamin fu
bring *v.* fesh; fess; **bring out** rank oot; **bring to mind** fess back; **bring up** fess up
bristle *n.* birse
brittle *adj.* bruckle; freuch
broad *adj.* braid
broke *v. pt.* brook, bruik; brak;

bruk
bronchitis *n.* broncaidis
brood *n.* cleckin; brodmell
brooding, broody *adj.* (of hen) *adj.* clockin
broom *n.* (brush) beesom; besom; (shrub) breem
broom-bush *n.* breem-buss
broom-handle *n.* besom-shaft
brother *n.* brither; breeder; bridder; broder (A2)
brother-in-law *n.* gweed-brither, -breeder, -bridder
brought *v. pt.* brocht; foosh. *cf.* **fesh**
brow *n.* broo
brow-band *n.* (in harness) broobin
brown *adj.* broon
bruise *n.* birse; malagruze
brush *n.* beesom; besom; *v.* sweesh
brushwood *n.* hag
brute *n.* breet
Buchanhaven native *pr. n.* Buchaner
Buchan Observer, **the** *pr. n.* the Buchanie
bucket *n.* backet
Buckie native *pr. n.* Bucker
build *n.* book, bouk; **of small build** sma-bookit, -boukit; **of lean build** nairra-bookit; *v.* big(g); **built** biggit
builder *n.* bigger
building *n.* biggin
building-ground *n.* seet
bulk *n.* book, bouk
bulky *adj.* (muckle-)bookit, -boukit
bull *n.* bul
bullock *n.* (young) stirk; (older, castrated) stot

bully *v.* bullyrag
bumble-bee *n.* bumbee; in Buchan, (Auchmacoy) bummer
bump *n.* doosht; *v.* (up and down) dyst
bumpkin *n.* gillieperous; gileepris (hard g)
bun *n.* (floury) bap; (glazed, with sugar on top) heater; (plain) soft biscuit, softie
bundle *n.* (loose, untidy) fushach
bungle *v.* bucker
bungler *n.* footer
buoy *n.* bowe
burden *n.* birn; (of a discourse) owercome
bureau *n.* buroo
burgh *n.* broch
burgler *n.* hoosebrakker
burial *n.* beerial
burial place *n.* (reserved in grave-yard) lair
buried *ppl.* beeriet; yirdit
burly *adj.* buirdly; muckle-bookit, -boukit
burn *v.* burn; *pt., ppl.* brunt; brent

(G1); plot; **burning brightly** (of fire) reevin
burst *v.* birst; (asunder) rive; **bursting** *ppl.* burssen
bury *v.* beery; yird (doon)
bush *n.* buss; (stunted) scrog
bushel *n.* bushle; bussle
business *n.* buzness
bustle *n., v.* steer; feerich; hash
busy *adj.* thrang
but *conj.* bit
butter churn *n.* kirn
butterfly *n.* butterflee (R); buttery (M1)
butterhand *n.* clapper
buttocks *n. pl.* dowp, doup; (vulg.) dock, doke; hurdies
buy *v.* buy; coff (G1)
buzz *v.* bizz; (of thoughts) ream
buzzing *n.* bizzin
by *prep.* by, b'; (used of time) gin; **by seven o'clock** gin seyven o'clock; **by the time that** gin
by-and-by *adv.* belyve
byway *n.* bywye

— **C** —

cackle *v.* keckle
cairn *n.* carn; cyarn
calf *n.* caaf, caafie; **calves** *n. pl.* car
calk *v.* (fix guard on horse's hoof) caak, cauk
call *v.* ca, caa
call on *v.* cry on; cry in by; cry tee
callous *adj.* scorie-hornt
calm *adj.* (of the weather) lown
calve *v.* caav

came *v. pt.* cam
candle *n.* cannle, cunnle
Candlemas *pr. n.* Cannlemas
candy *n.* gundy
cane *n.* (West Indian) spaingie; spainyie
can not *v. neg.* canna
canvas *n.* cannas
cap *n.* (man's) bonnet; caip, kep; (woman's) mutch

capable *adj.* cawpable
capacious *adj.* capawshus
capering *adj.* (of children) royd, royt
caprice *n.* maggot
card *n.* (playing) cairt; **to play cards** cairt; *v.* (wool) caird
care *n.* tent; (anxiety) cark; **not a care in the world** nae cark nor care; **take care** tak tent; *v.* car; raik; **don't care at all** carna doit; **take care** ca canny
careful *adj.* carefu; tenty
carefully *adj.* tentily
care of, take *v.* notice
caress *v.* daat, dawt
cargo *n.* cargie
carouse *n.* ran-dan; **on the carouse** oot on the ran-dan
carp *v.* yarp
carpenter *n.* jyner; vricht, wricht
carriage *n.* kerridge
carrier *n.* cadger
carrion crow *n.* hoodie(-craw)
carry *v.* cairry; cairt; (loads) cadge; (something heavy) humph; **carry-on** cairry-on; on-cairry
cart *n.* cairt; (mounted on springs) spring-cairt; *v.* (corn in from field) lead
carter *n.* cairter
carting *n.* (corn, hay) leading
cartload *n.* cartil
case, in *conj.* case be; (in neg. context) for fear
cast *v.* cast; *pt.* ceest, keest
castle *n.* castell
cast-off *adj., n.* aff-cast
castrate *v.* cut; lib
casual dress *adj., n.* go-ashores
catch *n.* (of fish) shot; **a good catch**
a cran-the-net; *v.* cleek; (with the hand) kep; (fish with the hands) guddle; **catch sight of** twig; **catch up with** win up wi
catechise *v.* catecheese
catechism *n.* carritch(es); catechis
cattle *n. pl.* beas' (C); bestial (A2); kine (A); kye; nowt; (disease; in the hindlegs) crochle; (to call to cattle) treesh
cattle binding *n.* (iron) bowsell; (retaining rod for binding) slider; (rope or chain on binding to attach sell to a stake) thrammle
cattle fold *n.* bucht
cattleman *n.* bail(l)ie; bylie; cattlie (S)
caul *n.* kell; seelyhoo
cause to *v.* gar
causeway *n.* causey; cassie
cautious *adj.* canny; cowshus
cease *v.* devall; jeho(y)
centipede *n.* meggie-monyfeet
certain *adj.* siccar
chafe *v.* chaff
chaff *n.* caff; **chaff mattress** caff-bed; caff-seck
chain *n.* chine; (by which pot hung over fire from crook) links; (to bind cattle) sell
chair *n.* cheer
chairman *n.* cheerman
chalk *n.* chack; *v.* caak, cauk
challenge *v.* dip; (for repayment of a debt) caak, cauk
chamber *n.* chaamer, chaumer (esp. for sleeping place for farm servants in Banff and Buchan); **to live in a chamber** to chaamer, chaumer

chamber-pot *n.* chantie, chanty, chuntie; dirler

change *v.* cheenge; chynge

changeable *adj.* changefu

changeless *adj.* cheengeless

channel *n.* (narrow) trink(ie)

chap *n.* billie; chiel; stock; (effect of cold) hack

characterless *adj.* eedle-oddle

charge *n., v.* chairge

charity *n.* chairity

Charles *pr. n.* Chae; Chairlie

charlock *n.* skellach

charmed with *phr.* teen wi

chat *n., v.* blether; crack; newse; *v.* ca the crack

chatter *n.* jaa, jaw; *v.* bledder; blether; gab; jaa, jaw; yammer

chatter-box *n.* gab

chattering *n.* gabbing

chatting *n.* chirr-wirrin (S)

chatty *adj.* crackie; newsy

cheap *adj.* chaip, chape

cheapjack *n.* chaip-john

cheat *v.* chait, chate; jink; snype, swick; (in marble-playing) foodge; *ppl.* snypit; swickit

cheating *n.* chaitry

checked *adj.* (of a pattern) chackit

cheek *n.* chik

cheek-by-jowl *adv.* cheekie-for-chowlie

cheeks *n. pl.* chafts

cheep *n.* chowp; peek; **not a cheep** nae a chowp

cheerful *adj.* blithe(some), blyth

cheery *adj.* canty

cheese *n.* chyse; (a round) kebbuck (soft) hangie

cheese press *n.* chessel; chesset

chemise *n.* sark

chequered linen *n.* chack

cherry *n.* chirry

cherry tree *v.* (wild) gean

chest *n.* kist; **get it off your chest** redd yer crap; teem yer crap

chew *v.* chaw

chewing-gum *n.* chuddy

chicken *n.* chucken; chucknie; **chicken soup with leek** cock-a-leekie

chickweed *n.* chuckenwort

chiefly *adv.* feckly

child *n.* bairn; geet; (small) eeshan (M2); (young) etsleel (B1); littlin; little een; wean

childhood *n.* bairnheid

chilled *adj.* chilpit; stervin o caal, stervin wi the caal

chilly *adj.* airish; caaldrife

chimney *n.* chimley; lum

chimney-corner *n.* ingle-neuk

china *adj., n.* cheena

chink *n.* bore

chinless *adj.* soo-moo't

chinwagging *n.* chirr-wirrin (S)

chipping *n.* (granite) chuckie-steen

chives *n.* size

choice *n.* wale

choir *n.* kyre; kire

choke *v.* smucht; (on food) worry

cholic *n.* belly-thraw

choose *v.* chyse; wale; wyle

chop *v.* chap

christen *v.* kirsen

christening *n.* kirsenin

Christmas *n.* Eel; Yeel

Christmas pudding *n.* dumplin

chuckle *v.* keckle

chummy *adj.* chuff

chunk *n.* skelp
church *n.* kirk; **at church** *prep. phr.* kirkit; **church-gallery** laft
Church of Scotland *pr. n.* the Aul Kirk
churchyard *n.* kirk-yaird
churl *n.* carl; nabble, nabal
churlish *adj.* nabble, nabal; **churlish man** tike
churn *v.* (butter) kirn
chute *n.* (conveying corn to elevator) shakkin-spoot
cinder *n.* shunner
circumspect *adj.* douce
cirrus clouds *n. pl.* (high) mackerels' backs an meers' tails
city *n.* ceety
civil *adj.* ceevil
clad *adj.* cled
clairvoyant *adj.* fey
clamber *v.* rink
clatter *n.* reemis(h)
claw *n.* claa; clook; faach, fauch (B1); **seize with the claws** cleek
clawed *v. pt.* clew
clean *v.* dicht; (a byre) muck
clear *adj.* clair; *v.* (out) redd (oot); (your throat) pyocher, redd yer throat; (up) redd up; (of weather) upple
clench *v.* steek; **clenched fists** steekit nieves
clever *adj.* clivver; fell; heidie; lang-heidit
cliff *n.* scaar, scaur
climb *v.* clim; *pt.* clam(b), clum; sclim; speel, speil
clinch *v.* (settle) clench
clod *n.* (of earth) knibloch
close *v.* dit

close by *adv.* aside
close together *adv.* curduddoch (J)
cloth *n.* claith; cloot; (very thin) flinrikin; (made of hards) harden; (sackcloth) harn
clothe *v.* claithe; clead
clothes *n. pl.* claes; clyes; cleadin; duds; graith; (second best) scuddlin claes
clothes peg *n.* pin
cloud *n.* clood; (small clouds flying before the wind) pack-merchants
cloudberry *n.* aiv(e)rin
clover *n.* clivver. *cf.* **clever**
club-foot *n.* clog-fit
clumsy *adj.* gaakit, gawkit; **clumsy person** hoffin; howfin; hurb
cluster *n.* dossie
clutch *n.* (of eggs); settin; *v.* claught; clootch
coal *n.* (live) eyzle; kwile
coal-dust *n.* coal-coom
coarse *adj.* coorse; grofe
coat *n.* kwite, kwyte; (dreadnought) fer-nothing; (old-fashioned) surtoo, surtout
coating *n.* (thin) yim
coax *v.* tice wi
coaxing *ppl., adj.* fraiky
cobbler *n.* sooter, souter
cobbler's wax *n.* rosit
cobblestone *n.* causey; cassie
cobweb *n.* moosewob; wob; **covered in cobwebs** wobby
cod *n.* (of medium size) sprag
coffin *n.* kist; **to put in a coffin** *v.* kist
cohabitee *n.* bidie-in
coin *n.* (of little value) doit; bodle (J); plack

coir yarn *n.* sparty tow
cold *adj.* caal(d); caaldrife; (as ice) jeel; (of weather only) fresh; (bitter) stervation; (of the wind) snell
colewort *n.* kail, kale
collapse *v.* (with drink, exhaustion, illness) fooner
collar *n.* (of iron, as instrument of punishment) jougs
collecting-box *n.* (offertory plate at church door) brod; (with long handle, passed round church) ladle
collection *n.* rickmatick; (of small objects) smyteral
colourful *adj.* (highly) kennelt
colt *n.* cowt
comb *n.* kaim, kame
come away *imp.* c'wa
comely *adj.* gatefarrin
come to *v.* (recover) weer tee
comfort *n.* easedom
comfortable *adj.* bien
comfortless *adj.* bienless
common *n.* (small) loan; (village green) loaning (S)
common-sense *n.* gumption; mense, minse; rum(mil)-gumption; rumigumshun
commotion *n.* stramash; tirravee
communicant *n.* commeenicant
company *n.* (musical or convivial) core
compared with *prep.* byes; forbye; till
compel *v.* gar
complain *v.* compleen; crowp; peek (peevishly) girn; peenge; yarp; **complaining feebly** goranichy (B1)

complaint *n.* compleent
completely *adv.* fair
comrade *n.* billie
conceited *adj.* bigsie; concaited; full
concern *n.* concairn; *in phr.* **the whole concern** the hail rickmatick
condescending *adj.* skichent
condition *n.* condeeshun; precunnance; (in good ~) clear
conduct *v.* conduck
confident *adj.* croose, crouse; **brisk and confident** croose i the craw
confound *v.* confoon; dag; deg; **confound it** dag it; dozen't
confuse *v.* dammer
confused *adj.* (of things) throwder; (of people) daivert; doilt, dylt; (mentally) dottelt; raivelt
confusion *n.* (state of) kirn; mixter-maxter
congeal *v.* jeel
congregated *v. pt.* congregat
connect *v.* conneck; *ppl.* conneckit
consciousness *n.* (recover) come alist
considerable *adj.* gey
consideration, under *phr.* throw-han
consort (with) *v.* colleague (wi)
constipated *adj.* corkit
constipation *n.* dry-darn
constitution *n.* constiteetion
constrained *adj.* hudden doon; hudden in aboot
constrict *v.* hank
contempt *excls.* of footers; tchach, tchoot; terms of (used of a person) scadden; scoot; skate;

splewin; (for someone of dirty habits) sklype; (for fellow of low character) slung; (for worthless type) slype; (puny, worthless type) tarlich; (foul-mouthed, vulgar type) tink

contemptible *adj.* dirten

contend *v.* conten

contest *n.* (esp. curling) bonspiel

continual *adj.* conteenwal

continue *v.* conteena (B1), *pt.* conteenit; hud

contradict *v.* conter; cwanter

contradictory *adj.* contermin't

contraption *n.* whigmaleerie

contrary *adj.* contermashious; contermin't; cwanter-kine

contribute *v.* contreebit

control, beyond *phr.* oot o han; nae tae hud nor bin'

controversial *adj.* kittle; kittlesome

convenience *n.* convainience

conversation *n.* a blether; news(e); spik; (low, muttered) toot-moot

conversation lozenges *n. pl.* readin sweeties

converse *v.* collogue; **conversing intimately** corrieneuchin

convey *v.* convoy

convince *v.* goy (B1)

convolvulus *n.* creepin-eevie. *cf.* **slow**

cook *v.* keuk, kyeuk

cool *adj.* cweel, kweel

copse *n.* shaw (J)

copy down *v.* tak aff

coracle *n.* currack

cord *n.* (used to pull cleaning-rag through a rifle) pul-throwe

corker *n.* beezer; binder; bummer

cormorant *n.* scrath

corn *n.* corn; oats; **corn chest** cornkist; bruise-box; **corn husk** sheelock

cornbin *n.* bing

corner *n.* neuk; (esp. of the eye and mouth) wick; **having corners** neukit

corn spurrey *n.* yarr

corps *n.* core

corpse *n.* corp

correct *v.* correck

corresponding to *ppl.* confeerin tae

corrugated iron *n.* sheet iron; tin-can

corsets *n. pl.* steys

cost *in phr.* **cost them a lot** pyke their pooch

cottage *n.* (for farmservants) bothy; (two-roomed) but-an-ben

cottager *n.* (in tied farm cottage) cottage; **farm cottage** cotter-hoose

cotton-wool *n.* caddis. *cf.* **fluff**

cough *n.* hoast; (deep-seated) kirk-yaird hoast; (catarrhal) pyocher; blocher; (whooping) kink-hoast; *v.* (bark) bouch; clocher; pyooch; (huskily) craighle

could *v. pt.* cud; cwid; *neg.* cudna; cwidna

coulter *n.* (iron cutter at front of plough) couter

count *v.* coont

countenance *n.* coontenance

counter *n.* (shop) coonter

country *n.* kwintra; kwintry

courage *n.* spunk

course *n.* coorse; **of course** of coorse; an coorse (A2)

court *n., v.* coort
courteous *adj.* mensefu
cover *n.* hap; (thin) scriffon;
striffin; *v.* hap; *ppl.* happit; (over)
hap up
cow *n.* coo; *pl.* kye; (suckling
calves) sooker; (name for a cow)
Crummie
coward *n.* coord(ie); coof
coward's blow *n.* coordie-lick
cow-dung *n.* sharn; (liquid) sharn-
bree
cower *v.* coor; coorie, coory; corrie;
crulge (doon)
cowrie shell *n.* (small) kysie;
calfie's mooie; Johnny Groatie
cowshed *n.* byre; (division between
stalls) traivis, trevis
crab *n.* partan; (small, greenish,
found in shore pools) (B) grindie;
grindie tocher
cracked *ppl.* crackit
crafty *adj.* sneck-drawin (A2)
crag *n.* heuch
cram *v.* pang; stech
crash *n.* reemis(h)
cravat *n.* graavit, grauvit
crazed *adj.* dylt, doilt
crazy *adj.* gyte; **drive him crazy**
raise him wull
cream *n.* ream; crame (S)
cream pot *n.* stoopie (B1)
crease *n.* lirk, lurk; *v.* crunkle; *ppl.*
crunkelt; gruggelt
creature *n.* craitur, cratur
credit *v.* crydit
creditor *n.* craver
crept *v. pt.* crap
crested *adj.* tappit
crevice *n.* bore

criminal *n.* ranegill
cringe *v.* creenge
crinkle *v.* crunkle
cripple *n.* laimiter
crippled *ppl.* crochle; crochly;
hypal (B1)
crisis *n.* creesis; bit; **in a crisis** at
the bit
critic *n.* creetick
critical *adj.* lang-nebbit
criticise *v.* creeticise; misca; redd
up (somebody)
criticism *n.* (severe) kail throwe the
reek
croak *n., v.* crowp; craik
crockery *n.* lame
croft *n.* craft
crop *n., v.* (of land) crap; *n.* (of
bird) crap
cross *adj.* crabbit; cankert
cross-beam *n.* (in rafters) baak,
bauk; spur-baak, -bauk
crouch *v.* coorie, coory; corrie;
crulge (doon)
crow *n.* craw; corbie; (hooded)
hoodie(-craa)
crowberry *n.* knowpert
crowd *n.* (small) boorach(ie),
bourach, bing; (noisy) clamjamfrey, clanjamfry; crood;
(confused, noisy) currieboram;
mardle, merdle; mengyie;
(confused) smarrach; swarrach; *v.*
crood
crowded *adj.* thrang
crown *n.* croon; (of a woman's cap)
cockernony, *v.* croon
cruel *adj.* ill; ull
crumble *v.* murle
crumbly *adj.* bruckle

crush *v.* pran
crusty *adj.* nibawa
crutch *n.* oxter-staff, oxter-stav
crutches *n. pl.* dooble-legs
cry *v.* (weep) greet, *pt.* grat; **cried his head off** roared an grat; (call out) scrie, scry; (esp. when dancing) hooch; (scream) walloch; (cry out) yammer, yaummer
cry-baby *n.* bubbly-bairn
cuckoo *n.* gowk. *cf.* **fool**
cud *n.* kweed
cuddle *v.* delt
cup *n.* (of tea) shallie (o tay) (old term)
cupboard *n.* aamrie; (wall-) press
curb *v.* pit the haims on

curdle *v.* yirn
curds *n. pl.* curds; **curds and whey** croods an fy; yirnt milk
curiosity *n.* keeriosity; (inquisitiveness) ill-, ull-fashence
curious *adj.* keerious
curlew *n.* whaap, whaup
curl papers *n. pl.* (hair in) curlie wurlies
currant *n.* curran
currant bun *n.* curran bap
curry favour *phr.* hud in wi; treesh; *ppl.* in-huddin
curse *v.* (swear) ban
curt *adj.* nippit
curtsey *n.* beck; *v.* bob
cut *v.* cut; *pt.* cuttit; clip; sned; (nip off) stoo

—— D ——

daffodil *n.* daffie
dagger *n.* dirk
dainty *adj.* denty; *n.* (delicacy) flagarie
dairy *n.* dyrie, diry
daisy *n.* gowan
dally (wi) *v.* tig (wi)
dam *n.* dem
damage *n.* scaith; *v.* (suffer) get the flacht
damn *n.* (euphemism) dang
damp *adj.* (of the weather) mochie
dance *n.* dunce; dince (S); hooch (S); *v.* dunce; caper; (slow Highland dance) strathspey; (Highland) walloch
dandle *v.* (a child) diddle (B)
dangerous *adj.* fell; (from

supernatural causes) uncanny
dangle *v.* dauchle
dare *v.* daar, daur; **dare not** daarna; dursna; *pt. used as pr.* durstna
darling *n.* dawtie
dark *adj.* murky; dairk (J); (very) pitch-dark; pick-mark
darkness *n.* mirk; markness; (extreme) pitch-dark; pick-mirk
dart *n.* dert
dash *v.* (hurry) skelp; (noisily) blatter; (down) ding, *pt.* dang, dung; (about) flee aboot; **at a dash** at a spinner
dashing *adj.* swashy
daub *v.* clart; skaik; sclarry (J)
daughter *n.* daachter (A2); dochter

(A1); dother

daughter-in-law *n.* gweed-dother etc.

David *pr. n.* Daavit

dawdle *v.* dachle; dackle

dawn *n.* skreek o day

day *in phr.* **day's work** darg; **day labourer** darger; **every day** daily-day

daze *v.* dozen

deacon *n.* deykon, dykon

dead *adj.* deed, deid

deadly *adj.* deidly; fell

deaf *adj.* deef, deif

deafen *v.* deeve, deave

deal *n.* dale; transack; *v.* dale; **deal with** sort; tak throw han

dealer *n.* (itinerant) cadger

dealt (wi) *v. pt.* deelt (wi)

dear *adj.* (expensive) daar

death *n.* daith; deeth (A2), deith (J); the hinner-en

death-throw *n.* deid-thraw

death-watch beetle *n.* chackie-mull

deceased *ppl.* worn awa

deceitful *adj.* forty-faal

deceive *v.* mislippen; fugle (B1)

decent *adj.* dacent, daicent; dassint; douce

defame *v.* ca for aathing; misca; (vilipend) wilipen

defeat *n.* defait; *v.* bleck; bauchle (B1); defait, *ppl.* defait

defecate *v.* cack; kich; drate *(pr., pt., ppl.* dritten)

defer *v.* defar

deformed *ppl., adj.* mishachlt

defraud *v.* snype

degrade *v.* degraad; **degrading** *ppls.* degraadin, degraadit

dehorn *v.* dodd

dehydrated *ppl.* druchtit

dejected *adj.* doon i the moo; disjaskit; blue

deliberate *adj.* deleebrate; *adv.* deleebrately; designtly

delicacy *n.* flagerie

delighted *adj.* trickit (S)

delve *v.* dell

demented *ppl.* demintit

demon *n.* deevilock

denial *n.* na-say

dent *v.* cloor, clour

deny *v.* na-say

departing *adj.* wa-gaan, wa-gaun

departure *n.* wa-gaan, wa-gaun

depend (on) lippen (tae) (B1)

dependable *adj.* siccar

depressed *adj.* doon

deprived (of) *ppl.* runtit (o)

describe *v.* descrive, descryve

deserving *adj.* wordy

desire *n.* (slight) inklin; *v.* sik, seek

desirous *adj.* keerious

desk *n.* dask

destitute *adj.* nace; but hoose an haa

destroy *v.* connach; misaacre, missaucre

destruction *n.* crockaneetion; gowf(f); wrack

detain *v.* deteen

Devil, the *pr. n.* Aul Nick; Clootie; Cloots; the Earl o Hell; Hornie; Nicky Cloots

devil *n.* deevil; deil; fient; sorra

devious *adj.* forty-faal

devour *v.* (greedily) gluff

dew *n.* dyow

dexterous *adj.* nacky

dialect *n.* leid
diarrhoea *n.* skitter(s); (suffering from) lowss
didn't *interrog.* didnin?
die *v.* dee, *pt.* deet; slip the timmers. *cf.* **do**
difference *n.* odds
difficult *adj.* ill; ull; (of a task) kittle, kittlesome; (of words) lang-nebbit, -nibbit
difficulty *n.* diffeekwalty (accent second syllable); fyke; snorl
dig *v.* cast; dell; howk; **dug** *ppl.* cas(s)en; howkit
digest *v.* disjeest
dignity *n.* deegnity
diligent *adj.* eident
din *n.* remis(h)
dinner *n.* dainner, denner; **provide dinner** *v.* denner
diphtheria *n.* diphthairy
direction *n.* airt; **in all directions** aa the airts
dirtied *ppl.* dirten
dirty *adj.* barkit; clorty; fool; muckit; yirdit; *v.* fyle; daidle (S)
disagreeable *adj.* (of weather) drabbly
disappoint *v.* disappynt; begeck; miscomfit (B1)
disappointed *ppl., adj.* nicket; hingin-luggit
disappointment *n.* begeck; hertscaad (B1)
disbelieve *v.* misdoot
discharge *v.* (any missile) fire
discomfit *v.* pit oot
disconsolate *adj.* doon i the moo; disjaskit
discord *n.* dispeace

discount *n.* discoont; (returned to the buyer) luckpenny
discourage *v.* dachle; dackle (C)
discourse *n.* discoorse; say-awa
discuss *v.* tak throw-han; dip
disdainful *adj.* sanshach
disembowel *v.* (deer carcase) gralloch
disfurnish *v.* displenish
disgust *n.* scunner; *v.* backset; scunner; (nauseate) skaichen, skaiken; (feel disgust) ug; (excl. of) feech, feich; **disgusted with** scunnert o/wi; skaikent; uggit
disgusting *adj.* fusome; ugsome; scunnerfu; scunnersome
dish *n.* (for serving) ashet
dish-cloth *n.* dish-cloot
dishevel *v.* toosle, toozle, tousle
dishevelled *adj.* hudd(e)ry
dishonesty *n.* oonhonesty
dismal *adj.* darksome; oorie
dismiss *v.* skail, skale
disordered *ppl.* agee; ill-shooken up; (in the mind) fey
disorderly *adj.* ramshackle; **in a disorderly way** over the bows
disperse *v. tr., intr.* skail, skale
display *n.* (fine) brevity, braivity; *v.* kythe
displease *v.* miscomfit
displeased, looked *phr.* his face wis trippin him
disputatious *adj.* din-raisin
dissatisfied, to be (with) *v.* ail (at)
distaff *n.* rock
distant *adj.* oot-by
distinct *adj.* clair
distorted *adj.* bogjavelt; bogshaivelt

distress *(excl. of)* feech; *v.* vex

district *n.* districk; (thirled to a mill or in which anyone carries on business) sucken

distrust *v.* mislippen

disturbance *n.* strush(ie); stramash

ditch *n.* dutch (G, M1); sheuch; stank

diversion *n.* (entertainment) divert

divested (of) *ppl.* runtit (o)

divide *v.* pairt; (in two) haaver

do *v. inf.* tae dee; adee; dae (S, J); *(pr. tense* I, you, we, they div; he, she, it dis; *imp.* dee/dae); **do not so badly** dee awa; **much to do** muckle adee

dock plant *n.* docken

doctor *n.* physeeshun

document *n.* dockiment

dodge *n.* ginkum; ginkmen (B1); *v.* jink; jook, jouk

doer *n.* deester (often contempt.)

doesn't *v. neg.* disna; *interrog.* disna, disnin

dog *n.* fulp; tike, tyke; doag (J); (bitch) bick, bik

doll *n.* dall

domicile *n.* doomsil

done *ppl.* deen, dune; daen (S). *See* **fatigued**

donkey *n.* cuddy

don't *v. neg.* dinna; *interrog.* divnin

doormat *n.* bass

dotage *n.* (in one's) dytit, doitit; donnert

double *adj.* dooble

double-jointed *adj.* dooble-jyntit

doubt *n.* doot; *v.* doot, misdoot

doubtful *adj.* dootfu

doughball *n.* twenty-minute-sweemer (B)

dovecot *n.* doocot

down *adv.* doon

downcast *adj.* disjaskit; blue (A1)

down-draught *n.* (in chimney) flan

downfall *n.* dooncome; doonfa

downpour *n.* doorpoor

downright *adv.* doonricht; evendoon

down with *phr.* hoot awa wi

down yonder *adv.* doonby

dowry *n.* tocher

doze (off) *v.* dover (ower)

dozen *n.* dizzen

draggle *v.* trachel, trachle, trauchle

drain *n.* (small open) stripe; (in cowshed) greep; (in street gutter) syre; *v.* (boiled solids) bree; (to last drop) dreep

drain-cover *n.* brander

dram *n.* skite; (in the morning) mornin; tootie

draught *n.* dracht; (of air) drucht

draught-board *n.* dambrod

draughts *n. pl.* (the game) draachts

draw *v.* draa; *ppl.* draan; (on a pipe) lunt

dread *n., v.* dreed, dreid

drench *v.* drook; *ppl., adj.* drookit

drenching *n.* steepin

dress *n.* (loose) slip; *v.* busk; rig; (for a journey) buckle; turse; (to go out) rank; (smartly) trig

dressed up *ppl.* trickit up; triggit oot; (showily) cockit up

dressing-down *n.* dixie; hanlin; sedarin

dribble *v.* dreeble

dribblet *n.* (small quantity of liquid) jibble (contempt. term)

drift *n.* (snow) wraith
drill *n.* (furrow with ridge on top) dreel
drink *n.* dracht; (of spirits) donal(ie); (small quantity) lab(b)ach
drip *n.* dreep; *v.* dreep; sype
dripping *n.* dreepin; **dripping enclosure (for sheep)** dreepin-penn
drive *n.* gurr; *v.* ca, caa; (animals, esp. poultry) hish; (~ in) yark in
drizzle *n.* sma weet; smirr
drizzly *adj.* dribbly; (with fog) muggly
drone *v.* bum
drop *n.* (sometimes of alcohol) drap; *v.* drap
drought *n.* drooth, drouth; drucht
drove *v. pt.* dreeve
drown *v.* droon; *ppl.* droont
drowsy, become *adj., v.* drow
drubbing *n.* nizzin
drug *n.* drog
druggist *n.* droggist
Drumlithie *pr. n.* (nicknamed) Skite
drummer *n.* (town) drumster
drunk, drunken *adj.* foo, fou; drucken; (very) bleezin; as foo's a buckie; greetin foo; (incapably) styterin foo; (wildly) fleein

drunkenness *n.* druckenness
dry *adj.* (sapless) foggy; (used of cows which have stopped giving milk) eel; yeld; *v.* (stooks) win
dryer *n.* (of grain) dryster
dry out *v.* skurken
dry up *v.* gizzen
duck *n.* deuk, dyeuk; *v.* jook, jouk
dull *adj.* dreich; ducksie (A)
dulse *n.* (edible seaweed) dilse
dumbfounded *ppl.* dumfoonert
dumbstruck *ppl.* dusht
dun *n.* craver
dung *n.* muck; sharn; (liquid) sharn-bree; (on the hind-quarters of cattle or sheep) knapdarloch
dungarees *n. pl.* dungers
dunghill *n.* midden; **moisture from dunghill** midden-bree; **top of the midden** midden-tap
duplicitous *adj.* dooble
dust *n.* dist; stue, styoo; (flying) stoor, stour
duster *n.* dister
dusty *adj.* stoorie, stourie
dwarf *n.* ablach
dwell *v.* dwaal, dwall
dwelling-house *n.* dwallin-hoose; firehoose
dyer *n.* dyester
dying (for) *ppl.* mangin (for)

—— **E** ——

each *adj.* ilk; ilka; ilky; ulkie
eager *adj.* ettlin; fain; gleg; yivvery
eager, to be *adj., v.* ettle; fidge (B1)
ear *n.* lug

earl *n.* yarl
earlier *adj.* earer
early *adj., adv.* airly; air; ear
earn *v.* airn

earnest *n.* (given on striking a bargain) arles; **in dead earnest** in gnappin earnest (B1)

earrings *n. pl.* lug-babs

earth *n.* airth; (also the earth) yird; **covered in earth** yirdit

earthenware *n.* lame

earwig *n.* forkie-(tail); horny-goloch

ease *n.* easedom

Easter *n.* Pase, Pess; Pesch

easy *adj., adv.* aisy (S); **no easy job** nae mowse job; **take it easy** hud doon the deece; lat the theats slack

easy-going *adj.* easy-osy; **easy-going person** sug

eat *v.* aet; **eaten** *ppl.* aeten, etten; (voraciously) gaap; (noisily and greedily) hamsh, humsh

eaves *n. pl.* easin, eezen(s)

edict *n.* edick

edify *v.* edifee; **edifying** *ppl.* edifeein

educate *v.* eddicat

education *n.* eddicashun

eerie *adj.* oorie

effect *n.* effeck

egg *n.* aig; (state of egg with young bird partially formed) gorbelt; *v.* (someone on) eik him up (A2)

egg shells *n. pl.* egg shallies

eight *adj.* acht, aucht; aicht, echt

eighteen *adj.* achteen; aichteen, echteen

eighty *adj.* achty; aichty, echty

either *adj., conj., pron.* edder; edderan (can be used at end of sentence as in Eng.)

elbow *n.* elbick, elbock, elbuck

elder *n.* (of the Church) eller; elyer

elder-tree *n.* boortree, bourtree; elyer

elevated *ppl., adj.* liftit

eleven *adj.* aleyven; eleeven, eleiven

else *adv.* anse

elude *v.* jink

embarrassed *ppl., adj.* affrontit; **deeply embarrassed** black affrontit

ember *n.* emmer; eyzle

embrace *v.* oxter

emotional *adj.* (showing emotion) great-hertit

empty *adj., v.* teem; toom (G1, J, M)

enamel *adj.* nammle

enclosure *n.* close, closs; (for poultry) crive; ree

encouragement *n.* hertnin; cuttins (usually in the neg., *e.g.* nae/sma cuttins)

end *n.* en; eyn; hinner-en; hint; (of yarn) thrum; *v.* en, eyn; *ppl.* eynt; **end of harvest, of the year** the back eyn; **make ends meet** get eyns tae rug the gidder

endearment (term of) *n.* (for children) chowter; smowt

endeavour *v.* mint

endless *adj.* eynless

end-ridge *n.* en-, eynrig

endure *v.* dree; thole

energetic *adj.* fersell

energy *n.* birr; spunk; virr; (great) rake; *adj.* (lacking) fen(d)less; thowless

engage *v.* (a farmhand) fee

engine *n.* engeen; ingine

English *adj.* suddron, sooth-kwintra
enlist *v.* list
enough *adj.* aneuch; aneu; enew
entangle *v.* insnorl; raivel; *ppl.* insnorlt; raivelt
entertainment *n.* a divert; enterteen-ment
enthralled *adj.* thirlt
enthusiasm *n.* (fit of) feerich
entice *v.* goy; tryst; tyce
entitle *v.* enteetle
entrails *n. pl.* (animal) harigals; monyfaalds, monyfaulds
entrance *n.* (at ground-floor level) low door
entrance-hall *n.* trance
entrap *v.* insnorl
equal *adj., adv.* (shares) eeksy-peeksy; -picksy; *n.* marra, marrow; *v.* peer wi
equipped *ppl., adj.* riggit oot
errand *n.* eeran
escape *v.* win oot
escapade *n.* ploy
escort *v.* convoy
Eskimo *n.* Yakki (deriv. from Yaqui) (B)
especially *adv.* espeeshully
estate manager *n.* grun offisher
evasive behavour *n.* hunker-slidin
even *adv.* aiven, ayven; eyven; **even with** upsides wi
evening *n.* even; een; (from twilight to bedtime) forenicht; **in the evening** at even, at een
ever *adv.* iver, ivver
everlasting *adj.* iverlaistin
every *adj.* ilk; ilka; ilky; ulkie
everybody *pron.* aabody
everyone *pron.* aabody; **everyone**

else aa ither body
everything *n.* aathin(g)
everywhere *adv.* aawye; aa gate
evil *adj.* coorse
eviscerate *v.* (of deer) gralloch
ewe *n.* yowe; (from one to two years old) gimmer
exaggeration *n.* hose an sheen
exalt *v.* heeze
example *n.* spyack, spyauck; **for example** likein
exceedingly *adv.* byous; feerious; fell; terrible
excel *v.* ding
excellent *adj.* braw; capital; rare
except *prep.* 'cep; 'cepin; excep; **except for** hud awa fae
exchange *v.* cowp; hooie; niffer; trock, troke
exciseman *n.* gaager, gauger, gager
excite *v.* flocht; raise; **in a state of excitement** flochtit; raist
excited *ppl., adj.* kittelt up
excitement *n.* (nervous) picher
exclamations (of surprise) goshie; heth; jings; loshins; loshtie (be here); loshtie-goshtie guide's; meggins alive; megstie me; michty me; (blood) sang; saal, saul; (troth) trogs; (of doubt, contempt) hoots; (of soothing and endearment) weel-a-wins, -wuns
excrement *n.* kich
excusable *adj.* exkeesable
exercise *n.* exerceese
exercise-book *n.* exerceese-beuk
exhaust *v.* jabb
exhausted *ppl.* deen; foonert; for-fochen; forjeskit; jabbit; wabbit
exhibition *n.* exhibeetion

129

expanse *n.* (of ground) sklyter
expect *v.* expeck; **expected** expeckit
expenditure *n.* (costly) hairrial, herrial
expensive *adj.* daar
experience *n.* expairience; *v.* pree
expound *v.* expoond
expression *n.* (e.g. of emotion) ootlat

extraordinary *adj.* byordnar; byous; exterordnar; ondeemas; unco
extremely *adv.* unco
extremity *n.* hinner-en
exult *v.* craa, craw
exultant *adj.* vantie, vauntie
eye(s) *n.* ee(n); **eyes like burning coals** eyzly ee't
eyelash *n.* brier; winker

—— **F** ——

face *n.* face; phizog; **facial expression** mudgeon
fact *n.* fack
fad *n.* aivis
fade away *v.* weer awa
faded *ppl.* cassen
failed *adj.* stickit
faint *n.* dwaam, dwam; fant; swarf; *v.* fant; swarf; tak a dwam
faint-hearted *adj.* chucken-hertit; henny-hertit
fair-haired *adj.* tow-heidit
fair play *phr.* fair hornie
faith *excl.* fegs; heth
faithful *adj.* faithfu
fall *n.* (sudden and heavy) clyte; (heavy) doosht; (with a bump) dird; (downfall) doon-come; (heavy) sklyte; sklyter; (light, of rain, snow) skiffin; *v.* fa; (with a thud) dyst; (with a bounce) dird; (heavily) sklyte, sklyter; (of heavy rain, snow) ding; (of light rain, snow) skiff; (sound of fall into water) plype; (of rain) onding
fall asleep *v.* (fisher term) to catch

her
fall out *n.* cast-oot; strive, *pt.* streeve
fall over *v. intr.* cowp
fallow land *n.* faugh
fall to *v.* fa tee
false *adj.* faase, fause
family *n.* faimly
famished *adj.* faimished
famous *adj.* faamous
fan *n.* (for winnowing corn) winnister
fancy *n.* maggot; (romantic) noshun (o); (foolish) whigmaleerie
fancy cake *n.* fancy
fancy work *n.* fineerin
far *adv.* hine; **far off** hine awa; **far gone** sair come at
fare *v.* faar, faur; (quite well) turn ower; **fare badly** misthrive
farewell *int.* faar-ye-weel
farm *n.* fairm, ferm; toon, toun
farm cottage *n.* cottar hoose
farmer *n.* fairmer
farmhouse *n.* fairmhoose; firehoose
farmhand *n.* fairm-servan

farming *n.* fairmin
farmservant *n.* fairm servan; (very experienced) docknell
farmstead *n.* steadin; toon, toun
farm tools (implement for clearing ground of roots etc) (Eng.) grubber; (for pulling turnips) neep-click; (for slicing turnips for fodder) neep-hasher; (for pulling turnips) neep-pluck; (for hoeing turnips) neep-rinner; (horse-hoe for weeding) shim; (skimmer for surface soil and weeds) skreefer; (small rake) smiler; (for removing turnip roots) tailer; (for removing turnip tops) tapner; (for twisting straw ropes) thrawcrook, thrawheuk; (for tilting loose sheaves off old-style reaper) tilter
farmworker's bag *n.* chackie
farmyard *n.* closs
farrier *n.* fairrier
farther *adv.* farder; (away, along) yont
farthing *n.* fardin
fast *adj., adv.* faist; *n., v.* fas(t)
fasten *v.* faisten; cleek; hank
fastidious *adj.* dorty; **over-fastidious** pernickety
fat *adj.* stoot; *n.* creesh; **fat person** fatty-bannocks
fatal *adj.* fattal
fate *n.* weird
father *n.* fadder; faither (C1, F)
father-in-law *n.* gweed-fadder, -faither
fathom *n.* faddom
fatigue *n.* harassment (A2); *v.* jabb; jaap, jaup
fatigued *ppl., adj.* deen; dylt;

daivert; jaapit; jabbit; tasht; typit; wabbit
fault *n.* faat, faut
fault-finding *n.* fittie-fies; (fretful) girn; *adj.* grumlie
favour *n.* faavour; **in favour with** (esp. with God) far-ben wi
favoured *adj.* faavourt; faart; **well-favoured (good-looking)** weel-faart; **ill-favoured (ugly)** ill-faart
favourite *adj.* faavrit, fauvrit
fear *n.* fear; ferr (S)
feast *n.* (of farewell or completion) foy
feather *n., v.* fedder
fed up (of) *adj.* doon; scunnert (o/wi)
feeble *adj.* dwebble; dweeble; dweebly; dweemly-dwamly; shilpit; thewless; *v.* (grow feeble in mind) doit
feed *n.* aet; **a good feed** a gweed aet; rim-rax; *v.* mait, *ppl.* maitit; (from a pail) cog; (with oats) to corn
feeding-bag *n.* (for horses) moo-bag; mou-bag
feel *v.* fin, *pt.* fan
feign *v.* feingie
felloes *n. pl.* (of wheel) fillies
fell out *v. pt.* streeve
fellow *n.* chiel; billie; folla; steel (B1); stock; (of low character) slung; (worthless) slype
felt *v. pt.* fan
fence *n.* palin; (of furze bushes) fundyke
ferment *n.* barm
fern *n.* fairn; bracken; breckan
fetch *v.* fesh; fess, *pt.* feese, feish,

foosh

Fetterangus *pr. n.* (nicknamed) Fishie

fettle *in phr.* **in fine fettle** in richt bone

fever *n.* fivver

few *adj.* fyow, fyou; *n.* fyow; a twathree

fewer *adj.* fyower

fibrous *adj.* stickly

fiddle (with or about) *v.* ficher; footer; **fiddly job** ficher; footer

fidget *v.* fyke; fidge (B); fyaach

field *n.* feedle (A, A2), fiedle; park (A); (for sowing turnip seed) patcher; (division of a field) wynin

fifty *adj.* fifety

fifteen *adj.* fifeteen, foifteen (A2)

fifteenth *adj.* fifeteent

fight *n., v.* fecht; pilget; shangie; sharrie; (with cudgels) a staffy-nevel job

fill *n.* sairin; **get your fill of** get yer sairin o; *v.* ful, full (rhymes with gull); *ppl.* fullt; bowden

film *n.* (membrane) scriffan; (thin) yim

final(ly) *adj., adv.* feenal(ly)

find *v.* fin

Findochty *pr. n.* (locally) Finechty

fine *adj.* braw

fine-looking *adj.* buirdly

finely *adv.* brawlies

finery *n.* braivity; (esp. of dress) braws; flagerie

finger *n.* finger (rhymes with singer); **the little finger** crannie; **finger tips** finger-eyns

finicky *adj.* jinipperous

finish *n., v.* feenish

finished *ppl., adj.* throw

fir-cone *n.* (fir-)yowe; yowie

fire *n.* ingle; (blazing) ingle-lowe; (small, blazing, coal or peat) cutchack; (big) bevie; (flame-less, of red-hot embers) greeshach (A1)

fireside *n.* ingle; ingle-cheek

firewood *n.* firewid; kinlin

firework *n.* squeeb; (primitive, home-made) poother-deevil

first rate *adj. phr.* bencape

fish *n.* (ungutted) rounder; (useless small species found in harbours) buddick; (take-home parcel of fish in the fishing industry) fry; *v.* (catch with hands in stream) guddle

fisher-boy *n.* fisher-loon

fisher-girl *n.* fisher-quine

fishing-line *n.* (hand) hanlin

fishing-rod *n.* waan

fish roe *n.* raan

fist *n.* nieve, niv; **fistful** nievefu

flabbergast *v.* stammygaster

flagged *ppl.* (of floor) flaggit

flagon *n.* stoop

flame *n.* lowe

flannel *n.* flannen

flap *v.* flaff; flaffer; wap

flash *n.* (of lightning) flacht

flattened *ppl.* (of crop) laid

flatter *v.* fraise; fleetch; **given to flattery** fraisie

flea *n.* flech

fleam *n.* (for bleeding of horses) fleem

flexible *adj.* wamfle

flick *v.* wheech

flicker *v.* flicher
flight *n.* (of birds) flacht; flicht;
  take flight tak sheet
flighty *adj.* flichty
flinch *v.* flench
flint and steel *phr.* flint an fleerish
flirt *v.* daff
float *n.* (for fishing) bowe
flock *n.* (of sheep) hirsel; (of birds)
  flacht
flog *v.* soosh
flood *n.* (of river, stream) spate;
  speet; speeth
floor *n.* fleer
flop *v.* flap
flour *n.* (wheaten etc.) floor
flourish *v.* fleerish
flower *n.* flooer, floor; (artificial)
  gumfleer, -floor
flowering currant *n.* (blossom
  appearing before the leaves) son-
  afore-the-father. (A name applied
  to other plants.)
fluff *n.* caddis
flukeworm *n.* (on the lung of
  sheep) the hooze
flung *v. pt.* flang
flurry *n.* flocht
flutter *v.* flaff; flaffer
fly *n., v.* flee
flywheel *n.* (of a spindle) whorl
foal *n.* foalie
foam *n.* faem, faim; *v.* ream
fodder *n.* fodd(e)rin
foe *n.* fae
fog *n.* lichen
foggy *adj.* (fog with drizzle)
  muggly
fold *n.* lirk, lurk; (of sheep) faal(d),
  faul(d); *v.* faald

folk *n.* fowk *(gen.)*; folk (G, M)
folly *n.* madden-dreem
fondle *v.* daat, dawt; delt
food *n.* mait; meat (J); **off his food**
  aff o's mait; **able to take food**
  mait-haill
fool *n.* feel, fule; gapus; gaak,
  gawk; gaakie; gillieperous,
  gileepris (hard **g**); gock; gowk;
  gomeril; gype; haveral; neip-heid;
  styoomer; sumph; tawpie;
  (outstanding) dunderheid; *v.*
  begowk; **fool's errand** feel's
  eeran; Prile eeran
foolish *adj.* feel; daft; fulage (B1);
  gockit; gowkit; gypit
foolishness *n.* feelness; gypery
foot *n.* fit; *v.* **to foot it** fit it; **footed**
  fittit
foot-and-mouth *n.* (disease) fit-an-
  moo
football *n.* fitba
Footdee *pr. n.* (old fisher district of
  Aberdeen) Fittie; Futtie
footing *n.* precunnance
footpath *n.* roddie
footstep *n.* fitstep
for *prep.* tae
force *n.* birr; virr
forceful *adj.* fersell
foreign *adj.* fremd; fremmit
forequarter *n.* (of an animal) spaal,
  spaul
foreshadow *v.* foreshaida
Forfar *pr. n.* Farfar
forget *v.* foryet; *v. pt.* foryat
fork *n.* (of a tree, in the road etc)
  glack; (used in farming) graip; *v.*
  graip
form *v.* fack (B1); *n.* (bench) furm

forsake *v.* forhooie, furhooie
forth *adv.* furth
fortune *n.* fortin
fortunate *adj.* chancy
fortune-teller *n.* (female) spay-wife; **tell fortunes** *v.* spay
forward *imper.* (instruction to a horse) gee up!
foul *adj.* foosome, fousome
found *v. pt.* fan; *ppl.* fun(d). *cf.* **fin**
foundations *n. pl.* foons, founs
fountain *n.* funtain
fountainhead *n.* funtainheid
four *adj.* fower
fowl *n.* (of the the first year) earock
fox *n.* tod
fragile *adj.* (feeling) aa egg shallies
fragment *n.* skirp
Fraserburgh *pr. n.* nicknamed The Broch; Faithlie
Fraserburgh native *n.* Brocher
fraud *n.* snype
freckled *adj.* ferny-ticklt
freckles *n. pl.* fern-tickles
freeze *v.* jeel
freight *n.* fraacht
fresh *adj.* caller
fret *v.* chirm
fretful *adj.* cankert; capernicious
Friday *n.* Freday
friend *n.* freen
friendly (with) *adj.* chief (wi)
fright *n.* fleg; gast; (Abdn. city and coastal) fear
frighten *v.* fleg; fley; frichten; (Abdn. city and coastal) fear; *ppl.* fleggit; fleyt; feart
frivolity *n.* (piece of) flagerie
frivolous *adj.* freevolous

frog *n.* poddick; puddock
frolic *n.* hyze; ploy; splore
frolicsome *adj.* daft
from *prep.* fae; (much less common) frae
front in (of) *adv.* afore; *prep.* afore; anent
frost *n.* freest; (hoar) rime; *v.* freest
frost-nail *n.* pike, pyke; sharp
frown *v.* froon
frugal *adj.* canny
fruit slice *n.* curran daad
fugitive *n.* (from the gallows) rin-the-wuddie
full *adj.* fou, fu; ful, full (rhymes with gull)
full up *ppl.* (after eating) bowdent
fulmar *n.* mallie
fumble *v.* fummle
fume *v.* feem
funeral *n.* beerial; (refreshment) dregie
furious *adj.* feerious
furnish *v.* plenish
furniture *n.* furnitur; plenishin
furrow *n.* fur, furr; sheugh; (open furrow between two ridges) mids; (shallow) scart; *v.* (set up the first furrow when ploughing a field) feer. *cf.* **feerin**
further *adj.* farrer
furthest *adj.* farrest; **furthest out** farrest ootbye
fury *n.* rampaage
fuss *n.* fyke; adee; (great) mineerum; a wark; (outcry) scronach
fussy *adj.* fashious; perjink

— **G** —

gabble *v.* yab-yabble
gable *n.* gaivel (G); gale (M); (top stones on gable) tablin
gadfly *n.* cleg; gleg
gaiters *n. pl.* cweetikins; queetikins
gallery *n.* (in church) laft
gallows *n.* wuddie, wuddy
game (ball-) sappy sodgers; (catching) leavie-oh; (selection) pye; (marbles played against a door) doorie; (playground) jyne-on; (seashore) rocky-on; (team game for boys) hucky-ducky (S); (for two with a stick) pooin the sweer-tree; (tag) tackie, takie; tik-an-tak
gamekeeper *n.* gamie; (the work) keeperin
gander *n.* ganner
gang *n.* gyang
gaol *n.* jivvle
gap *n.* (in wall or fence) slap
gape *v.* gaap, gawp
garden *n.* gairden; (on farm) yard
Gardenstown *pr. n.* (local) Gaimrie
Garioch *pr. n.* (pro. Geery; Gerry)
garments *n. pl.* (outer, usually untidy) bullaments
garter *n.* garten
Gartly *pr. n.* (local) Gairtly
gas *v.* (talk idly) lyaag; laig
gasbag *n.* blether; bleeter; gab
gate *n.* yett
gather *v.* gaither; gedder; gether; gidder
gatherer *n.* (of grain to make

sheaves, usually female) gaitherer; gedderer; lifter
gaudy *adj.* skiry, skyrie; galliart (B1)
gave *v. pt.* gae (M, A2); gya; gied, gid
Gavin *pr. n.* Ga'in
gawp *v.* gowp, goup; gype
generation *n.* ashun
generous *adj.* fraachty; gweedwillie, gweedwullie
genial *adj.* humoursome
gentility *n.* genteelity
gentle *adj.* douce
George *pr. n.* Dod; Geordie
get *v.* get; win; **get off** win aff; **get out** win oot; **get even with** win tee wi; **get away** swithe; **get on with something** hing in; **get over** (recover from) cower; **get ready** (esp. dress to go out) rank; **get up** rise, *pt.* raise, rase
gewgaw *n.* flagerie
ghastly *adj.* gash; ugsome
g(h)illie *n.* gheelie
ghost *n.* ghaist(ie); boodie; wreith
ginger-beer *n.* ginch-breid
girl *n.* (young) deemie; lassickie, lassockie; quine
girlfriend *n.* blon; laas
give *v.* gie
give me *phr.* (when someone chooses a particular thing) chaps me
glad *adj.* gled; gledsome; blythe
glance *n.* glent; skance; went; twig;

v. twig
Glasgow *pr. n.* Glaisga
glass *adj., n.* gless
gleam *n.* flacht; leam; glaik
glen *n.* cleuch
glide *v.* snoove
glimpse *n.* glint (M); went
glitter *v.* (gaudily) skire
gloomy *adj.* dowf; drumly
glossy *adj.* sleekit
glove *n.* glive (A2); (without separate division for the four fingers) doddy-mitten
glow *n., v.* glowe; lowe
gluttonous *adj.* gutsy
gnaw *v.* gnaave, gnauve
go *v.* gae; gang; ging; gyang (A, A1); gaan, gaun (coastal); (reach a place) win; **go away** *excl.* g'wa; *v.* win awa; **go off something** tak a scunner till; **go on** hud awa; **go over** owergae; **go your way** gang yer gait; **go up and down** dyst; **as you go by** i the byg(y)aan
goad *n.* (for driving horses or cattle or directing corn to the scythe or binder) gaad, gad; **one who uses a gaad** gaadsman
goal *n.* (in children's games) dell
God *pr. n.* Gweed; *(euph.)* dyod; nyod; od; frequently *good* in expletives, *e.g.* good be here; good al meggins (prob. *euph.* for God Almighty); **God grant** Gweed sen; **God knows** Gweed kens; **God preserve us** Gweed keep's aa, Gweed preserve's
godly *adj.* gweedlie
going *ppl.* gaan, gaun; gyaan,
gyaun; **going about** *ppl.* agyaan; **going on** *ppl.* agyaan
goings-on *n. pl.* ongaans, ongauns
gold *n.* gowd
golden *adj.* gowden
golf *n.* gowf
golfer *n.* gowfer
gone *ppl.* geen, gane
good *adj., n.* gweed, guid; geed (F); (very) capital
good-for-nothing *n.* ranagant; hurb; wally-draigle; warridrag
good-hearted *adj.* gweedwully
good-humoured *adj.* canty
goodies *n. pl.* chit-chow; galshachs, galshochs; perlyaag
good-looking *adj.* weel-faart, -faurt
goodness *excl.* gwestie, gweeshtie, gweeshtens
goodness knows *excl.* Gweed kens
goodness sake, for *excl.* for ony faavour!
goodnight *int.* gweednicht
goodwill *n.* gweed-wull
gooseberry *n.* grozart
gorge *v.* stech
gosh *excl.* goshie; jings
gossamer *n.* slammach
gossip *n.* claik; clash; (chat) crack; (person) kimmer; claik; sclave; *v.* claik, clash; crack; sclave; sclaver
got *v. pt.* gat; gowt
Gourdon *pr. n.* Gurdon
gown *n.* goon
grab *v.* glammach, glammoch; mitten
grain *n.* (freed from husks) shillans; (threshed) thrash; (particle) sinacle (B1)
grain-loft *n.* corn-laft

grain prices *n. pl.* (fixed for the year) fiars
grand *adj.* gran; (very smart) fantoosh
grandchild(ren) *n. (pl.)* oe(s)
grandfather *n.* granda; deydie (B); lucky daddy (A2)
grandmother *n.* grunny; lucky minnie
grasp *v.* glammach, glammoch; lat glammoch at; fist (B1)
grasping *adj.* nabble, nabal
grass *n.* girse, girss; (coarse) sprot; (near the sea) bent; (long, left standing in winter) fog; (long, thin) ling (J); (any tall, thin, withered stalk) windle-strae; (crested dogstail) windlestrae
grassland *n.* green
grassy *adj.* girssy
grave *n.* greff; (earth) mools
gravel *n.* graivel; (compacted) chad
gravelly *adj.* chaddy
gravestone *n.* lair-steen, -stane
grease *n.* creesh
great *adj.* gryte; muckle; meikle; (considerable) gey
greedy *adj.* gutsy; **greedy person** guts; (mean) hungry
green *n.* (village) loaning (S)
greenish *adj.* greenichtie
grey *adj.* hyaave; (turning) grizzelt; (streaked with) lyart
griddle *n.* (circular iron plate with bow handle for baking) girdle
gridiron *n.* brander
grief *n.* dool
grievances, expressed their *phr.* shook their craps

grim *adj.* door, dour
grimace *n.* murjin, murgeon; mudgeon
grindstone *n.* grinsteen
grip *n.* grip; purchase; *v.* grup; **in the grip of** i the thraws o
groan *n., v.* grain
groom *n.* (in charge of horse) strapper; shalt-loon
grope *v.* grape
ground *n.* grun; (large piece of wasteland) gleebrie; gliberal (B1)
group *n.* boorach(ie)
grow *v.* growe; sproot
growl *n., v.* gurl; gurr
grub *n.* (of cranefly, eating germinating grain) tory; *v.* (of birds) dorb
gruel *n.* stoorum
gruesome *adj.* gash
gruff *adj.* strunge
grumble *v.* grummle; girn; mump
grumbling *adj.* grumlie; nyattery
grunt *v.* gruntle
guano *n.* (fertiliser) gwana
guard *n., v.* guaird, gaird
guernsey *n.* (seaman's jersey) gansey; ganjie
guess *v.* jaloose, jalouse
guffaw *n.* gaff, gauff; guffa
guide *n.* (example) spyaack
gull *v.* gow
gullet *n.* wizzen
gumboil *n.* gumbyle, gumbile
gunpowder *n.* gunpoother
gusset *n.* gushet
gust *n.* (of wind) flan; (sudden) howder

— H —

habit *n.* haibit

had *v. pt.* hid; hed (A2); **had not** hidna

haddock *n.* haddie; (split open, salted, dried in the sun) speldin; (dried without being split) widdie

haft *n.* (of knife) heft

hag *n.* (withered) runt

hair *n.* (haircut) snod-in-aboot; (cut with a bowl) bowel-crappit

hairpins *n. pl.* oots-an-ins

hairy *adj.* nep

half *adj., n.* haaf

half-holiday *n.* haafie

halfpenny *n.* maik

halfpennyworth *n.* maikst

half share *n.* haaver

halfway *adv.* mids; half-roads; **a halfway point** the mids

halfwit *n.* haveral

hall *n.* ha

halt *v.* hult

halter *n.* helter

halve *v.* haaver

hammer *n., v.* haimmer, hemmer; *n.* (heavy) mell

hand *n.* han; *v.* rax

hand's breadth *n.* han-breed; spang

handcart *n.* hurlie

handful *n.* hanfae; (what two cupped hands can hold) gobbinfae; gowpenfu; (of unthreshed corn/hay) ripp

handkerchief *n.* hankie; naipkin

handle *n.* hannle; lug; *v.* hannle (carelessly) toosht

handless *adj.* smeerless (B1)

handline *n.* (for catching cod) ripper

handloom *n.* han-leem

handsel *n., v.* hansel

handsome *adj.* weel-faart, -faurt

handwriting *n.* vreet; vreetin

hang *v. tr., intr.* hing

hanging *n.* hingin

hangman *n.* hangie

happy *adj.* seely

harangue *n.* lay-aff

harbour *n.* hairbour, herbour

hard *adj.* (difficult) ill; ull; **hard-pressed** sair dung, sair made; **hard struggle** sair fecht; **hard at work** i the tag; **hard-working** hard-vrocht; **hard to please** dorty; fashious; **hard up** *adj.* deft; grippit (R)

hare *n.* bawd; maakin, mawkin; myaakin

harelip *n.* hare-shard

harm *n.* hairm; skaith; *v.* hairm

harmless *adj.* hairmless; ulless-gweedless

harness *n.* graith; taikle; (for attaching harness at front of cart shaft) foreslings; (part of britchin, for attachment to rear of cart) hin-slings; (fitment on cartshaft) slider

harnessed *ppl.* (of a horse) drachtit

harp *n.* herp

harrow *n.* harra

Harry *pr. n.* Hairry
harsh *adj.* maroonjus
harvest *n.* hairst; (opening of) moo o hairst; *v.* win, *pt.* wun
harvest home *n.* meal-an-ale
has *v.* his; **has not** hisna
hash *n.* (of potatoes and salted fish) hairy-tatties
hasp *n.* hesp
haste, hasten *v.* hist; swithe
hasty *adj.* ramsh
hat *n.* (deerstalker type worn by gillies and grieves) pickiesay; **top hat** lum-hat
haughty *adj.* heich-heidit
haunch *n.* hinch
haunt *n.* howff
have *v.* hae; hiv; **have not** hinna, *pt.* hid, *ppl.* haen, hin
hawk *v.* (clear throat) haach
hay *n.* hey; (built into a stack) *ppl.* stackit; (gathered row of hay) winraa
haycock *n.* cole; (large) tramp-cole
hay-gatherer *n.* tummlin-tam
haymaker *n.* hey-makker
hay-shed *n.* hey-hoose (S)
haystack *n.* hey-ruck; hey-soo
haze *n.* gull
head *n.* heid; knowe; napper; pow; riggin; **head-first** heelster-heid; **head over heels** heels ower gowdie; heelster-gowdie; hyster-gowdie
head for *v.* ca for
headmaster *n.* heid(maister)
head-stall *n.* heid-stall
headstrong *adj.* heidie; ramshackle
heal *v.* haill
healthy *adj.* hale; hale an fere; (and active) kneef

heap *n.* dossie; hullock; hape (S); (large) kyarn; (loose heap or stack) rickle
heard *v. pt.* hard
heart *n.* hairt, hert
heartburn *n.* hertscaad; watter-brash
hearth *n.* ingle; chimbly-chik; hairth (J)
heat *v.* het, *pt.* het
heathen *n.* haythen
heather *n.* hedder
heave *v.* haive; heeze
heaven *n.* hivven; heeven (C)
heavy *adj.* wachty
heed of, take *v.* reck; tak tent
heifer *n.* quake, quaik
height *n.* heicht, hicht
heighten *v.* heichen
held *v. pt.* heeld, *ppl.* hudden
hell *n.* the ill pairt
hello *int.* ay, ay
helping *n.* sairin
hempen *adj.* himpen
hen *n.* hen; chucken, chuckney; (free-range) gaan-aboot hen; (not exceeding a year old) yearock
hen-pecked *adj.* hudden-doon
hen-run *n.* ree
herdsman *n.* herd
heretic *n.* heretick
herring *n.* herrin; heerin; **herring fever** herrin fivver
herself *pron. (also* **by herself**) hersel
hesitate *v.* dachle; dackle; swither
hiccup *n.* esk; *v.* esk; yist; **get hiccups** tak the esk
hide *v.* hod, *pt.* hid, *ppl.* hodden

hiding *n.* sack ful o sair beens

high *adj.* heich, hich; (of wind) reevin

highland *adj.* hielan(t)

Highlander *n.* Hielander; (sometimes disparaging) teuchter

hill *n.* ben; hull

hillock *n.* hullock; (small) knablich (A2); **top of a hillock** knowe-heid

himself *pron.* (also by himself) himsel

hinder *v.* hinner

hint *n.* sleumin

hip-joint(s), aching *adj., n.* hippit; hip-grippit

hired-hand *n.* fee't man

hiring fair *n.* feein-fair; feein-mairket

his *adj.* his; 's

hit *v.* hit, *pt.* hat

hoard *v.* hain

hoar-frost *n.* rime

hoarse *adj.* hairse; roopy, roupy

hobble *v.* fuffle; hirple

hobnail *n.* tacket; **hobnailed boots** tackety beets

hoe *n., v.* hyow(e); *v.* (turnips) single

hoist *v.* hyste

hold *n.* had; hud, haud; hid (S); purchase; *v.* hud; hid (S); **hold your tongue** hud yer tongue

hole *n.* bore

hollow *adj.* boss; halla; *n.* howe; sheuch; (small, scooped out of ground for use in game of marbles) kyp(i)e; **hollow-backed** *adj.* howe-backit

holm *n.* howm (J)

home *n.* hame; doonsit (B1); (belonging to) *adj.* hamel(t)

home farm *n.* hame-fairm

homely *adj.* hamel(t); haimal(t)

homesick *adj.* hamesick

homespun *adj., n.* hamespun; hodden; **grey homespun** hodden grey

homewards *adv.* hameward; hamewith

honest *adj., adv.* (fair-)furth-the-gate

honey *n.* hinny

hoof *n.* hiv

hook *n.* heuk, hyeuck; (used on fishmarket floor) lowrie

hoop *n.* (child's) gird

hop *v.* hap

hope *v.* howp

hornless *adj.* doddit; hummel, hummle; hummel-doddie

horrible *adj.* ugsome

horrify *v.* horrifee

horse *n.* (small) garron; (walking in furrow) furrer; fur-beast; (landside) lanner; (disease affecting legs) grease

horse-hoe *n.* (small plough for weeding) shim

horse-trough *n.* horse-troch

hot *adj.* het; (scalding ~; ~ and sweating) plottin; **hot foot** het fit

hotel *n.* hottle

hot water bottle *n.* pig

hour *n.* oor

hour-glass *n.* san-gless

hourly *adv.* oorly

house *n.* hoose; (the laird's) the Hoose, the Big Hoose, the Place; (temporary, for shepherds)

sheilin; (removal) flittin
houseful *n.* hoosefae, hoosefu
house-room *n.* hooseroom
housewife *n.* hizzie
housewifery *n.* hizzieskep; hoosewifeskip
how *adv.* fit wye; foo; hoo; **how
are you** fit like
however *adv.* fooivver; hooever;
hoosomever; hoosomediver
hubbub *n.* gilgal (hard g)
hullabaloo *n.* heelabalow
humble *adj.* hoomble
humble-bee *n.* foggie-bee
humbling *adj.* heemlin
humid *adj.* blobbie-like
humiliate *v.* mortifee; *ppl.*
mortifeet
humour *n.* eemur; teen; **fit of ill
humour** *n.* tig

hump *n.* humph
hunchbacked *adj.* humphie-backit
hundred *n.* hunner
hundredweight *n.* hunnerwecht
hunger *n.* hunger (**ng** as in singer)
hungry *adj.* hungert; (very) yamph;
yap; **hungry-looking** yappy;
hungry for *adj.* yivvery
hurdle *n.* (for penning sheep, used
as a gate) flake
hurricane *n.* heerican
hurry back *imp.* hist-ye-back
hurry off *v.* scoot; skirt
hurt *v.* (severely) missaacre,
missaucre; (severely, fatally) pran
husband *n.* man; goodman (A2);
gweedman; *v.* hain
husk *n.* (corn) sheelock
hussy *n.* hizzie
hypocrite *n.* heepocreet

— I —

I *pers. pron.* A; Aw; I
ice-cream *n.* (between two wafers)
slider
icicle *n.* ice-tangle
idea *n.* adaya; noshun
idiot *n.* eediot; gapus
idle *adj.* orra
idle frolics *n. pl.* idelties
idleness *n.* idlety; idleseat; idleset
if *conj.* gin; gif (B1); **if only** *conj.*
gin (M2)
I'll *pron. with v.* Aw'se; I'se
ill-fated *adj.* weirdless
ill-humour *n.* bung
ill-humoured *adj.* cankert
ill-natured *adj.* ill-gruntit; ill-

naturt; nabble
illness *n.* (a fit of) drow
ill-tempered *adj.* nyattery
ill-use *v.* ill-, ull-eese
ill-will *n.* ull-wull
imagination *n.* imaiginashun
imagine *v.* imaagine, imaigin;
jaloose, jalouse
immediately *adv.* immediantly
imp *n.* buckie; deevilock
implements *n. pl.* leems
improve *v.* impruv
improvement *n.* impreevement
impudent *adj.* impident; (of the
tongue) ill-hung; **impudent
person** smatchet

in *prep.* i
incapable *adj.* feckless
incidental *adj.* overly
incidentally *adv.* in the bygaan,
    bygaun; bygyaan
incline *n.* brae
inconsequential *adj.* sma drink
inconvenience *v.* pit aboot
indeed *adv.* awat; deed; fairly; faith
indigestion *n.* belly-rive
induce *v.* gow (ower)
induct *v.* induck
industrious *adj.* eident
infect *v.* smit
infectious *adj.* smittin
infested *adj.* hotchin
inflamed *ppl., adj.* (by cold) frostit
influence *n.* moyen; **through your**
    influence in the leethe o ye
influenza *n.* inflooensie
infuriate *v.* raise
infuse *v.* mask
ingenious *adj.* jinipp(e)rous
inhalation *n.* (of air) gluff
inherit *v.* heir; fa heir till
inheritance *n.* heirskip
inhibited *adj.* hudden-doon
injury *n.* scaith
injustice *n.* oonjustice
inlet *n.* (narrow and rocky) gwite
inn *n.* chynge-hoose
innermost *adj.* benmaist
inner workings *n. pl.* intimmers
innovatory *adj.* new-fanglelt
inquire *v.* inquar
inquiry *n.* inquary
inquisitive *adj.* ill-, ull-fashent
inquisitiveness *n.* ill-, ull-fashence
inside *adv.* ben; in-by(e); *prep.* ben
insipid *adj.* saarless, saurless;

warsh; wersh
insist *v.* threep
instinct *n.* enstinck
instrument *n.* enstrument
intelligence *n.* smeddum
intelligent *adj.* lang-heidit
intend *v.* ettle, *ppl.* ettlin; mint
intention *n.* mint
inter *v.* beery; yird
intercept *v.* kep
interdict *n.* enterdick
interesting *adj.* interaistin
interfere *v.* enterfere
interment *n.* beerial
intestines *n. pl.* intimmers; mony-
    faalds
intimate *v.* intimat; forquant
intimate (with) *adj.* chief (wi);
    thrang (wi); (esp. in favour with
    God) far ben (wi)
intimidate *v.* coonjer
into *prep.* intil
intoxicate *v.* deleer
intoxicated *ppl.* glorious
inventory *n.* inveetor
Inverurie *pr. n.* In'rurie
invitation *n.* inveet
invite *v.* bid; inveet; seek
irregular *adj.* (in appearance)
    shammelt
irresponsible *adj.* haaf-hung-tee
irritable *adj.* sanshach; short i the
    trot
irritation *n.* aggravation
Isabella *pr. n.* Beldie
island *n.* inch
it *pron.* it; 't; hit
itch *n., v.* yock
itchy *adj.* yockie
ivy *n.* eevie

— J —

jacket *n.* jaicket; (woman's loose) vrapper
jade *n.* (woman) jaad, jaud; bizzar (J)
jail *n., v.* jile
jalopy *n.* shan-dre-dan
jam *n.* jeely; **jam jars** jeely pigs
James *pr. n.* Jamie; Jeems(ie)
Janet *pr. n.* Jinse
janitor *n.* jannie
January *n.* Janwar; Janiwar
jar *n.* (earthenware) pig
jasmine *n.* jassamine
jaundice *n.* the jandies
jaunt *n., v.* jant
jaunty *adj.* jinkie
jaw *n.* jaa, jaw
jaws *n. pl.* chowks
jeer *n.* fleer (J); *v.* jamph; lant
jelly *n.* (table) shoggly-wullie
jellyfish *n.* (stinging) scalder; (harmless) slivvery-doctor (B)
jeopardy *n.* jipperty
jerk *v.* (gently) tit; (strongly) yark; (repeatedly) joggle
jersey *n.* maasie (G); (seaman's) gansey; ganjie
Jew's harp *n.* trump
job *n.* jot; a wark; (troublesome, fiddly) footer; (involving much detail) scutterie jobbie; **a job of work** a jot wark
jocular *adj.* vokie; vyokie
jog *n., v.* cadge

joggle *v.* joogle
John *pr. n.* Jock
join *v.* jyne; (together, esp. roughly in sewing) ranter
joiner *n.* jyner; vricht
joint *n.* jynt; (segment) lith
joist *n.* jyst
joke *n.* (funny story) bar; (at someone's expense) rise; **make fun of** tak the rise o; *v.* fun joking; *adj.* (normally used in the neg.) **no joking matter** nae jeesty; nae mowse; nae a mowse concairn
jolly *adj.* jelly
jolt *v.* daad, daud; (severe) junny
journey *n.* traivel
jovial *adj.* joco
judge *v.* jeedge
jug *n.* joog; stoop, stoup; stowp; (whisky) jorum
juice *n.* bree
juicy *adj.* sappy
jumble *n., v.* jummle
juniper *n.* etnach
junk *n.* rottacks
junk food *n.* galshachs, galshochs perlyaag
just *adv.* jist; joost (A2)
just after *prep.* (of time) the back o
justice *n.* joostice
just like *prep.* siclikes
just now *adv. phr.* enoo, eenoo; eynoo; eyvnoo; iv noo; iv now

— K —

kail stalk *n.* kail runt
keen *adj.* gleg, glegsome; keerious; **keen on** teen wi
keep *v.* kep; (away) hud oot ower; (clear of) hud redd o; (in with) hud in wi
keeper *n.* (of farm at weekends) catcher; toondie, toondy; toonkeeper
keep in with *phr.* hud in wi
keep up *v.* keep tee
kennel *n.* cooch
kennel-attendant *n.* dog-dirder
kept *v. pt.* keepit
kettle *n.* byler (R); **a different kettle of fish** a different Maggie Rennie (B)
kill *v.* fell
kilted *ppl.* kiltit
kind *adj.* douce; kine; *n.* (nature, sort) kine
kindle *v.* kennle
kindling *n.* kinlin; kennlin

kindly *adj.* couthie
king *n.* keeng
kingdom *n.* keengdom
kiss *n.* smeerich; smoorich
kitchen *n.* kitchie; but-the-hoose
kitchen-maid *n.* kitchie-deem
kite *n.* (plaything) draigon; (bird) gled; gleed
kitten *n.* kit(t)lin
knave *n.* (in cards) munsie
knife *n.* futtle; whittle; (large) gullie
knight *n.* knicht
knit *v.* shank; wyve
knitting *n.* wyvin
knitting-needle *n.* weer
knitting-wool *n.* worsit
knob *n.* knag
knock *v.* ca; chap; knack; knap; (about) cadge
knoll *n.* knap, knowe
knot-hole *n.* navus-bore
know *v.* ken; wat; **I know** awyte; I ken; *neg.* kenna; dinna ken; watna

— L —

labour *n.* laabour, lawbour
lack *v.* wint
lad *n.* callant; laad; loon
ladle out *v.* lave (B1)
lady's man *n.* a bit o a lad
lag *v.* trytle
lain *ppl.* lyen
lamb *n.* (little) lammie; (male with only one descended testicle) rig-lamb; (pet brought up on the

bottle and summmoned by the call 'sick') sick lamb
lament *v.* willieway
laminate *v.* skelve (B1)
lamp-lighter *n.* leerie
lancet *n.* fleem
land *n.* lan; (exchanged) excamb; (low-lying, beside river) haagh, haugh
landmark *n.* prop

land on *v.* licht (on)
landowner *n.* laird
landside *adj.* (side of plough next the unploughed land) lanside
lane *n.* (narrow) wynd
language *n.* leid
languor *n.* langer
languish *v.* dwine
lanky person *n.* stilpert
lantern *n.* (han-)booet; booit
lap *v.* lab; lapper; lerb
lapwing *n.* pee-weet (M, R); peesie (-weep) (S); teuchat, teuchit
larch *n.* larick
large *adj.* bookit, boukit; muckle; meikle
lark (about) *v.* hollach (aboot)
lash *n.* whang
last *adj., n., v.* laist, lest; hinmaist
last out *v.* (of people) store the kin
latch *n.* sneck
late *adv.* ahin
laudanum *n.* lodomy
laugh *n., v.* laach, lauch, *pt.* leuch; (loudly) gaff, gauff; (heartily) bicker; **to be laughed at** laachen at; **how I laughed** fit I leuch
laughter *n.* laachter, lauchter
launch *v.* lench
Laurencekirk *pr. n.* Lowrenkirk
lavatory *n.* wattery
law *n.* laa, law
lawful *adj.* laafu, lawfu
lawn *n.* green
Lawrence *pr. n.* Lowrin
lawyer *n.* laavyer, lawvyer
lay *v.* plank
lay hold of *v.* claaght, claught
laziness *n.* sweirty
lazy *adj.* latch; sweer, sweir

lea *n.* (unploughed land) ley; **lea-corn** ley-corn
leader *n.* heid-bummer
leaf *n.* (of potato, turnip etc.) shaw
lean-to *n.* lean-tee
leap *v.* lowp, *pt.* lowpit; lape, *pt.* lap
learn *v.* lairn; leern
learned *adj.* leernt
learning *n.* lairnin; leernin; lear
lease *n.* (of a farm) tack; **leased farm** tack; *v.* set
leather strap *n.* (formerly used by school teachers for punishment) tag; tawse
leave *n.* (of absence) afflat; *v.* lea, ley (A1); lave (S); (one home for another) flit; (in the lurch) lanter; **take one's leave** weer awa
lectern *n.* laiteran; lettrin
left, turn *imper.* (instruction to a plough horse in Buchan) hi
leftovers *n. pl.* orrals
leg *in phr.* **pull my leg** draa ma leg
legless *adj.* shankless
leisure *n.* leasure, leesure
lemonade *n.* ale (also used of other aerated waters)
lend *v.* len
length *n.* lenth; linth
let *v.* lat; lit; lut; *pt.* lat; leet; loot; *ppl.* latten, lutten; **let alone** latten be; **let it be known that** lat licht that
let *v.* (land, property) set
let-down *n.* snipe, snype
lethargic *adj.* oonfersell; smeerless; thowless
letter-be *n.* (the one who feeds in the straw in rope-twisting) latter-oot

liberal *adj.* fraachty, frauchty; leebral; (extravagantly) lordlifu; *n.* Leebral

library *n.* leeberary

licence *n.* leeshens, leeshins

lick *n.* (of fluid) lerb

lie *n.* lee; (big) whapper; *v.* lee, *ppl.*, *n.* leein; **without a word of a lie** onleet; *v.* (in bed etc) lig (lit.)

lift *n.* (in a vehicle) hurl; *v.* heeze; luft; (up) heft; (with effort) heist, hyste

light *adj., n., v.* licht; **indirect light** borrat licht; **make light of** lichtlifie

light-fingered *adj.* tarry-fingert

light-headed *adj.* litchie

lighthouse *n.* lichthoose

lightning *n.* lichtnin; (streak of) flacht o fire

liked *v. pt.* liket, likit

likely *adv.* lickly; belike

likened (to) *ppl.* lickent wi

liking (for) *n.* noshun o

limp *adj.* (from weakness) waffle; *v.* hirple; clench (A2); crochle;

line *n.* (fishing snood made of horse hair) tippen

lingo *n.* linga

linnet *n.* lintie

liquid *n.* bree

liquor *n.* (from Eng. *naphtha*) naftie, naphtie

listen *v.* hearken

listless *adj.* oonfersell; smeerless; heepochondreech (B1)

litany *n.* leetiny

literary *adj.* leeterary

litter *n.* (brood) cleckin

live *v.* (at an address) bide, *pt.* bade; bed(d); stop

livelihood *n.* liveliheid; throw-beerin

lively *adj.* croose

livestock *n.* beas'

living being *n.* leevin

load *n.* lade, laid; (two or more cartloads, barrowloads) fraacht, fraucht; draacht, draucht

loaf *v.* sorn

loathsome *adj.* scunnerfu; scunner-some

lobster *n.* (fisher term) labster

loch *n.* (small) lochan

lock *n.* (of hair) tait

loft *n.* laft

loiter *v.* lyter

long *adj.* lang; **the long and the short of it** the reet an the rise o't

long ago *phr.* lang syne; than an awa

long (for) *v.* green (efter); mang (for)

long-gone *adj.* lang-geen, -gane

long-legged *adj.* lang-leggit; **long-legged person** stilpert

look *n.* leuk; scance; (evil) scook, scouk; vizzy; **backward look** vizzy backart; *v.* leuk; scance

look after *v.* tak aboot

look for *v.* sik, seek

look out *v.* (search and find) rank oot; **on the look-out for** on the haik for

loosen *v.* lowssen

Lord *excl.* lod; losh; loshins; loshtie; **Good Lord guide us** loshtie-goshtie guide's

lordship *n.* lairdskip

lorry *n.* larry

lose *v.* loss; tyne, tine, *pt. ppl.* tint
loss *n.* (by cheating) snipe, snype
lost *in phr.* **get lost** flee up
lot *n.* (situation) billet; **the whole lot** the hale jing-bang
loud *adj.* lood
louse *n.* loose
lousy *adj.* loosie
lout *n.* fang; fleep; flype; (rough) gillieperous; gileepris (hard **g**)
love *n.* luve; *v.* loo, loe
lovely *adj.* bonnie, bonny
low *adj.* laich, laigh; lyaach; **low-lying ground** laigh

lowland *adj.* lallan
lowlands *n. pl.* laalands, lawlands
loyal *adj.* leal
lucky *adj.* chancy; licky
lug *v.* humph
lumbago *n.* lumbaga
lumber *n.* rottacks
lump *n.* (large, of cheese, beef etc) kneevlick; knyte; fang; (also used as mild insult) knibloch
lungs *n. pl.* (human or animal) lichts
lychnis floscuculi *n.* raggit robin (S)

— **M** —

Macduff native *pr. n.* Duffer
mad *adj.* gyte; wid; wud
madam *n.* muddim
madden *v.* raise
madness *n.* madden-drim, -dreem; (sudden) wudden-dream
magic *n.* glamour; glamourie
magnet *n.* lodesteen, lodestane
magpie *n.* pyot
manners *n. pl.* mainners
mainpin *n.* docknail
maintain *v.* (assert) hud, haud oot
majority, the *n.* the feck
make *v.* mak; fack (B1); (cause, compel) gar; **make known** lat licht; **make no difference** mak nae odds
maker *n.* makker
makings (of) *n. pl.* makkins o
malcontent *n.* (female) peekin-eevie
mallet *n.* mell

malt *n.* maat, maut
maltreat *v.* ill-eese; ill-guide
man *n.* maan; maanie; carl; chiel; (little) mannikie; (little, old) carlie; (form of address) min
manage *v.* tak aboot
manager *n.* (of farm) grieve; (of an estate) grun offisher
manger *n.* foresta
manly *adj.* byoordly; beerdly; buirdly
manner *n.* menner; *pl.* menners; **well-mannered** weel-mennert; **ill-mannered** ill-mennert
mantel-shelf *n.* chumla; chumlay
manure *n.* muck; (on the surface) tapdress; **manure-barrow** *n.* muck-barra; **manure distributor** *n.* (horse-drawn) bone davy
many *adj.* mony; **many a one** mony een
marble *n.* (glass) bool; (game of

147

marbles played against door)
doorie

March *n.* Mairch

march *n., v.* mairch, merch

mare *n.* mear, meer

Margaret *pr. n.* Marget; Muggie

market *n.* mairket, mercat; (agric.)
mart; mairt

marking substance *n.* (for sheep)
keel

marriage *n.* mairrage, mairritch;
(paraphernalia) bucklins (A2)
married woman *n.* kimmer

marrowbone *n.* marra-been

marry *v.* mairry; mairry on (to),
ppl. mairrit; wad, *pt.* waddit

marsh *n.* stank

Martinmas *n.* Martimas

marvel *n.* mervel

mash *v.* chap; **mashed potatoes**
chappit tatties

masquerade *v.* guise

mass *n.* (great crowd) mengyie;
(seething) hotter

master *n., v.* maister

match *n.* (stick) spunk; (equal)
marra, marrow; **not matching**
marless; *v.* peer wi

matter *n.* maitter; **doesn't matter**
maksna, disna mak; **no matter**
deil-ma-care

maximus *n.* (gravest error in Latin
prose composition) maxie

May *n.* Mey

me *pron.* ma

meadow *n.* ley

meal *n.* brose; **meal-chest** *n.*
girnal; (farm-servant's) meal-kist;
meal-bunk (S); mealer (S)

mealy-mouthed *adj.* mealy-moo't,
-mou't

mean *adj.* dirten; (shabby) wheetie;
(unsporting) skicy (children's
word); (tight-fisted) hungry;
meangie; near the been; nar (B1);
mean person *n.* hunger; a
hungry Angus

meander *v.* wimple

meanness *n.* near-beg(y)aanness;
near-begaunness

means *n.* moyen

meant *ppl.* meent

measles *n. pl.* the mirrles

measure *n., v.* mizzer;
measurement *n.* mizzerment

measures (grain, six bolls) chalder;
(fourth part of a boll) firlit;
(fourth part of a peck) lippie,
leepie; (liquid, equal to Eng. pint)
mutchkin

meat pie *n.* braddie; bridie

meddle *v.* mell; middle

medicine *n.* feesick

meet *v.* (by chance) kep

meeting *n.* (arranged) tryst

melancholy *adj.* darksome; dowf;
oorlich

mellow *adj.* maamie, maumie,
mawmie

membrane *n.* scriffan

memorial *n.* prop

men *n. pl.* mannies; mennies; men;
chiels

mend *v.* sort; (patch) cloot; (by
coarse darning or sewing) ranter

mention *v.* moo-ban (B1); *in phr.*
not to mention forbyes

mercy *n.* leenity; merciment

merry *adj.* blithe(some), blythe;
mirky

mess *n.* kirn; queeger; soss; (disgusting) sotter; (wet or dirty) slorach; (scattered) splutrich (B1)

mess about *v.* pleiter; (at domestic work) scuddle; scutter

messenger *n.* (sent ahead of bridegroom to summon bride) sen

mettle *n.* spunk

middle *n.* mids; (of the night) riggin o the nicht

midge *n.* midgie; midgeck

mid-ridge *n.* mid-rig

midst *n.* mids

midwife *n.* howdie

might *n.* micht; *v.* micht; mith; **might not** *v. neg.* minna; mithna; mithnin

mignonette *n.* meeninit

migraine *n.* megreem

mildew *n.* mildyow

milk *n.* (jet from a cow's teat) strin

milk-cow *n.* milker; **preparation of milk** milkness; **milk-strainer** *n.* search

mill *n.* mull; (stone hand-mill) quern

miller *n.* mullart, mullert

million *n.* meelyin

millionaire *n.* meelyinaire

mind *n.* myn

minister *n.* meenister; minaister (A2)

minnow *n.* minnon, bandie

minute *n.* meenit

mire *n.* (bog) lair; (mud) dubs; gutters

mirror *n.* gless

mischief *n.* ill-tricks; mischeef; (a bit of) protick; **mischief-maker** *n.* buckie

mischievous *adj.* ill-trickit; **mischievous boy** nickum

miser *n.* hunger (**ng** as in singer)

miserable *adj.* oorlich

miserly *adj.* nar (B1); near-beg(y)aan, near-begaun; grippy

mishap *n.* mishanter; scavie (B1)

mismanage *v.* mislippen

misshapen *ppl., adj.* mishachelt

missionary *n.* missioner

mist *n.* haar; (thin, cold) gull; (in a billow) folm

misty *adj.* mochie

mistake *n.* mistak

mistaken *ppl.* misteen, mistaen

mix *v.* kirn; mell

mixture *n.* mixter; mixter-maxter; queeger

mix-up *n.* quigger

moan *n., v.* main

mob *n.* kinallie

mock *v.* jamph; scowff

mockery *n.* jamphin

moderate *adj.* (in price) canny

moderately *adv.* middlin

modern *adj.* modren

moist *adj.* sappy

mole *n.* mowdie(warp), mowdiewart; **molecatcher** *n.* molie

Monday *n.* Monanday

money *n.* bawbees; siller; tin (A); (just enough to pay one's way) rin-watter

monkfish *n.* (Buchan) caithick; (Moray Firth) oof (B)

monologue *n.* say-awa

monument *n.* moniment

mood *n.* teen; bin; **bad mood** ill teen; **in the mood for** on for

moody *adj.* maggotive
moon *n.* meen, mune; **moonlight** *n.* meenlicht, munelicht
moor *n.* meer, muir; (peat moor) moss
moorcock *n.* muircock
mooring-pot *n.* paal
moorland *n.* muirlan
mope *v.* mump
more *adj.* mair; **more than** *prep.* passin
morose *adj.* strunge
morsel *n.* glammach, glammoch
mortgage *n.* wadset
moss *n.* fog; (alpine club) stag-moss
moss-covered *adj.* foggit
mossy *adj.* foggy
most *adj., n.* most; the feck
mostly *adv.* maistly; feckly
moth *n.* moch
moth-balls *n. pl.* moch-baas
moth-eaten *adj.* moch-aeten; mochie
mother *n.* midder; mither; mammy; (pet name) minnie
mother-in-law *n.* gweed-mither
mould *n.* moold; (a mould for ball, spoon etc.) caam, caum
mould-board *n.* cleathin
mouldy *adj.* foostie; fooshtie; foostit
mount *v.* munt; **mounted (on)** *ppl.* cockit (on)
mountain *n.* ben
mountain-ash *n.* rowan; rodden; rantree; (berry) rodden
mourn *v.* murn
mourning clothes *n. pl.* murnins
mouse *n.* moose
moustache *n.* mowser

mouth *n.* gab; maa, maw; moo, mou
mouthful *n.* moofae, moufu; gnap (large) rive; (of food or drink) howpie
move *n.* meeve; (jolting) hotter; *v.* meeve; muv (B1); gee, jee; (hurriedly) fudder; (quickly and noisily) bicker; binner; (with rocking motion) jow; (with friction) hirstle, hurschle, hursle; (awkwardly or jerkily) hodge, hotch; (smoothly) snoove; **on the move** on the ca; **move house** flit
moved *adj.* (emotionally) affeckit
movement *n.* (quick) binner; (jolting) hotter
mow *v.* maw
mucus *n.* (nasal) snotter(s)
mud *n.* dubs; clort; glaar, glaur; gutters; lair; slabber; (alluvial, left in tidal rivers) sleek; slich
muddle *n.* queeger
muddled *adj.* throw-idder; throwder; (mentally confused) raivelt
muddy *adj.* dubby; dubbit; (of water) drumly; plytery
mud-spattered person *n.* drablich
muggy *adj.* mochie
multitude *n.* multiteed
multure *n.* (miller's fee) moolter, moulter; mooter, mouter
mumble *v.* mum; mummle
mummer *n.* guiser; guizard (J)
mumming, to go *v.* guise
murder *n., v.* muther
murmur *n.* chirm; myowte; *v.* chirm; (plaintively) chunner
museum *n.* musaium

music *n.* meesic; **musical tones** airels
mussel *n.* (shelled) sheelter (B)
must *v.* maan, maun; *neg.* maana, mauna; beet, *pt.* beed
mute *n.* dummie

my *poss. pron.* ma
my goodness *excl.* my cert; my certie
myself *pron.* (also by myself) masel; masellie; ma nainsel

— **N** —

naked *adj.* nakit; nyaakit
napkin *n.* nepkin
nappy *n.* hippen
narrative *n.* say-awa
narrow *adj.* nairra, nerra
nasty *adj.* naisty
national *adj.* naitional
native wit *phr.* mother wit
natty *adj.* jinipperous
natural *adj.* naitral
natural herbage *phr.* natur-girss
nature *n.* natur, naitur
nauseated (by) *ppl.* ska(i)kent (wi)
near *adj.* nar
nearly *adv.* nearhan; naarhan; geylies
neat *adj.* nait; nacket; snod; **neat person** nackety
necessary *adj.* necessar
necessity *n.* needcessity
neck *n.* (to one side) gyke-neckit
need *n.* needcessity; *v.* need; *neg.* needsna, *pt.* nott, *pt. neg.* nottna
ne'er-do-well *n.* neer-dee-weel
neglect *v.* mislippen; negleat
neigh *n.* (of horses) nicher
neighbour *n.* neebour; neeper, neiper
neighbourly *adj.* neiper-like
neither *conj., pron., adj.* naither,

nether; nedder; nedderin
nephew *n.* neffy
nervous *adj.* nervish
nest *n.* (of wild bees) bike
nestling *n.* cheeper; gorbal; gorblin; gog (S)
never *adv.* niver, nivver; ne'er
nevertheless *adv.* natheless; still-an-on
next *adj.* neest, neist; neesht
new *adj.* (quite) spleet-new
Newburgh *pr. n.* (near Ellon) Neebra
newly *adv.* new; newlins
news-starved *adj.* news-gizzent
New Year's Eve *n.* Hogmanay
niggardliness *n.* near-beg(y)aan-ness; near-begaunness
niggardly *adj.* near-beg(y)aan; near-begaun; *adj., adv.* scuddy
night *n.* nicht; **last night** the streen; **overtaken by night** nicht-boon, nichtboun
nimble *adj.* swack, swak; swippert, swyppert; swuppert
nitwit *n.* gapus
no *adj.* nae, *e.g.* nae wark
no *adv.* na; **no thank you** na thenk ye
nobbly *adj.* knablick

noise *n.* (loud) dirdum, dundeerie, min(n)eer, mineerum
noisy *adj.* raachle, rauchle
nominated *v. pt., ppl.* nominat
none *pron.* neen, nane
nonsense *n.* blethers; blickers; buff; havers; stite, styte
noose *n.* mink
Norway *pr. n.* Noroway (A2)
Northern Lights, the *pr. n.* the Merry Dancers
northland *adj.* norlan
nose *n.* cooter, couter; neb, nib; niz; nob; snoot
nosebleed *n.* bleedy cooter
not *adv.* nae, *e.g.* she's nae gaan; no *e.g.* she's no gaen (C1, G1, S); the Deil., *e.g.* the Deil he did; fient a, *e.g.* **not one** fient een; **not likely** fient afears; **not a bit** fient hait; deil a nip **not at all**

excl. fie na
notch *n.* hack; nick
nothing *n.* naething; nocht; (absolutely) naither eechie nor ochie; **a mere nothing** *n.* wanwurth
notion *n.* noshun; (foolish) gee; **to take a notion** *phr.* tae tak a tig
nought *n.* nocht
now *adv.* noo; **just now** aenoo; eenoo, eynoo; eyvnoo; ivnoo; **now and then** fyles; noo an than; noo an aan; noos an aans
nowadays *adv.* nooadays
nowhere *adv.* naewye
nuisance *n.* bucker; scutter
number *n.* nummer; a wheen; a curn; a puckle; (large number) a gweed curn; dose; hantle; spreeth
numskull *n.* gapus

— **O** —

oak *n.* aik
oatcakes *n. pl.* (ait) kyaaks; cyacks; bannocks (S); (in a round) kyaak o breid; (taken as dessert in bowl of milk) breid; (crumbled into milk) murly-tuck, snap-an-rattle; (buttered by thumb) thoomb-piece
oaten *adj.* aiten
oat husks *n. pl.* (used for sowans) sids
oatmeal *n.* aitmeal, meal; (quantity received from the mill at one time) maillyer; (when boiled thicker than gruel, with butter and

honey) brochan; (~ or peasemeal mixed with boiling water or milk) brose; (mixed cold with water) crowdy; (with boiled milk) knotty tams; (pudding) mealie puddin; (pancakes) saatie-, sautie-bannocks; (cooked with onion, dripping and seasoning) skirlie; (~ ball given to children during baking) sooie
oath *n.* aith; charge
oats *n. pl.* ait(s); corn; (fermented husks of ~ boiled) sowans
obedient *adj.* obaidient
object *n., v.* objeck

oblige *v.* obleege
obliged *ppl.* behudden; obleeged;
  not obliged onbehudden
obstacle *n.* bunkert
obstinate *adj.* stockit; thraan,
  thrawn
occasional *adj.* antrin
occasionally *adv.* fyles
occupy *v.* occupee
October *n.* Jocktober
odd *adj.* orra; (peculiar) unco
oddity *n.* ferlie; (untidy person)
  track
odd-job man *n.* (on farm) orra man
odd-job boy *n.* (on farm) orra loon
odour *n.* waff
of *prep.* o
off *adv., prep.* aff
offence *in phr.* **take offence at**
  someone tak the gee wi
offend *v.* miscomfit; offen
officer *n.* offisher
officiate *v.* offeeshyat
often *adv.* afen; aft; aften
oh *excl.* och
oh yes *excl.* hoot ty
oil *n.* ile
oil-cake *n.* ile-cake
oil lamp *n.* ily(-lamp); (old-
  fashioned) cruisie, crusie
oil-skin *adj. n.* ile-skin
oily *adj.* eely
ointment *n.* saa, saw
old *adj.* aal(d), aul(d)
old age *n.* eild; eld (C1)
older *adj.* aaler, auler
oldest *adj.* aalest, aulest
old-fashioned *adj.* aal-farran(t)
on *prep.* on; o
once *adv.* eence; ance (G1); **once**

upon a time eence on a day
one *adj.* ae; *n.* (numeral) een; **the**
  one (contrasted with the other)
  the teen; the taen (S)
onion *n.* ingan
onslaught *n.* dirdin
ooze *n.* glaar, glaur
open *adj., v.* apen; **open air** the
  furth
open air, in the *phr.* thereoot
opening *n.* slap
opinion *n.* opeenion; opingan
opinionative *adj.* heidie; noshunate
opportunity, at every *phr.* at aa
  hans
opposite *prep.* anent; fornent
ordain *v.* ordeen
ordeal *n.* throw-come
order, out of *prep. phr.* agley
ordinary *adj.* ordinar
ornament *n.* (showy) furligorum;
  (fantastic and useless)
  whigmaleerie; (elaborate
  architectural ornamentation)
  furlimafaals
ostentatious *adj.* vantie, vauntie
other *adj., n., pron.* idder; ither;
  odder; **the other** (contrasted with
  the one) the tither
ought *v.* ocht
ounce *n.* unce
our *pron.* oor; wir
ours *pron.* oors
ourselves *pron.* (also **by ourselves**)
  oorsels; wirsels
out *adv.* oot
out of *prep.* oot o; (bed, a cart etc.)
  ootower; **out of favour with** oot
  wi; **out of things** oot amint (S);
  out of the way ootby

outbreak *n.* ootbrak
outcast *n.* ootlin
outcry *n.* (querulous) scronach (A2)
outdo *v.* cow(e)
outfield *n.* ootfeedle
outfit *n.* rig-oot
outgoing *n.* (departure at end of season) ootgang
outhouse *n.* oothoose
outlay *n.* ootlay, ootlie
outlet *n.* ootlat; (at spring) stroop
outlines *n. pl.* rinnins
outmost *adj.* ootmaist
outrageous *adj.* maroonjus (A)
outside *adv.* ootby; thereoot
outspoken *adj.* tongue-betroosht
outstanding thing of its kind *n.* beezer; binder
outward(ly) *adj., adv.* ootwith, -wuth
over *adv.* ower; (past) by; by wi't; **over against** *prep.* fornent
overall *n.* vrapper; wrapper
overboiled *ppl.* (of potatoes) throwe the bree
overburden *v.* (yourself) forfecht (yersel)
overcast *adj.* owercassen
overcome *adj.* (by emotion) great-hertit; *v.* ding

overdo *v.* forfecht yersel
overflow *v.* jibble ower; ream
overheated *ppl.* stecht
overjoyed *ppl., adj.* liftit
overlay *v.* owerlay
overlook *v.* owerleuk
overnight *adv.* owernicht
over-particular *adj.* jinipperous
overrun (with) *adj.* hotchin (wi)
overseer *n.* (of farm) grieve; owersman
overtake *v.* owertak
overturn *v. tr.* (turn upside down) folm; *tr., intr.* cowp; whummle (J); **overturned** *ppl.* (sheep) cowpit
overwrought *adj.* wrocht-up
owe *v.* acht, aucht; awe; **owing** awin
owl *n.* oolet (A); hoolet; howlet (G1)
own *adj.* ain; nain; nown; **hold your own** hud yer nain; **one's own self** yer nainsel; *v. pr. (in third pers. sing.)* acht; yacht; *ppl.* echt; yacht
ox *n. sing.* nowt; owse; (fattened for market) feeder; (killed at Martinmas for winter use) mart; mairt; **oxen** nowt; owsen

— **P** —

pacify *v.* peshifee
pail *n.* (wooden, for milking or herring guts) cog(gie), cogue
pain *n.* jip; pyne; (animal suffering pain) pyner; (*excl.* of) feech;

seized with pain (in the hips) (hip-)grippit
paint *n., v.* pent, pint; **painting the town red** oot o yer box
palace *n.* pailace

pale *adj.* gowsty
paling *n.* palin
pampered *ppl., adj.* (of farm animals) fence-fed
pane *n.* peen
pant *v.* blyaav; pech; (with heat or exertion) fob
parapet *n.* (of a bridge) lanstell
parched *ppl.* gizzent
parent *n.* paarent
parish *n.* pairis
part *n.* pairt; trail; (small) tait; (very small) nimp; nippock(ie); *v.* pairt; sinder, sinner; (the hair, or sheep's wool) shed
particle *n.* hait; sinacle (B1)
particular *adj.* parteeclar; (very) pernickety
particularly *adv.* freely; **particularly fine** freely fine
partin *n.* pairtin
partner *n.* pairtner
partridge *n.* pairtrick (M, C); paitrick (S, M1)
party *n.* pairty; shine; (for women) henshine
pass *v.* (something to someone) rax; (through or over) owergae; **pass the time away** fite the idle pin
passage *n.* closs; pass; throw-gang; (in a house) trance
passing, in the *phr.* i the bygaein; i the bygaan
past *prep.* by
pat *v.* (fondle) clap
path *n.* roddie; waakie
patron *n.* paatron
patronage *n.* paatronage
patronise *v.* paatroneese
pattern *n.* pattren

pause *n., v.* devall
pavement *n.* planesteens
pay *n., v.* pey
payment *n.* peymen
peace *n.* quaitness
peak *n.* snoot
peaked *adj.* (of a cap) snootit
pearl *n.* pairl
peas *n. pl.* piz
pease meal *n.* piz-meal; pizzers
peat *n.* (individual) cloddie; (pile of) stack; **peat-cutting** mossin; **peat dust** drush
peck *n., v.* (of birds) dorb
peculiar *adj.* unco
peddle wares *v.* cadge
peep *v.* keek; teet; **peep-bo** keek-a-bo; teet-a-bo
peevish *adj.* girnie; nibawa; nyattery; orpiet (A2); **peevish person** wittrel, witterel
pelt *v.* clod; daad, daud
pen *n.* (for cattle) pumphel
penholder *n.* penner
people *n. pl.* fowk; folk
perched (on) *ppl.* cockit (on)
perhaps *adv.* ablins; aiblins; mebbe
periwinkle *n.* buckie; wulk
perplexed *adj.* hobbelt
persevere *v.* hing in
person *n.* bodie; leevin; wicht
persuade *v.* gow (ower); perswaad
pertain *v.* perteen
pert girl *adj., n.* clip; (person) smatchet
perverse *adj.* camsteerie; contermin't; ill-gatit, ill-gettit
pester *v.* (with entreaties) deeve, deave
pet *v.* daat; dawt; *n.* daatie; tae-ee

Peter *pr. n. dim.* Patie
Peterhead native *pr. n.* Blue-moggener
petrol *n.* peetrol
petticoat *n.* kwite; quyte; *n. pl.* cotts; (made of wincey) winceys
pew *n.* (square) pumphel
phlegm *n.* haach
physical *adj.* feesickle
physically *adv.* body-bulk
physician *n.* physeeshun
piano *n.* peanny
pick *v.* pyke
Pict *n.* Picht
picture *n.* picter, pictur
piece *n.* (large) daad, daud; fordel (B1); knyte; (very small) nimp; nippock(ie)
pierce *v.* prob (*incl.* piercing of cow's stomach to release gas)
pig *n.* (fisher word to overcome taboo) grunter; Sandy Campbell
pigeon *n.* doo
pigeon-toed *adj.* pirn-taed
pigsty *n.* swine's hoose
pilfer *v.* pilk
pill *n.* peel
pillow *n.* pilla
pimple *n.* plook
pimply *adj.* plooky
pin *n.* preen; (or knob) knag; *v.* preen
pinafore *n.* peenie; (loose) slip
pincers *n. pl.* turkis
pinched *adj.* wainished-like
pine *v.* dwine
pine torch *n.* fir
pin-headed *adj.* preen-heidit
pinnacle *n.* toopachin, toopican
pipe *n.* (short tobacco pipe) cutty; (chain of tin pipe-lid) rackle
pitch-dark *n.* pick-mirk
pitcher *n.* craggin; pig; (wooden) stoop(ie)
pith *n.* fushen, fushon
pitiful *adj.* peetifu
Pitsligo *pr. n.* (nickname) Kyack
pity *n.* peety; *v.* meen; peety
place *v.* plank
plague *n.* pleege
plaice *n.* plashie; plash fluke
plaid *n.* faik; fayich; fyaaak
plain *adj.* (blunt) aff-han; (simple) hamal(t)
plank *n.* (of wood) plunk
plantation *n.* plantin
plaster *n.* plaister
playground *n.* playgrun; playgreen
plaything *n.* plaik
plead *v.* prig
pleasant *adj.* couthie; leesome; lichtsome; pleesint; plizzant
pleased *adj.* pleased, pleast; plaised (S, C1); **pleased with** teen wi
pleasure *n.* pleesur(e)
plentiful *adj.* raffy
plenty (of) *n.* rowth, routh (o)
pliable *adj.* weffle
plight *n.* plicht; pilget (B1); plisky (B1)
plod *v.* stowff
plough *n.* pleuch (A, M1); ploo; (projecting wing on sock) ploo-feathers; (handles) ploo-stilts; *v.* ear (A2); pleugh; ploo; (shallow furrows) ebb-ploo; brak-fur; (fallow land) fauch
ploughed land *n.* red-lan
ploughing *n.* earin (A2); plooin
ploughing marker *n.* prop

ploughman *n.* plooman
ploughshare *n.* sock
plover *n.* plivver
plump *adj.* sonsy
plum pudding *n.* dumplin; (boiled in a cloth) clootie dumplin
plunder *n.* herry; *v.* reive; (bird's nest) harry; herry
plunge churn *n.* plump churn
pocket *n.* pooch; pock (J); (inside) oxter-pooch; *v.* pooch
poet *n.* makar
point *v.* pynt
point of, on the *prep. phr.* aweers o; on the weers o
poison *n.* pooshan, pooshin; pyshon
poisonous *adj.* pooshinous
poke *v.* dab; pirl; powk
pole *n.* stang
polecat *n.* foumart
police *n.* pleece; pollis (J)
policeman *n.* bobby
polish *n.* (black polish) blake
politician *n.* politeeshun
politics *n.* poleetics
pond *n.* (for watering cattle) coble; stank
pony *n.* shalt(ie); shelt(ie); shult; (suffering from stringhalt) cleekit shalt
pool *n.* peel
poor *adj.* peer, puir
pope *n.* pape
porridge *n.* porritch; pottich; parritch (J) (plural in Doric)
Portessie *pr. n.* the Sloch
portion *n.* pairt; trail; (small) tait
position *n.* poseetion; (posture) powster
possess *v.* acht, aucht

possession *n.* acht, aucht
postman *n.* postie
pot *n.* pat; **went to pot** gaed worth
potato *n.* tattie; pitaatie (B1); **potato-masher** tattie-chapper; (pit for storage) tattie-clamp; **potato digger** tattie-howker; (implement) deevil; **potato harvest** tattie-howkin, -liftin (J); **potato foliage** tattie-shaw
potter *v.* plowter; plyter; scutter
poultice *n.* pultice; steepit loaf
pound *n.* (sterling) poond; pown; pund; (in weight) pun; pund
pounded oats *n.* bruised corn
pour *v.* poor
poverty *n.* poortith
powder *n.* pooder
power *n.* pooer
practical joke *adj., n.* hyze; rig
practise *v.* practeese
praise *n.* (high) reeze; *v.* reeze
pram *n.* coach
pranks, mad *n.* madden-dreem
prate *v.* gab
prattle *n.* gab
prattler *n.* a gab
prayers *n. pl.* gweed-words
precise *adj.* perjink; preceese; *adv.* preceesely
predicament *n.* frap; hobble
prefer *v.* prefar
preference *n.* prefairrance
pregnant *adj.* muckle-bookit, -boukit; in the faimly wye (A2); **make pregnant** *v.* bairn; nick
prejudice *n.* prejudeece
present *adv.* aside; *n.* praisent; (bought at a fair) fairin(g)
presentable *adj.* gatefarrin

presently *adv.* belyve
preside *v.* (at a Presbyterian Church court) moderate
press *v.* birse, birze
press on *v.* kneip on
press-stud *n.* dome
pressure *n.* (*esp.* from a crowd) birse
pretence *n.* mak-on
pretend *v.* mak on
pretentious *adj.* upsettin
pretty *adj.* bonnie, bonny; protty; **a pretty penny** a protty penny
pretty well *adv.* geylies
prick *v.* brob; job; **pricked** *ppl.* brobbit
prickly *adj.* jobby
prim *adj.* mim; mim-like; mim-moo't, -mou't; perjink; primpit
prime *n.* potestatur; pottiestattur
prince *n.* prence
principle *n.* prenciple
print *n., v.* prent
privilege *n.* preevilege
probably *adv.* belike
proclaim *v.* scrie, scry
procrastinating *ppl., adj.* aff-pittin
prod *v.* prob
prodigious *adj.* prodeegious
profit *n.* (high) rug
progress *n.* fordal, fordle
project *n.* projeck
promoter *n.* deester
proof *n.* preef, pruif

properly *adv.* the richt gate
prophesy *v.* prophesee
protect *v.* proteck
protest *v.* oot-cry
proud *adj.* poochle; prood; pridefu (J)
prove *v.* pruv
provisions *n. pl.* proveesions
provoking *adj.* angersome
prudent *adj.* canny
prune *v.* sned
prying *adj.* lang-nebbit, -nibbit
puff *n.* (of wind) waff; **puffed up** *ppl., adj.* (of a person) ful, full
pull *v.* poo, pu; tit; (forcibly) rive, *ppl.* rivven
pullet *n.* yearock
pulpit *n.* poopit
punch *n.* plowt
punctual *adj.* punctwal
puny *adj.* nochtie
pupil *n.* scholar
puppy *n.* fulpie
purple *adj.* purpie
purr *n.* (of a cat) three-threids-an-a-thrum; *v.* spin his/her thrums
push *v.* shiv; shive; putt; (push to) birse tee
puss *n.* bau(l)drins; bawdrons
put *v.* pit, *pt.* pat; **put away** pit past; **put by, put aside** *ppl.* pat tee; **put out** *ppl.* pitten, putten oot; **put together** *v.* ranter
puzzle *v.* bleck

— **Q** —

quaff *v.* skowf. *cf.* **scoof**
quake *v.* shak; trimmle

quandary *n.* swither
quantity *n.* a curn; sowd; wheen;

(large) gweed curn; feck; hantle; (small) bittock; pick; starn(ie); tait; tooshtie (very small) skirlie; (small, of liquor) skite; tootie; (tiny) stime, styme

quarrel *n.* cast-oot; faa oot; scashle; sharrie; split; strush(ie); throw-the-muir; tulzie; *v.* scashle; strive, *pt.* streeve, *ppl.* striven; threep

quarrelsome *adj.* camsteerie; din-raisin

quarter *n.* (of oatcake round) corter, korter; (of a year) raith

quart measure *n.* (with knobbed lid) tappit hen

queer *adj.* unco

quench *v.* (thirst) slack; slock, sloke; slocken, sloken

querulous *adj.* girny; orpiet (A2)

question *n.* quisson; *v.* back-speir

quibbles *n. pl.* fittie-fies

quick *adj.* faist; slippy

quick-tempered *adj.* short-i-the-trot

quiet *adj.* quait; **be quiet** hud yer tongue; hud yer wheesht

quietness *n.* quaitness

quit *v.* quat

quite *adv.* (completely) fair; *excl.* fairly

quiver *v.* chiver; trimmle

quiz *v.* backspeir

quoth *v.* quo

—— R ——

rabbit *n.* rubbit; ribbit (S); (used on board ship to avoid taboo word) mappie; (Russian) Roosian

rack *n.* (for fodder) haik

radish *n.* (wild) runch

rafter *n.* couple, cupple

rag *n.* (thin cloth) flinrikin; (worthless) peltin-pyock; *chf. in pl.* duds; **rags and tatters** tatterwallops

rage *n., v.* rampage, rampauge

ragged *adj.* duddie; raggit; **ragged person** tatterwallop

raging *ppl., adj.* ragie

ragweed *n.* weepies (J)

ragwort *n.* tansy

rain *n.* reyn; (light, good for crops) growin shoorie; (a heavy fall) onding; spleeter o weet; (fine)

smirr; smoocherin; *v.* (slightly) spirk; spit

rainbow *n.* (broken) a teeth in the sky

rainy *adj.* drappie; weety

rake *n.* (small) smiler; *v.* raik

range *v.* (roam) reenge

ransack *v.* raffle; rype

rascal *n.* a bit o a lad; limmer; scypal, skypal

rash *adj.* ramsh

raspberry *n.* risp; sivven

rat *n.* rottan

rather *adv.* gey; geylies; raither; redder; some; **rather cold** some caal

ravenous *adj.* yamph

ravine *n.* cleuch; glack

ray *n.* (of sun) blink

reach *v.* (a place) win
ready *adj.* redd
real *adj.* rale
really *adj.* ralely
reap *v.* cut; shear
reaper *n.* raeper, raiper
reason *n.* rizzon
reasonable *adj.* rizzonable
rebound *v.* skite
recently *adv.* newlins
recipe *n.* recaipt
reck *v.* (care) raik
reckon *v.* rackon
recline *v.* (lit.) lig
recognisable *adj.* (easily) kenspeckle
reconsider *v.* fell-think
recover *v.* weer tee; (one's health or spirits) cantle; (from) cower
recuperate *v.* recreet
red *adj.* reed, reid
red-cheeked *adj.* reid-chikkit
red-combed *adj.* reid-kaimed
redcurrant *n.* rizzar
red-headed *adj.* reid-heidit
red-hot *adj.* reid-het
reed *n.* sprot
reel *n.* (on which yarn or thread is wound) pirn
refer *v.* refar
refusal *n.* na-say
refuse *n.* orrals; *v.* refeese; na-say
regard *n., v.* regaird
register *v.* (for proclamation of banns of marriage) beuk
regret about, express *v.* remorse
regular *adj.* reglar
rein *n.* rine, ryne
related *adj.* sib
relationship *n.* sibness

relax *v.* rist; hud doon the deece; lat the theats slack
reliable *adj.* siccar
relief *n.* easedom
religion *n.* releegion
religious *adj.* releegious
remain *v.* bide
remains *n. pl.* hinner-en
remainder *n.* the lave
remark *n.* (quick-witted) upcome
remarkable *adj.* unco
remedy *n.* remeid
remember *v.* mynd; myn
remind *v.* mynd; myn
removal *n.* (from a tenancy) ootgang
renegade *n.* ranegill
renewal *n.* (replacement) retour
rennet *n.* yirnin
rent *n.* rint
repent *v.* remorse
replacement *n.* retour
replete *adj.* (after food) ful; ful up; stappit; weel-sairt;
reprimand *n.* owergaan, -gaun
reproof *n.* (severe) owergaan, -gaun
reprove *v.* repree
require *v.* requar, requair
reserved *adj.* poochle; puchal
resin *n.* rosit
resinous *adj.* firry; rositie
respect *n., v.* respeck
respectable *adj.* douce; wice-like; (of appearance) gatefarrin
respectful *adj.* mensefu
responsible *in phr.* **to be responsible for it** tae be the deed o't
rest *n.* rist; flap; (the remainder)

lave; *v.* rist; hud doon the deece;
lat the theats slack
resting-place *n.* ludgement
restive *adj.* reistin
restless *adj.* (of a horse) tittersome
retailer *n.* merchan
retch *v.* cowk, kowk
retort *v.* rebat
reveal *v.* kythe
revel *n.* splore
reverse *n.* revarse; (of a horse etc.)
  into reverse intae the britchin
rhododendron *n.* rhoddie
ribbon-ends *n. pl.* fattrels
rib-grass *n.* carl-doddie
riches *n. pl.* graith
rick *n.* ruck; (large, or hay or corn)
  moo; (small, of corn or hay)
  hooick; scroo
rick-yard *n.* stack-yaird
ricochet *v.* skite
rid *adj.* redd; *v.* redd; **get rid of**
  wun redd o
riddance *n.* reddance; **good
  riddance** gweed reddance; **off
  you go and good riddance**
  mirra-hine; merry-hyne
ridge *n.* rig; riggin; (on which
  plough is turned) fleed; (side)
  side-rig
ridiculous *adj.* rideeclous
riff-raff *n.* raff; scruff; warriedrags,
  towrags an swypins o the pier (B)
rifle *v.* rype
right *adj., n., v.* richt
righteous *adj.* richteous
right thing, do the *v.* dee the richt
  gate
right turn *phr.* (command to
  plough-horse in Buchan) wish

rigid *adj.* strait
rigmarole *n.* la(m)gamachie;
  linglairy (B1)
ring *v.* (of a tolling bell) jow
rinse *v.* sweel
ripple *v. intr.* bicker; pirl
risky *adj.* oonchancie
rivet *v.* clink
road *n.* (narrow) roddie
roam *v.* raik, rake; reenge
roar *v.* (of cattle) rowst, roust; rowt
  (G1)
roast *v.* birsel, birstle; roast; *ppl.*
  roasin, roassin; **roasting hot**
  roassin
Robert *pr. n.* (familiar form)
  Rob(bie)
rod *n.* (for stirring porridge)
  spurkle; spurtle; theevil; (in
  chimney for hanging pots over
  the fire) swey; (fishing) waan
rode *v. pt.* rade
roe *n.* raan
rogue *n.* widdiefu; (term of
  endearment for a child) rogie
roguery *n.* joukerie pawkerie
roll *n.* (morning) buttery-rowie;
  buttery; rowie; (floury) bap; *v.*
  rowe; wammle
roof *n.* reef; riggin
room *n.* (best) the room
roost *n., v.* reest
root *n.* reet
rope *n.* raip, rape; tow; (round
  eaves of a stack) eave raip; (ball
  of straw-rope) edderin; *v.* (twist
  ropes round a stack) edder; (used
  to lash a load on to a cart) girdin;
  (for hanging nappies) hippen-
  towie; (double ropes for skipping)

lundies
rope-twister *n.* thrawcruik;
  tweezlock; twiner
rose *v. pt.* rase
rough *adj.* roch; reuch (J); grofe;
  (unmannerly) menseless; (~ in
  manners) roch an richt; **rough
  character** ranegill
rough-and-ready *adj.* hull-run
rough-cast *v.* (a wall with mortar)
  (sneck)-harl; **rough-casting** *n.*
  harlin
round *adj., adv., prep.* roon
round-shouldered *adj.* roon-
  shoodert
rouse *v.* (to anger) roose
route *n.* gate
row *n.* gyang; raa, raw
row *n.* (rumpus) reerie; sta(r)shie;
  stushie; **make a row** kick up a
  reerie
rowan tree *n.* rantree; rodden tree
rub *v.* faach, fauch (B1)

rubbish *n.* pelt; perlyaag
ruddy *ppl., adj.* kindlin (J)
ruin *n.* gowf(f); (cause of) herrial
rule *n., v.* rowle
ruler *n.* rowler
rumble *v.* rummle; (of the stomach)
  womle
rummage *v.* reemish
rumour *n.* raiverie; reverie
rumpus *n.* ran-dan; rammie; reerie
run *v.* rin; skelp; (off quickly)
  skice, skyce; skite; uptail; (in
  excited or aimless fashion) fudder
runny jam *adj., n.* elbuck jam
rush *n.* (plant) rash; sprot; *v.*
  (forward impetuously) breenge;
  (of the wind) sough
Russian *adj.* Rooshian
rustle *n., v.* reesle, reeshle; (of grain
  indicating ripeness) buzzle
rust *n., v.* roost, roust; *ppl. adj.*
  roostin
rusty *adj.* roosty

— S —

saa *v. pt.* saw, *neg.* saana, sawna
Sabbath *n.* Saabath, Sawbath
sabre *n.* saabre
sack *n.* saick, seck; **sackcloth and
  ashes** harn bags an shunners
sad *adj.* doolsome; dowie; wae;
  waesome
saddle *n.* saiddle, seddle
safe *adj.* saff; (~ to deal with)
  chancy
sag *v.* seg
sagging *adj.* seggit
sago pudding *n.* (nicknamed)

birdies eenies; puddock's eggs
saint *n.* sant
saintly *adj.* santly
salary *n.* sailary
sallow *adj.* hyaave
salmon *n.* reidfish (to avoid taboo
  word at sea)
salt *n.* saat, saut; **worth his salt**
  wirth saat till his kail; *v.* (fish)
  roose; **salty** *adj.* saatie, sautie
salt-box *n.* saat-backet, saut-backet
salt-brick *n.* (for cattle) saat-lick,
  saut-lick

salter *n.* saater, sauter
salve *n.* saa, saw
same *adj.* **all the same** aa ae claith
sample *n.* swatch
sanctify *v.* santifee
sand *n.* saan
sand-eel *n.* sile; sunnel
sane *adj.* aa come; aa there
sapless *adj.* foggy
saps *n. pl.* flannen broth
Satan *pr. n.* Saatan, Sawtan
sate *v.* sair
satiate *v.* sair; stech; *ppl.* sick sairt
satisfy *v.* saitisfee; (*esp.* with food or drink) sair
Saturday *n.* Saiterday, Setterday
saucy *adj.* sanshach
saunter *v.* pammer, paumer
savour *n.* saar
saw *v. pt.* saa
sawdust *n.* saadist
saxifrage *n.* fou
scabbed *adj.* scabbit; scabby
scabby *adj.* scabbit
scald *v.* scaad, scaud; plot; (slightly) scam, scaum
scamp, *n.* fang; widdiefu
scan, *v.* scance
scandal *n.* ill-win
scandal-monger *n.* sclave
scarcely *adv.* jimp
scare *n.* gliff (B1); *v.* fley
scarecrow *n.* bockie, bokie; scare-craa, scarecraw; tattie-boodie (A); tattie-bootie (C); tattie-doodle (S); tattie-dulie (J)
scarf *n.* graavit, grauvit
scavenge *v.* scran
scheme *n., v.* skaim, skem
school *n.* skweel, squeel; skale (S);

schule (J); (attendance officer) wheeper-in
schoolmaster *n.* dominie
school pupil *n.* scholar
scientific *adj.* scienteefic
scissors *n. pl.* sheers
scivvy *n.* sciffie (S)
scoff *v.* scowff
scold *v.* ban; banter; coonjer; flyte, *pt.* flate; get on tae; gie intae trouble; (severely) bully-rag; rally on; scaal, scaul; seeg (G); tongue. *cf.* **flyte**
scolding *n.* bark-an-bowff; scaal, scaul; sedarin; sortin; (severe) dixie; kail-throwe-the-reek; owergaan, -gaun; (mild) ragie;
scoop *n.* (metal ~ for use with herring) sheil
scope *v.* scooth; scowth; scouth
scorch *v.* birstle; plot; scam, scaum; scorching, *ppl.* birstlin
scoundrel *n.* scoon(e)ral; (*joc.*) bleck
scour *v.* scoor
scowl *n., v.* glower; scool
scraggy person *adj., n.* sharger
scrape *v.* screeve
scratch *n.* scart; scrat; (large) screeve; *v.* claa; faach, fauch (B1); scart; scrat; screeve
scratching-post *n.* claain-post
scream *v.* skirl; skwaal
screech *v.* scraach, scrauch; skraich
scrimmage *n.* bicker; shangie
scrounge *v.* cadge; mooch; (of people and dogs) skweenge
scrounger *n.* moocher
scrubbing-board *n.* scoorin-buird
scurry *v.* skyce, skice

scythe *n.* robsorbie (from make of scythe); **scythe handle** sned

sea anemone *n.* pap

seagull *n.* (Buckie) gow; (M1) maa, maw; (Fraserburgh) myaave; (Gardenstown) pule, pyool; (Peterhead) scurry; (M1) scurry-waster; (A1, R) sea-goo; (M1) seamaa

search *v.* rake

season *n., v.* sizzon; *v.* (food) hire

seasoning *n.* kitchie

seat *n.* sate, **take a seat** sit doon; lean yersel doon; loot ye doon

seaweed *n.* (heavy with thick stalks, broad fronds) carlers; (coloured) dallies clysies; (dulse) dilse; (a species) tangles

second day's broth *phr.* yavil-broth

second thoughts, to have *v., n.* fell-think

second-year crop *n.* yavil

secret *n.* saicret; **divulging a ~** *phr.* lattin oot the pooder

secretly *adv.* stown-wyes

secure *adj.* siccar

sedge *n.* seg(g)s

see through a dodge *phr.* twig

seed *n.* sid

seek *v.* sik, seek

seemly *adj.* wice-like

seep *v.* sype

see to *v.* sort

see-saw *n.* coup-the-ladle

seething *adj.* hotchin

segment *n.* lith

seize *v.* cleek; mitten; nab

seizure *n.* jamaica, *in phr.* jist aboot hid a jamaica

select *v.* seleck, wale; wyle

selection *n.* wale; wylin

self *n.* sel

self-important *adj.* puchal, puchil (A2)

selfishness *n.* selfitness

self-righteous *adj.* unco-gweed

send *v.* sen

senna *n.* sinna

senseless *adj.* glaikit

sensitive *adj.* (of an issue) kittle, kittlesome; (of a person) thin-skinnt

sent *ppl.* putten

separate *v.* sinder; sinner; (used in curling) split

sergeant *n.* sairgint

serious *adj.* sairious

serve *v.* sair; ser; (~ a cow) bul(l)

serving *n.* sairin

set *in phr.* all set, riggit oot; set off, get roadit

setback *n.* backset; snipe, snype

settle *n.* deece, deese; *v.* sattle

settlement *n.* (usually at marriage) doon-sittin

seven *adj.* saiven; seiven; seyven; siven

seventeen *adj.* saiventeen; seiventeen; seyventeen

seventy *adj.* saiventy; seiventy; seyventy

several *adj.* (a) twa-three; a wheen

sew *v.* shoo, shew

sewing *n.* shooin, shewin

sewing-machine *n.* shewin-machine

shabby *adj.* orra; scabbit; (mean) wheetie

shadow *n.* shadda

shaft *n.* (of barrow, cart) tram
shake *n., v.* shak; shog; shoggle; shoogle; (roughly) cadge; (wave) wag; **no great shakes** nae great dell
shaker *n.* (in a mill) shakker
shaky *adj.* shakky; shoggly; shoogly; (from weakness) waffle
shall *v.* sall; **shall not** sanna
shamble *v.* baachle, bauchle
shanks' pony *n.* shanks' meer; waaker's bus
shape *v.* fack (B1)
shaped *ppl.* shapit
shard *n.* (of earthenware) lame
share out *n.* pairtin; pairt-oot (S); *v.* pairt; **badly shared out** ill-pairtit
shark *n.* (basking) muldoan, muldoon
sharp *adj.* (of mind) gleg; glegsome; (of tongue) ill-hung; (of the wind) snell
sharpen *v.* sharp
shatter *v.* chatter
shaved *v. pt., ppl.* shaven
sheaf *n.* shafe, shaif; shave; (last sheaf on top of a stack) heid(in)-shafe
shed *n.* lean-tee
sheep *n.* (female) yowe; (young, before first shearing) hog(g); (having died a natural death) braxy; (disease) braxy; (fluke worm on lung) the hooze; (hurdle for penning) flake
sheep-fold *n.* bucht; fank, faul(d)
shelf *n.* skelf; skelve (B1)
shell *n.* shall; *v.* sheel; **shell sand** shall san
shelly *adj.* shally

shelter *n.* biel; bield; leethe; lythe; scoog, scoug
sheltered *adj.* bieldy; lown; lythe
sheriff *n.* shirra
sherry *n.* shirry
shiftiness *n.* hunker-slidin
shiftless *adj.* fen(d)less
shilling *n.* shullin
shine *n., v.* shine; (gaudily) skyre
shingle *n.* chingle
shirt *n.* sark; sarkit
shiver *v.* chitter
shock *n.* an astonishment (A1); begeck; gliff; gluff; stammy-gaster; *v.* stammygaster
shock *n.* stook; **put into shocks** *v.* stook
shoe *n.* shee; *pl.* sheen, shune; shoon; **old shoe** baachle, bauchle
shoe-lace *n.* baachle-, bauchle-ban; lacer; pynt, pint
shoemaker *n.* sooter, souter; **shoe-maker's awl** ellieson; eshin; **shoemaker's last** sooter's deevil
shoot *v.* sheet
shop *n.* chop; shop; (small) shoppie
shop-assistant *n.* coonter-lowper
shop-keeper *n.* merchan
shopping *n.* messages; **do the shopping** go the messages
short *adj.* (and stocky) laichy-braid
shortcomings *n. pl.* shortcomes
short-tempered *adj.* capernicious
should *v.* sid; shud; sud; **shouldn't** sudna
shoulder *n., v.* shooder, shouder; shoother, shouther; (one higher than the other) shoother-the-win; (of an animal) spaal, spaul; **shoulder joint** shooderheid

shout (for) *v.* cry (on);
(incoherently) gollar
shove *v.* putt; shiv; shive
shovel *n., v.* sheel
show *n.* (fine) braivity, brevity; *v.*
kythe (B1); shaw
shower *n.* shooer; (sharp) blatter;
(heavy) spleeter o weet; (heavy,
putting a stop to work) lowsin-
shooer; (passing) scuff o rain;
(slight) shoorie
show off *n.* palaiver; *v.* cock
showy *adj.* skiry, skyrie
shrewd *adj.* lang-heidit; fell (J);
pawky
shrewdness *n.* smeddum
shriek *v.* scraich; skry; walloch
shrink *v. intr.* crine; (with age)
creep doon; *v. tr.* nirl, *ppl.* nirlt;
skurken
shrivel *v. intr.* crine; gizzen, *ppl.*
gizzent; *v. tr.* nirl, *ppl.* nirlt;
skurken; wizzen(t)
shroud *n.* shrood
Shrove Tuesday *pr. n.* Faster's
Eve(n), (Een); Fasten's Eve
shudder *v.* grue, groo
shuffle *v.* fuffle; scooshle; scushle;
sclaap; sclaup; shaachle; shauchle
shut *v.* (the mouth) dit; (the door,
your eyes) steek; **shut the door**
caa the door tee
shy *adj.* baach, bauch
sick *adj.* sick; seek (S); (of)
scunnert wi/o
sickly *adj.* gowsty; paewae; peelie-
wally
sickly-looking *adj.* fauchie
side-by-side *adv.* cheekie-for-
chowie

side ridge *n.* siderig
sideways *adv.* sidelins; sidiewyes
sieve *n.* riddel; sey; (with solid
base) blin sieve; wecht
sigh *n., v.* sich; sooch, soogh,
souch, sough
sight *n.* sicht; **a welcome sight** a
sicht for sair een
signature *n.* signaatur
silence *n.* seelence; **silenced** *ppl.*
dusht
silent *adj.* seelent
silver *n.* siller. *cf.* **money**
simmer *v.* hotter
simple *adj.* haimal(t); (of a person)
saft
simpleton *n.* nosy-wax (B1)
since *adv.* seen; sin; syne; *prep.*
seen; sin; *conj.* sin; **since then**
sinseen; sinsyne
sincere *adj.* aefaal(d), aefaul(d)
sing *v.* (of birds) chirm; (in low
tone without words) diddle
sing-song speech *adj., n.* sing-sang
singe *v.* scam, scaum; *sing., ppl.*
sung
sink *n.* jaa-hole, jaw-hole; *v.* (in
bog or mud) lair
sip *n.* sup(pie); bleb; *v.* (a small
amount) blibber; (noisily)
slubber; (take food or liquid *esp.*
with a spoon) sup
sister *n.* (*chf.* child's word) titty
sit *v.* (down) lean doon; (down with
a bump) dyst; **sit down!** *imp.* faal
yer fit; lean yersel doon; reest
site *n.* stance; seet
sitting *n.* (of eggs) laachter,
lauchter
situated *ppl.* sitiwat

situation *n.* (lot) billet; powster; seetivation

six *adj.* sax

sixteen *adj.* Saxteen

sixty *adj.* sixty

sixpence *n.* saxpence

skid *n.* skite

skilful *adj.* kittle; nacky; skeely

skill *n.* skeel

skim *v.* skum

skimmer *n.* (for surface soil and weeds) skreefer

skin *n.* bark; peelin; *v.* bark; flae; **skinned** barkit; **by the skin of his teeth** by the briers o his een

skulk *v.* scook, scouk

skull *n.* riggin

sky *n.* lift; welkin (M1)

skylark *n.* lav(e)rock; livrock

slab *n.* skelp

slake *v.* (thirst) slack; slock; slocken

slander *n.* ill-win; *v.* misca

slant *v.* sklent, sklint

slap *n.* sclaffert; (on the hand with a leather belt) the scud

slate *n.* sklate; sclait

slate pencil *n.* skaalie; skaillie; skeily

slater *n.* sklater

slattern *n.* trail

slaughter *n.* slaachter, slauchter

slaughter-house *n.* slaachter-, slauchter-hoose

slaver *n., v.* sliv(v)er

sledge *n.* sled; (heavy, used on farms) puddick, puddock

sleek *adj.* sleekit

sleight *n.* sleicht

slept *v. pt.* sleepit; **overslept** sleepit in

slice *n.* (of bread) sheave; (thin) skelf; *v.* hash

slid *v. pt.* sleed (S)

slide *n.* (children's) rone; (on ice) skip; *v.* (suddenly) skite

slight *adj., n.* slicht

slime *n.* (from fish, ill-smelling) goor

slip *n.* skite; *v.* skite; (awkwardly) sklyte, sklyter

slipper *n.* saftie

slippery *adj.* skitie; sliddery

slop *n.* slabber

slope *n.* brae; **situated on a slope** braeset; *v.* sklent, sklint

sloven *n.* trail

slovenly *adj.* strushel; struchlach (B1)

slow *adj.* slaa, slaw; latch; **slowly** *imp.* heely! **slow person** creepin-eevie. *cf.* **convolvulus**

slow-coach *n.* warridrag

sluggish *adj.* smeerless

slush *n.* snaa-, snaw-bree; slabber

slut *n.* limmer

sly *adj.* (*chf.* re humour) pawky; slee; sleekit; sneck-drawin (A2)

slyly *adv.* sleely

smack *n.* lick; skelp

small *adj.* sma; wee; *n.* (person) picht

small-holding *n.* huddin

smart *adj.* smert; (grand) fantoosh

smear *v.* clart; clort; sclarry (J); skaik; *ppl.* skaikit; (with tongue, *liter.*) sklaik

smell *n.* guff; (sharp, disagreeable) kneggum; (of fumes) yowder; *v.* smell about (like a dog) snowk

smiling *adj.* mirky
smithereens *n. pl.* crockaneeshun
smock *n.* (for working) vrapper
smoke *n., v.* rik, reek; **belch of smoke** reek-book, -bouk; (of a pipe) feuch; lunt
smoky *adj.* reekie; smeeky (G1)
smooth *adj.* smeeth; (and glossy) sleekit
smother *v.* smore
smoulder *v.* smuchter
smudge *n.* smad; smird
smut *n.* smad; smird
snack *n.* (portable) piece
snap *v.* (with the teeth) gnap; **snappy** *adj.* nibawa; snappus (A2)
snare *n.* girn
snarl *v.* girn
sneak *v.* sneck
sneaky *adj.* sleekit; thiefie
sneer *n., v.* jamph
sniff *n.* snifter; *v.* snifter; (noisily) snocher
snigger *v.* snicher
snivel *v.* sneevil
snod *adj.* tidy
snood *n.* (of horsehair, made by fishermen) tippen
snore *v.* snocher
snotty-nosed *adj.* bibbly-nibbit
snout *n.* snoot
snow *n.* snaa, snaw; snaave; snyaave (slight squally shower) fluffert; (heavy fall) onding; (driving) blin-drift, yowden drift; (melted) snaa-, snaw-bree; *v.* (in big flakes) flag
snow-flake *n.* (large) flag
snow-white *adj.* snaa-fite

snowy *adj.* snaavie (S)
snuff *n.* sneeshin
snuffle *v.* snotter; (like a dog) snowk
so *adv.* as; sae; that; **so much** as much; **it was so cold that** it wis as caal
soaked *ppl.* sypit
sob *v.* sab; (deeply) swult
sock *n.* ploughshare; (short) fit-sock; (with legs cut off) fittock
soft *adj.* saft; (spongy, *e.g.* of rotten vegetables) fossy; fosy, fozie
soft drink *n.* ale; dazzle
softness *n.* saftness
soil *n.* yird; (shallow) ebb land; (thin, poor) scaap, scaup; *v.* fyle
soirée *n.* siree
sold *v. pt., ppl.* selt; saal, saul
solder *n., v.* sooder, souder
soldier *n.* sodger
some *adj.* a puckle
somebody *See* **someone**
someone *pron.* some-een, some-ane
sometimes *adv.* fyles
somewhat *adj.* gey
son *n.* sin; **son-in-law** *n.* gweed-sin
song *n.* sang; (farmworker's) bothy ballad; cornkister; (silly) strood; strowd; stroud
soon *adv.* seen
sooner *adv.* seener; sheener, shuner (S)
soot *n.* sitt; (on pots) brook
sooty *adj.* (of pots) brookie
sore *adj., n.* sair
sorely *adv.* sair
sorrel *n.* soorocks
sorrow *n.* dool; sorra
sorrowful *adj.* dool; dowie;

sorrafu; wae; waesome
sorry *adj.* vexed; (extremely) ill-peyt; (for) wae for
sought *ppl.* socht. *cf.* **seek**
soul *n.* saal, saul; sowl
sound *n.* soon(d); myowte; *v.* soon(d); soun(d)
soup *n.* (made with offal) womble-brees
sour *adj.* soor; (of disposition) sturken; **sourness** *n.* soorness
south *adj., n.* sooth; **southern** *adj.* southron; suddron; sooth-kwintra
southernwood *n.* sudderinwid
sow *n.* soo
sow *v.* saw (S), *pt.* sew; shaw, *pt.* shew; shaave, shauv, *pt.* shew, *ppl.* shaaven, shauven
sower *n.* sawer
sowing machine *n.* broadcast
spacious *adj.* spaacious, spawcious
spade *n.* spaad, spad, spaud; (two-handed for cutting turfs, peats) flaaghter-spaad, flaughter-spaad
span *n., v.* spang
spanking *n.* buttock-mail
spare *adj.* (of figure) sober
spare room *n., adj.* spence
spark *n.* spirk; (from wood fire) flaesick
sparrow *n.* (house) spurdie; spurgie (O); sparry (J)
spate *n.* speet; speeth
spatter *v.* spairge
spawn *v.* spen
speak *v.* spik; (angrily/fretfully) nyatter, rally on; (ill of) misca; (again) rebat
special(ly) *adj., adv.* speeshal(ly)
speckle *v.* spraikle, *ppl.* spraiklt;

speckled (of cattle and sheep) brookit
spectacle *n.* (a sight) moniment
spectacles *n. pl.* glesses
speech *n.* (of an area) spik
speed *n.* nip; **at high speed** at a gweed lick; at the iverleevin gallop; at howdie haste
spelling-book *n.* spell-beuk, -buik
spend *v.* spen; waar, waur; wair, ware; (of time) hud
spider *n.* ettercap; nettercap; wyver; **spider's web** moosewob
spike *n.* (of a railing etc.) pyke, *ppl.* pykit
spill *v. tr.* jilp; *tr., intr.* skail, skale, skel; splyte; spull
spillings *n. pl.* spleeters; spullins; skaillies
spill over *v.* jibble ower
spindle *n.* spinnle; **spindly legs** spinnle shanks
spinning-bee *n.* rockin
spinning-wheel *n.* wheel
spirit *n.* gurr; speerit
spiritless *adj.* saarless, saurless
spiritual *adj.* speeritool
spite of, in *prep. phr.* mager, mauger
spit out *v.* splew
splash *n.* jilp; skirp; *v.* skite; skirp; spark; sperk, spirk; spurk (J); splyter
splash about *v. intr.* jilp; (in mud or water) plowter
splashings *n. pl.* spleeters
splatter *v.* daad, daud
splay-footed *adj.* skew-fittit; skyow-fittit
spleen *n.* melt; milt

splendid *adj.* (first rate) bencape; (excl.) capital; **splendidly** *adv.* brawly

splendour *n.* braivity

splinter *n.* skelb; skelf

splints, put in *phr.* scob

splutter *v.* splooter, splouter

spoil *v.* blad, blaud; connach; spile, spyle; *ppl.* bladdit, blaudit; (completely) connacht; geen tae potterlow

spoke *v. pt.* spak

sponge *v.* cadge; sorn

sponge-cake *n.* (in paper cup) sair-heidie

sponger *n.* cadger

spoon *n., v.* speen

spot *n.* (splash) spirk

spout *n.* spoot; (of teapot etc.) stroop(ie); *v.* (talk volubly) lay-aff

sprawl *v.* sprachle, sprauchle

spring *n.* spang; (elastic force) sprent; *v.* spang

sprout *n.* (Brussels) sproot; *v.* sproot; (of grain) breer

sprouting *n.* (of new grain) braird; breer

spruce *adj.* jinipperous

spue *v.* splew

sputter *v.* hotter

squall *v.* (scream) skwaal

square *adj., n., v.* squaar, squarr

squat *v.* (on the haunches) hunker

squeal *v.* skwyle, squile; squallach

squeamish *adj.* cackie-stammackit; **be squeamish** *v.* womle

squeeze *v.* birse, birze

squelch *v.* plowter; plyter

squint *adj.* gley; *n.* cockle-ee, gley; **eye with a squint** gleyed ee

squire *n.* laird

squirt *v.* skite

stack *n.* ruck; (steaming) het ruck; (thatched for winter) thackit ruck; (badly built and porous) wattert ruck; (foundation) ruck-foon; (support for off-centre stack) ruck-post; (stack ladder) ruck-ledder; (rectangle of hay/straw) soo

stack-yard *n.* corn-yard

staff *n.* (heavy) rung

staff-in-hand *adj.* staffy-nevel

stagger *v.* stacher, staucher; staamer, staumer, styte, stoit; styter, stoiter; stot; stotter

stake-fence *n.* palin

stale *adj.* wachy

stalk *n.* (of kail or cabbage) castock; runt; *v.* stilp

stall *n.* sta(a)

stallion *n.* staig

stalwart *adj.* beerdly, buirdly

stammer *v.* habber, hubber; mant

stamp around *v.* (noisily) haamer; pammer

stampede *v. intr.* (of cattle to avoid insect bites) prick

stand *v.* stan

star *n.* starn(ie)

starch *n.* stairch; stiffen; *v.* stairch

stare *v.* gowp, goup; gype

starling *n.* stirlin

start *n.* aff-go; *n., v.* stairt, stert **starting-time** *n.* (at work) yokin-time

starvation *n.* stairvation

starve *v.* stairve, sterve; knap (B1)

state *n.* (of excitement) feerich; **in a state** in a feerich

stately *adj.* (would be) pensy
statue *n.* staito (A2)
staunch *adj.* stanch; stainch, stench; stinch
stay *n.* stey; *v.* bide, *ppl.* bidden; stey; (at an address) stop
steading *n.* steadin; toon
steal *v.* nab; rype; stale, stail; stow; *ppl.* stowen
stealth, by *adv.* stown-wyes
steam *n.* stame; **steam-driven threshing-maching** stame-mull; stem-mull
steep *adj.* stey
steeple *n.* toopachin; toopican
steer *n. sing., pl.* nowt
steering-rod *n.* stang
step *n.* stap
stick *v.* stick, *pt.* stack, *ppl.* stucken
stick in *v.* persevere
stickleback *n.* (or minnow) bandy
stiff *adj.* satteral
still *adj.* (of weather) lown; *adv.* aye
stilt *n.* stilpert
sting *n.* stang; job; *v.* job; **stinging nettles** jobby nettles
stingy *adj.* grippy
stint *n.* stent
stipend *n.* steepin
stir *n.* steer; stur; *v.* gee; jee; kirn; pirl; steer; stur
stitch *n.* steek; *v.* (coarsely) ranter; steek
stock, take *phr.* tak taik
stocking *n.* hose; (sometimes used as a purse) moggan; (being knitted) shank; **footless stocking** moggan; **shoes and stockings** hose an sheen

stomach *n.* kite, kyte; stamach, stam(m)ack; *v.* stammack; wame; wime, wyme; (of a calf) yirnin
stomach-ache *n.* belly-thraw
stomp *v.* stodge
stone *n., v.* steen, stane; **stone's throw** steen-cast
stone-chat *n.* steen-chackert
stonecrop *n.* fou
Stonehaven *pr. n.* (to outsiders) Steenhive; (locally) Stonie
stony *adj.* steeny, stany
stood *v. pt.* steed
stool *n.* steel, steil; creepie; (square-shaped) buffet steel; (with short legs) cutty steel
stop *v.* stap
store *n., v.* fordal, fordle
stormy *adj.* (of weather) cankert; gurlie, gurly
story *n.* (tall tale) binder; (old and stale) caal kail het; (long, about nothing) lab(b)ach (R); (drawn out) la(m)gamachie; linglairy (B1)
stout *adj.* brosie; stoot, stout
straight *adj., adv.* eyven; stracht, straucht
straight, off the *phr.* agley; agee
straightaway *adv.* strachtwye, strauchtwye
straighten *v.* strachen; straichen; stracht, straucht; **straighten your tie** set yer tie eyven
straightforward *adj.* (honest) fair-furth-the-gate; stracht-oot-the-gate
strain *v.* (milk through a sieve) sey; **strainer** *n.* (of milk) seyer
strange *adj.* keerious; unca, unco

stranger *n.* ootlin; unco man; *n. pl.* the fremt; unco fowk

strangle *v.* worry

strap *n.* (leather – for punishment in school) tawse

straps *n. pl.* (buckled leather, worn below the knee by farm-workers) nicky-tams; waal-tams

straw *n.* strae; (loose, e.g. on field after harvest) strab; (bundle of) win(d)lin; **the last straw** the croonin shafe; *v.* (one's boots) strae (T), stra (R) yer beets

strawberry *n.* straaberry

straw-rope *n.* (ball of) clew, cloo

stray *v.* rake

streak *n.* spraing

stream *n.* burn; (small) strype

street *n.* causey; (narrow) wynd

street-sweeper *n.* scaffy

strength *n.* strenth, strinth

stretch *v.* rax; streek; streetch

strict *adj.* streck, strick

stride *v.* spang; sten(d) (A2)

strife *n.* sturt (C)

strike *v.* cloor, clour; clowt, clout; strick, strik; (sharply) wap

string *n.* twine; tow

strip off *v.* tirr

stripling *n.* callant

strive *v.* strive; *pt.* streeve

strode *v. pt.* strade

stroke *n.* straik, strake; (blow) daad, daud; (on the palm) paamie; sclaff; sclaffert; (sharp) wap (of good luck) raise-o-the-win; *v. pt.* strack

stroll *n.* taik; *v.* danner, dauner; dander, daunder

strong *adj.* baul (B1); beerdly,
buirdly; fere; kibble; stoot strang; (of wind) reevin; **strongly** *adv.* starkly

stronghold *n.* haald, hauld

strove *v. pt.* streeve, struve

struck *v. pt.* strack; *ppl.* strucken

struggle *n.* pilget; tyaave, tyauve; (hard) sair fecht; sair tyaave; ae pot an row; *v.* tyaave, tyauve; strive, *pt.* streeve; waachle, wauchle; warsle, warstle

stub *v.* (the toe etc.) stob

stubble *n.* stibble

stubborn *adj.* thraan, thrawn

stubbornness *n.* gee

stucco *n.* stookie

stuck *v. pt.* stack; *ppl.* stucken

stud *n.* tacket; **studded boots** tackitie beets

student *n.* colleeginer (A1); (first year) bajan

stuff *v.* stap

stumble *n., v.* hyter; styter, stoiter; (of a horse) snapper

stump *v.* stowff

stun *v.* daver

stunted *adj.* crynt; (in growth) settril; shargart; **stunted person** sharger

stupid *adj.* bleat; dylt, doilt; dytit, doitit; donnert; feel; gaakit, gawkit; gapus; glaikit; **stupid fellow** stirk. *See* **fool**

stupidity *n.* feelness; gaakitness, gawkitness; gypery

stupify *v.* daver; dozen

sturdy *adj.* buirdly; fere; kibble

stutter *v.* habber, hubber; mant

subject *n., v.* subjeck

substance *n.* graith

such *adj.* sic; siccan; **such and
  such** sic an sic; **such-like** *adj.*
  siclike
suck *v.* sook
sucker *n.* (of tree) sooker
suckling calf *n.* sookin caafie
sudden *adj.* suddent (C)
suddenly *adv.* in (on) a suddenty
suddenness *n.* suddenty
suffocate *v.* scomfish; skumfish
sugar *n.* succar
suit *n., v.* shoot; sheet, shuit
sulk *v.* mump; funk (B1); **sulky**
  adj. sturken; **look sulky** *v.*
  glumph
sullen *adj.* drumly; **sullenness** *n.*
  gee; soorness
sum *n.* soom; (large) sowd; (small)
  triffle; trifflie
summer *n.* simmer
summit *n.* toopachin; toopican
sumptuous *adj.* lordlifu
sun *n.* sin; **sunburned** *adj.* sin-
  brunt; din-skinnt
sunder *v.* sinder; sinner
sundown *n.* sindoon
sundry *adj.* sinry
sunk down *adj.* seggit
sunset *n.* sindoon
sunshine *n.* sunsheen
superannuated *ppl.* sooperanniwat
superior *adj.* skichent
superstition *n.* suppersteeshun; a
  fret
superstitious beliefs *adj., n. pl.*
  feart things
supervisor *n.* owersman
supper *n.* sipper
supple *adj.* soople, souple; swack,
  swak; **make supple** swacken

support *n.* stey
sure *adj.* seer; shair (S)
surely *adv.* seerly; shairly (S);
  fairly
surface *n.* (of water) screeth
surfeit *n.* forleithy (B1)
surliness *n.* soorness
surly *adj.* strunge
surmise *n.* sleumin
surpass *v.* cow(e)
surprise *n.* astonisher; (excl. of)
  goshie; govie-dick(s); jings;
  loshins; loshtie (be here); loshtie-
  goshtie guide's; meggins alive;
  megstie me; michty me; serve's
survive *v.* (as a race) store the kin
  (*chf.* used in *neg.*)
suspect *v.* jaloose, jalouse; suspeck
suspense *n.* tig-tire; **in suspense** in
  captire
suspicious *adj.* (giving rise to
  suspicion) ill-thochtit
swagger *v.* cock
swallow *n., v.* swally; (quick(ly))
  scoof, scouf
swarm *n.* hobble; smarrach;
  swarrach
swathe *n.* (cut by scythesman) bout
sway *v.* swey; swye; swig (J);
  (influence) swye
swear *n.* sweer, sweir; *v.* sweer;
  ban; (vehemently) sweer blue
  lowes (B)
sweat *n., v.* swat, *pt.* swat, swattit;
  swate (A2); swite, swyte; (state of
  sudden heat) feem
swede *n.* swad; Swaddish neep
sweep *v.* swipe, swype
sweet *n.* (round) sweetie-boolie; *pl.*
  galshachs, galshochs; smachrie

173

sweetheart *n.* lad; jo (J)
sweet-seller *n.* (female) sweetie-wife
swell *v. tr., intr.* swall; hive, *ppl.* hoven
swept clean *ppl., adj.* besom-ticht
swerve *v.* jink; jouk
swift(ly) *adj., adv.* swith
swig *n., v.* scoof, scouf; waach, wauch
swill *v.* sweel
swim *v.* sweem; soom (C)
swimmer *n.* sweemer
swindle *v.* swick
swindler *n.* swick

swing *n., v. tr., intr.* showd; sweeng; swey
swing-boats *n. pl.* (at the carnival) showdin-boats
swingle-tree *n.* swingle-, sweengle-tree
swirl *v.* sweel
swish *v.* sweesh
swivel *v.* sweevle
swollen-headed *adj.* swall-heidit; swale-heidit (S)
swoon *n., v.* swarf
sword *n.* soord; swoord; soward
Synod *n.* seenit
syrup *n.* seerup

— **T** —

table *n.* brod; buird
tackle *n.* taikle
tag *n.* (game) tackie, takie; tik an tak
tail-board *n.* (of cart) back-door
tail end *n.* tail-eyn
tailor *n.* tyler; tylie; (itinerant) whip-the-cat
take *v.* tak, *pt.* teuk, *ppl.* teen; taen (S); **take care of** tak aboot; **take it easy** lat the theats slack
talk *n.* blether; jaa, jaw; (idle, silly) clashmaclavers, clish-ma-claver; gypery; (intimate) collogue; (low, muttered) toot-moot; (foolish) yaam; yaum (R); *v.* jaa, jaw; blether; (nonsense) blether; haver; (idly and at length) lyaag; laig; (volubly) lay-aff; (excitedly) (yab-) yabber; *adj.* (given to unwholesome talk) kyaard-

tonguet; **talking about** on aboot
talkative *adj.* crackie
talking-to *n.* dixie; hanlin; sedarin
tall *adj.* (and agile) strappin; **tall person** traleel; (lanky, ill-shaped person) trypal
tangle *n.* snorl; (of objects) wumple
tangled *ppl., adj.* raivelt
tantalise *v.* tantaleese
tap *v.* tig
tapioca *n.* (nicknamed) puddock's eggs
tardy *adj.* latch
tare *n.* teer
tart *adj.* satteral
tassle *n.* tossil; toshil
tasteless *adj.* saarless, saurless; wersh
taught *ppl.* taacht, taucht
tavern *n.* cheenge-hoose; chynge-

hoose

tea *n.* tay; (sly cup) fly-cup; fly; (made in the cup) tinkie's maskin

teach *v.* lairn; leern

teacher *n.* missie (S)

team-picker *n.* (in games) chyser

teapot *n.* taypot; (earthenware) trackie

tear *n., v.* rive; (rip) teer

tear-stained *adj.* begrutten; grutten

tease *n.* tarraneese; *v.* tarraneese; *tr.* banter

tease out *v.* tase oot (S)

teaspoon *n.* tayspeen; **teaspoonful** tayspenfae

teat *v.* tit; pap; **blind teat** blin tit

tedium *n.* langer

teetotum *n.* tottum, totum

tell-tale *n.* clipe, clype

temper *n.* birse; dander; teen; **bad temper** ill teen; **get angry** get yer dander up

temples *n. pl.* (of the head) haffets

tent *n.* tint

term *n.* (at school) raith

tern *n.* (Arctic) tarick

terrified *ppl.* terrifeet

terrify *v.* terrifee

testament *n.* tasment; tastement; tesment

tether-peg *n.* baikie

than *conj., quasi-prep.* nor

thank *v.* thank; thenk (S)

that *adj., pron.* aat; thon; yon; *conj.* at

thatch *v.* thack; theek (J); (by means of stob or stake) stob; (rope-thatch with a cloo) swap; **thatched** thackit; stobbit

thaw *v.* thow

thawing *ppl.* (of weather) fresh

the *def. art.* e; the

themselves *pron.* (*also* **by themselves**) theirsels

then *adv.* syne; than

thereupon *adv.* syne

these *adj., pron.* aat; thase; thon; yon; thae (S, J, C)

thick *adj.* (of water) drumly; **thick with** thrang wi

thief *n.* reiver

thigh *n.* (lower part of human thigh) hoch, hough

thimble *n.* thummle

thin *adj.* (of a person) skinny; wainisht-like; **thin legs** spurtle-shanks; **thin person** skinnymalink

thing *n.* (the very) the verra dunt

thingummybob *n.* thingumboob; thingumenderry

thirst *n.* thrist; **thirsty** *adj.* droothy, drouthy; thristy

thistle *n.* thrissle, thristle

Thomas *pr. n.* Tam

thorn *n.* stob

those *adj.* (*or* **these**) aat; thon; yon; thae (S, J, C)

thought *n., v., pt., ppl.* thocht

thousand *n.* thoosan(d)

thrash *v.* ledder; lick; aam, aum; creesh

thrashing *n.* ledderin; lickin; limerin; peelin

thread *n.* threid; (unbleached) whitet-, whitie-broons; **losing the thread of his thought** aff his stotter

threat *n.* threet

threaten *v.* thraten; threet; threeten

threatening *adj.* threetnin; (of weather) cankert; gurlie, gurly; (supernaturally) uncanny

threshing-mill *n.* thrashin-mull

threw *v. pt.* ceest

thrill *v.* thirl

thrived *v. pt.* thrave

throat *n.* craig; thrapple; witters

throb *n., v.* stoond, stound

throng *n.* thrang

throttle *v.* thrapple

through *adv., prep.* ben; throw

throw *n.* (heavy) doosht; *v.* fung, haive; thraw; (with a bump) dyst; (down with a thud) doosht; (of rope or fishing line only) shyve

throw off *v.* (a coat) cast

thrush *n.* mavis (M)

thud *n.* dird

thumb *n.* thoomb

thumb-rope *n.* thoomb-raip

thump *n., v.* dird; dunt

thunder *n.* thunner

Thursday *n.* Fiersday

thwarted *ppl.* stickit

tickle *v.* kittle

ticklish, tickly *adj.* kittlie, kittly

tidy *adj., v.* trig

tidy up *v.* snod

tie *v.* (tightly) hank

tight *adj.* ticht; **tighten** *v.* tichen; **tight-fisted** *adj.* grippy; near the been; **tight-fitting** *adj.* nippit

tile hat *n.* (black) lum hat

till *conj.* ontill, oontill

timber *n.* timmer; **seasoned timber** wun-timmer

time off *n.* afflat

time-serving *adj.* time-sairin

timid *adj.* bauch

timorous *adj.* arch (**ch** *gutteral*)

tinful *n.* mulfa

tingle *v.* dirl; thirl

tinker *n.* caird; cyaard; gate-ganger; tinkie; tinkler; kyaard

tinware *n.* fite iron

tipple *n.* bleb

tipsy *adj.* foo, fou, fu; far on; weel on

tiredness *n.* tire

tithe *n., v.* teind

title *n.* teetle

tittle-tattle *n.* claik; clash

to *prep.* tae; (*usu.* before a vowel) till; tull

toad *n.* ted

toadstool *n.* puddock-steel

toast *v.* birsel, birstle

tobacco *n.* tobaacca; (unconsumed in pipe) dottle; **tobacco pouch** spleuchan, splochan

today *adv., n.* the day

todo *n.* adee

toe *n.* tae

together *adv.* thegidder; thegither

told *ppl.* bidden; *v. pt., ppl.* taal, taul; telt

tolerance *n.* merciment

tolerate *v.* bide; thole; tolerat

Tomintoul *pr. n.* Tamintowl

tomorrow *adv.* the morn; **tomorrow night** the morn's nicht

tongs *n. pl.* tyangs; (hinged wire-tightener in fencing) taings

tongue-tied *ppl., adj.* tongue-tackit

tontine *n.* tamteen

too *adv.* an aa; tee; tae (S)

took *v. pt.* teuk; tyeuk

tool *n.* teel

toothache *n.* teethache
tootle *v.* (on a wind instrument) tweetle
top *n.* tap; (spinning) peerie; (card with pin passing through, resembling a teetotum) tipperteen; *v.* tap; **top man or woman** tapster; **over the top** (in behaviour) throw the bows
topsy-turvy *adv.* tapsalteerie
torch *n.* (paraffin torch used at sea) bubbly
tore *v. pt.* rave. *cf.* **rive**
torment *v.* tarraneese
torture *v.* (as a martyr) martyreese
totter *v.* styter; (from age) tite, tyte
touch *v.* lightly tap; (lightly in passing) scuff
touched *ppl., adj.* affeckit
touchy *adj.* kittle
tough *adj.* teuch, tyeuch
tousle *v.* tossle; toosle; **tousled** *adj.* toosy, tousy
towel *n.* tool
tower *n., v.* toor, tour
towering *ppl., adj.* toorin
town *n.* toon
town-dweller *n.* toonser
toy *n.* plyaak
trace *n.* theat; **kick over the traces** kick ower the theats; (the slightest) sinacle (B1)
tractor *n.* (Field Marshall diesel) pom-pom
train *v.* (animals to go in traces) track
tramp *n.* gangrel; trump; (with quarters on farm in exchange for work) quarterer
transaction *n.* transack

trash *n.* pelt; trag; trock, troke
travel *n., v.* traivel
travelling people *n. pl.* tinkies
treacle *n.* traikle, trykle
treacle toffee *n.* claggum; claggieleerum
tread *v.* treid (J)
treat *n.* cheery-pyke; gallshach, galshoch; trait; *v.* (harshly) ool; **harshly treated** oolt
treble *v.* threeple
tremble *v.* chitter
trench *n.* sheugh
trencher *n.* truncher
trestle *n.* mason's mear
trick *n.* aivis; begeck; gaa, gaw; (of the weather) widder-gaa; ginkum; ginkmen (B1); rig; jink; (mischievous) plisky; *v.* begeck; begowk; **to play a trick on** tae hae a hyze wi; tae play a rig; tak the rise o
trickery *n.* joukerie pawkery
trickle *v.* treetle
tricky *adj.* (of a task) fykie; kittle, kittlesome; quirky
trifle *n.* triffle; trifflie; (worthless) quinkins
trifling *adj.* nochtie, noughtie
trim *adj.* jinipperous
trip *v.* hyter
triple *adj.* threeple
triplet *n.* threeplet
trollope *n.* limmer
trot *v.* tite, tyte; treetle
troth *excl.* trogs
trouble *n.* fash, dispeace; trebble; tribble; **troublesome thing** tribbler; *v.* fash; **don't trouble yourself** dinna fash yer thoomb,

yer heid; **make trouble** raise din
trouble-maker *n.* din-raiser
trouble-making *adj.* din-raisin
troublesome *adj.* fykie
trough *n.* troch
trousers *n. pl.* breeks, briks; (of thick cotton) moleskins; troosers; **trouser braces** galluses; **trouser fly** spaver
trout *n.* troot
trowel *n.* trool
truant *n.* fugie (rhymes with budgie); true (the skweel); **truant officer** catcher (S)
truce *n.* (in games) parley, after the cry 'parleys-on'
trudge *n., v.* traik; trail
trust *v.* lippen tae; troo
truth *n., int.* trowth; **truthful** *adj.* trowthfu
trysting-tree *n.* covin-tree
tuck up *v.* (skirts, sleeves etc.) kilt
Tuesday *n.* Tyesday
tug *n., v.* rug; tit; yark
tumble *n., v.* tummle
tumbledown *adj.* tummle-doon
tumbler *n.* (glass) tummler
tumult *n.* shirrameer; shirramineer
tune *n.* teen; (lively, on the bagpipes) port; (lively) rant; spring
turf, a *n.* a divot; truff
turkey-cock *n.* bubbly(jock)

turn *n.* (to play etc.) shottie; *v.* (over) wummle; whummle; (of a river) wumple; (inside out) flype; (sudden) jink; twine; **turn and twist** weemple an wample
turncoat *n.* turnkwite
turnip *n.* neep; **turnip-slicer** neep-hasher; **turnip-lantern** neepie-lantrin; **turnip-hoeing** neep-rinnin; **turnip and potato soup** lefts an richts; **turnip watch** neep waatch
turret *n.* toopachin; toopican
Turriff *pr. n.* Turra
twelve *adj.* twal
twelve-month period *n.* towmon(d); twalmont(h)
twenty *adj.* twinty
twice *adv.* twise
twig *v.* (of shrub or bush) cowe
twilight *n.* gloam; gloamin; gloomin
twine *n.* (strong) tow
twirl *n., v.* birl
twist *n.* crook; thraw; *v.* kinsh; thraw, *ppl.* thrawn; twine
twitch *v.* tit
two *adj.* twa; **two-faced** *adj.* dooble; **two-handed** *adj.* twa-han
type *n.* teep
tyrant *n.* tirran

—— U ——

udder *n.* aidder; ether
ugly *adj.* ill-, ull-faart
umbrage *n.* umrage

umbrella *n.* umberella
un- *prefix* on-; oon-
unaware *adj.* onwuttin

unbaptised *ppl., adj.* oonbapteest
uncanny *adj.* eldritch; oonchancie
uncaring *adj.* ooncarin
unceasing *adj.* oondevallin
uncivil *adj.* oonceevil
uncommon *adj.* ooncommon
uncontrolled *adj.* oon o han
uncouth *adj.* hull-run
uncover *v.* tirr
undamaged *adj.* clear
undecided *adj.* i the deid-thraw; **to be undecided** *v.* swither
under *prep.* oonder; ooner
under-cattleman *n.* little bailie
underground *adj., adv.* oondergrun
undermost *adj.* naithmaist
underpants *n. pl.* (long) draars; draavers
undershirt *n.* semmit; linder; linner; sarket, sarkit
understand *v.* oonerstan, *pt., ppl.* unnersteed
undertake *v.* tak in han
undertaking *n.* oonertakkin
undigested *adj.* ondisjeestit
undoubtedly *adv.* oondootitly
undress *v.* tirr
undulate *v.* wammle
unearthly *adj.* eldritch; uncanny
uneducated *adj.* unedicat
unending *adj.* oonendin
uneven *adj.* shammelt
unexpected *adj.* oonexpeckit
unfair *adj.* (used by children) skicie
unfeeling *adj.* onfeelin
unfortunate *adj.* misfortnat
unfrequented *adj.* lown
ungenerous *adj.* ill-willie; (used by children) skycie
ungrateful *adj.* peyed-thankless;

pickthank; pykethank
unhappy *adj.* oonhappy
unheeding *adj.* onheedin
unintelligent *adj.* preen-heidit
unkempt *adj.* hudd(e)ry
unkind *adj.* ill; ull; **unkindly done** ull-deen
unknown *adj.* oonkent; unco
unlawful *adj.* oonlawfu
unless *conj.* onless, oonless
unload *v.* unlade; (a catch of fish) liver
unmannerly *adj.* menseless
unmethodical *adj.* ramshackle
unmindful (of) *adj.* onmynit (o)
unnatural *adj.* oonnaitral
unpleasant *adj.* (in behaviour) ull-farrant
unprincipled *adj.* oonprenciplt
unquenched *adj.* oonslockent
unreasonable *adj.* oot o theat
unrighteous *adj.* oonrichteous
unroof *v.* tirr
unruly *adj.* (of children) royd, royt
unsettled *adj.* (of weather) tittersome
unsociable *adj.* saachen, sauchen
unsought *ppl., adj.* unsocht
unsporting *adj.* skycie
unstable *adj.* oonstable
unsteady *adj.* (of a table, etc) shoogly
untidy *adj.* strushal, strushel; ill-shooken up; struchlach (B1); throw-idder; throwder; **untidy person** eeshich (B1); ticket; track; wallydraigle
until *conj.* or; ontil, oontill
untiring *adj.* ontirin
untroubled *adj.* oonfasht

unwashed *ppl., adj.* oonwaashen
unwell *adj.* oonweel; paewae; **to be unwell** *v.* ail
unwilling *adj.* oonwullin; sweer, sweir
unworked *adj.* (of land) unvrocht
unyoke *v.* lowse
up *adv.* up; hup
upbringing *n.* upfessin, -feshin
uphold *v.* uphud
upon *prep.* upo
upper hand *n.* wheep han
uppermost *adj.* eemaist; **upper part** (of field) eemaist wynin
uproar *n.* collieshangie; dirdum; gilgal (hard **g**) (B1); rammy; reerie; remishin; rippit; shirrameer; shirramineer; sta(r)shie; stramash; stushie
uprooted *ppl., adj.* (by the wind) win-casten
upset *v. tr.* kittle; vex; (overturn) cowp; (a plan) cowp the creels
upwards *adv.* upwuth
urine *n.* strang; (stale, used as detergent) maister; **urine jar** maister-pig
urinate *v.* pish
urination *n.* rin-oot
us *pron.* hiz; huz
usage *n.* eesage
use *n.* eese (*pro.* eece); **full use of** *phr.* weelins; *v.* eese (*pro.* eeze); **used to it** eest wi't; **useful** *adj.* eesefu; essfu
useless *adj.* eeseless; feckless; **useless person** footer
usual *adj., adv.* eeswal(ly)
utmost *adj.* itmaist
utter *v.* moo-ban
uvular 'r' *n.* (sounded in throat) burr; hurl in the throat; *v.* to use the uvular 'r' burr

— V —

vacant *adj.* vaacant, vawcant
vagrant *n.* gangrel; gyangrel
vain *adj.* full; vantie, vauntie
valentine *n.* valinteen
valley *n.* strath; (narrow) glen; howe
valuable *adj.* vailyable
value *n.* vailye; (something of little value) wanwurth; (something of no value) tinkler's curse
vanish *v.* vainish
vapour *n.* vaapour, vawpour
variable *adj.* immis (B1)
vegetation *n.* growthe
vehicle *n.* viackle; (old and rickety) shan-dre-dan
venomous *adj.* veeperate
very *adj., adv.* fair; foo; gey; verra; unco
vessel *n.* veshel; (drinking) pint-stowp,-stoup
vestige *n.* sinacle
vetch *n.* (tufted) fidgick; **wild peas** fidgick piz
veterinary surgeon *n.* ferrier
vibrate *v.* dirl; tirl
vibration *n.* dirl, tirl
vicious *adj.* veeperate; veeshus

view *n.* (range of vision) vizzie; (mental attitude) opingan

vigour *n.* fushen, fushon; vigour; **lacking vigour** fushenless

vilify *v.* (vilipend) wilipen

village *n.* clachan; toon; (with parish church) kirkton; **village green** loaning(s)

violence *n.* (to person or property) bangstrie

violent *adv.* veelent

violin *n.* fiddle

virago *n.* randy

vision *n.* veesion

visit *n.* veesit; *v.* (briefly) ca in by; cry in by

visitor *n.* veesitor; (the first to meet a marriage party or call on New Year's Day) first-fit

voice *n.* vice, vyce

voluble *n.* lairge

vomit *n.* splewin; *v.* byock (B1); kowk (A); spue; splew

vouch *v.* vooch

vow *v.* voo

vulgar *adj.* grofe

— **W** —

waddle *v.* shochle; waachle, wauchle

wade *v.* wide, wyde

wager *n., v.* waager, wauger

wages *n. pl.* waages, wauges; (farmhand's) fee; (in advance) sub

wagon *n.* (two-wheeled, open) bogie

wail *v.* walloch

waistcoat *n.* waskit; weskit; (sleeved) shafter, shaftit weskit; (under-jacket) fecket

wait *v.* bide; wyte; *imp.* heely

wakeful *adj.* waakrife, waukrife

waken *v.* waaken, wauken

walk *n.* waak(ie), wauk; traivel (S); (stroll) taik; (long, wearisome) trail; *v.* waak, wauk; leg, shank it; traivel; (noisily) clamp; (awkwardly) fuffle; (unsteadily) hyter; (hand-in-hand, arm-in-arm) link; (clumsily) haamer;

(aimlessly) pammer; (in mud or water) plyper; (slowly) stodge; (with a spring) stot; (with heavy, swinging gait); slewie (B1); (in a stumping way) stumpart, stumper; (in flat-footed way) sclap, sclaup

walker *n.* waaker, wauker

walkway *n.* waakie

wall *n.* wa; (of stone) dyke; (dry-stone) dry steen dyke; (built of sods) feal dyke

wall clock *n.* (with pendulum) wag-at-the-wa

wall-cupboard *n.* press

wall-eyes *n. pl.* ringel-een

wallow *v.* (in mud) slocher

wand *n.* gad, gaad; waan

wander *v.* rake; stravaig; wanner; (in speech) raivel

want *v.* wint; wunt; sik

wares *n. pl.* gibbles; waares

warm *adj.* waarm; *v.* (before the fire) beek; bek; byke; (warm, dry

181

weather, good for growth) forcie
warped *ppl.* gizzent
warrant *v.* warn
was *v. pt.* wis, *neg.* wisna
wash *n.* waash; (quick) cat's dicht;
v. waash, *pt.* weesh(t); *ppl.*
waashen
washing-line *n.* claes tow
waste *n.* waistry; wastry
waste away *v.* dwine
water *n.* watter
water-closet *n.* wattery
waterfall *n.* linn
water-glass *n.* (for preserving eggs)
watter-gless
water-hen *n.* beltie (G1)
watering-can *n.* rooser
water tap *n.* stroop
watery *adj.* (of flavour) waable,
wauble
wave *n.* waav; (at sea) jaa, jaw; *v.*
wag
way *adv.* wye; wa; wan; **come
away in** come yer was ben; **in
the direction of Kintore** Kintore
wye/wan; *n.* gate; wye
weak *adj.* feckless; saft; waffle;
waik; wyke; **weak-minded
person** *n.* saftie
weakly *adj.* sober
weakness *n.* waikness; wykeness
wealth *n.* gear; **accumulate wealth**
fog
wealthy *adj.* walthy
wean *v.* speen; spen
wear *n., v.* weer; **wear yourself out**
ca yersel deen
wearied *ppl.* dylt; wabbit; weariet
wearisome *adj.* dreich; langsome
weary *v.* jaap, jaup

weasel *n.* futrat, futtrat; **weasely
person** futtrat
weather *n.* widder; wither; (warm,
dry, good for crops) forcie;
(conducive to growth) growthie
weather-beaten *adj.* din-skinnt. *cf.*
sunburned
weave *v.* wyve
weaver *n.* wabster
weaving *n.* wyvin
web *n.* (spider's) (moose)wob; (of
small spiders) slammach; (woven
fabric) wab
wed *v.* wad, *pt.* waddit; mairry
wedding *n.* mairritch, mairrage;
waddin
weed *n.* wide, wyde
week *n.* wik; ook, ouk; **a week
today** this day ook
week-end *n.* wik-en
weigh *v.* wye, *pt.* wyt
weighed down *ppl.* wechen doon
weighing machine *n.* (steelyard
type) steilert
weight *n.* wacht, waucht; wecht;
(for fastening horse in stall)
sinker
weighty *adj.* wachty, wauchty;
wechty
weird *adj.* uncanny
weld *v.* (by hammering) clink
we'll *pron.* with *v.* we's
well *adj.* weel; *adv.* brawlies;
brawly; brulies; weel; *int.* aweel;
weel; wale (S); *n.* waal
well-bred *adj.* mensefu
well-built *adj.* kibble
well-favoured *adj.* weel-faart,
-faurt
well-fed *adj.* brosy; sair-maitit

well-known *adj.* weel-kent
well-loved *adj.* leal-loved
well-mannered *adj.* weel-mennert
well-off *adj.* foggit; weel-geddert
well-to-do *adj.* bien; geddert
went *v. pt.* gaed, gid
wept *v. pt.* grat, *ppl.* grutten; (noisily) roared an grat
we're *pron. with v.* we's
were *v. pt.* war; wur, *pt. neg.* warna
west *adj., adv.* wast; **western** *adj.* waster; **westward** *adv.* wastlins; wastward
wet *adj.* wat; weet; plytery; (of weather) drabbly; *v.* drabble
wether *n.* (castrated ram) wedder
wetting *n.* steeping
whack *n.* skelp
whale *n.* whaal, whaul
what *adj., pron.* fat, faat; fit; fut; **what a lot of** fat a; **what sort of** fatna; **what-do-you-call-it** fat-ye-ca't
whatever *adv., conj.* farivver
wheedling *ppl., adj.* fraiky
wheel *v.* (a barrow) rowe
wheeze *v.* clocher; whazzle; wheezle
whelk *n.* wulk
whelp *n.* fulp
when *adv., conj., pron.* fan, faan; fin
where *adv.* faar, faur; whaar (G1), whaur
whereas *conj.* forbyes
where else *interrog. adv.* faar idder
wherever *adv., conj.* farivver
whether *conj.* fidder; fudder; futher; gin
whey *n.* fy

which *pron.* whilk; *rel. pron.* whilk; fit (S)
whiff *n.* waff
while *conj., n., v.* fyle; (little) fylie; wee; whilie; whylock; **stay a while** bide-a-wee
whim *n.* gee; maggot; **full of whims** maggotive
whimper *n., v.* girn
whin *n.* fun, funn; **whin mill** fun mull
whine *v.* peenge; yammer
whinny *n.* nicher
whip *n., v.* fup; wheep; whup
whip-hand *n.* fup-han
whipper-in *n.* dog-dirder
whirl *v.* furl; **whirly** *adj.* furly
whirr *n.* birr
whisk away *v.* wheech
whiskers *n. pl.* fuskers; **whiskered** *ppl.* fuskert
whisky *n.* fusky; whusky; the cratur; **small whisky bottle** cutter
whispering *n.* fusperin; toot-moot (B1)
whistle *n.* fustle; (of the wind) sough; (whistling sound) wheeber; *v.* fustle; sough; wheeble; wheeple; (in a low tone) sowff
whit, not a *phr.* dag the bit
white *adj.* fite
whitlow *n.* futlie (beelin)
Whitsunday *n.* Wutsunday
whittle *v.* fite; futtle
whizz *v.* wheech; wheek
who *pron.* fa, faa; wha (G1)
whole *adj. n.* hail(l), hale
wholesome *adj.* halesome

whom *pron.* wham
whooping cough *n.* kinkhoast
whore *n.* hooer, hure
whorl *n.* (flywheel on spindle) forl
whose *pron.* whase (G1), whause
why *adv.* foo; fit wye; hoo
wicked *adj.* ill; ull; wicket
widow *n.* weeda; widda; widdie (J)
wife *n.* goodwife (A2); gweedwife; kimmer; wife
wight *n.* wicht
wild *adj., adv.* wil; wudden; wull; (unfrequented) bosky; (of children) royd, royt
wild-like *adj.* wull-like
wild mustard *n.* skellach
will *n.* (testament) tasment; tastement; tesment; wull; *v.* wull, *neg.* winna; wunna
William *pr. n.* Weelum; Wull(ie)
willing *adj.* redd; wullin
willow *n.* saach, sauch; (abounding in willows) sauchy; **willow wand** saach-waan, widdie-waan
wind *n.* win; (gust) flan; (sudden gust) howder; (off the sea) oot-win; (high) reevin win; **break wind** *v.* pump; let off
wind *v.* (a rope) kinsh; (of a river) wimple
windbag *n.* gab
windfall *n.* capshun
wind instrument *n.* tooteroo
window *n.* windae; windy (J); winnock (A1)
window-catch *n.* windae-sneck
window pane *n.* lozen
windy *adj.* winny
wing *n.* weeng
wink *v.* blink

winnow *v.* winny; (for the first time) cuff
winnowing machine *n.* fan; fanner
wipe *v.* dicht; *n.* dicht; dirrum-dicht
wire *n.* weer; **wire-tightening lever** peer-man
wise *adj.* wice, wyce
wish *n., v.* wiss; wuss
wishbone *n.* thocht-been
wisp *n.* wusp
wit *n.* wut; **wits** *n. pl.* wuts
witch *n.* carlin(e)
with *prep.* wi
wither *v.* widder
withered *adj.* (of flowers) wallant
without *prep., conj.* athoot; wi-oot; withoot; on (used with *pt. ppl.*); **without being** on-been; **without having** on-hed; **without doing** on-deen etc.
witness *n.* wutness
wizened *adj.* foggie
wobble *v.* waable, wauble
wobbly *adj.* waable, wauble
woe *n.* wae
woe-begone *adj.* hingin-luggit
woeful *adj.* waefu
woe-is-me *phr.* wae's me
woman *n.* umman; wife; wifie; *pl.* weemen; (married) kimmer; (old) carlin(e); *(derog.)* besom; (of doubtful character) kiltimmer; (of ill repute) runk; (loose-tongued) randy; (dirty, untidy) trail; (loose) vyaig; (worthless) baggerel
womb *n.* wyme
won *v. pt.* wan
wonder *n.* ferlie; winner; *v.* winner; wonner, *ppl.* winrin
wonderful *adj.* winnerfu

wood *n.* (substance) timmer; (trees) wid; wud; (small) widdie; shaw (J)
wooden *adj.* timmer; widden
wood pigeon *n.* cushie-doo
wood-shaving *n.* flaesick, flezick; spell
wood-turner *n.* (maker of caaps) caaper, cauper
wool *n.* oo; woo; (knitting) worsit; **wool-bag** *n.* worsit-bag
word *n.* wird; **words** *n. pl.* langidge
work *n.* wark; (day's work) darg; (messy or difficult) scutter; *v.* darg; wark, *pt. reg.*, also vrocht, wrocht; (in a flurried way) foorich; (in a slovenly way) kirn; (clumsily) haamer; (at high pressure) hash; (vigorously) link at; (messily) plowter; plyter; (at domestic chores) scudge, skudge; (awkwardly, messily) scutter; (vigorously) timmer on/up; (ineffectually) tooter; (strenuously) tyaaave, tyauve; (hard) yark; **start work** yoke, yoke intae; **set to work** wire intae; **stop work** lowse; **at work** *prep. phr.* ayoke
worker *n.* warker; wirker
work-house *n.* peer(s)-hoose
working period *n.* yokin
world *n.* wardle; warl(d); wordle
worldly *adv.* wardly
wordly-wise *adj.* warly-wise
worm *n.* wirm
wormwood *n.* wormit
worn *adj.* tasht
worn out *ppl., adj.* forfochen; forjeskit; foonert; (with hard work) fochen-deen; puggled; sair awa wi't; sair come at
worried *adj.* pit/pitten oot; vext
worse *adj.* waar, waur; **the worse for wear** waar o (*or* i) the weer
worst *adj., n.* warst
worsted *adj., n.* wirsit, worsit; (fine, from spun wool) fingerin
worth *n.* wirth
worthless *adj.* orra; weirdless; (anything worthless) *n.* wa-cast
worthy *n.* woorthy; *adj.* wordy
would *v.* wad, wid, wud; **would not** wadna, widna, wudna
wound *n.* hagger; sair; *v. pt.* wun
woven *ppl.* wivven
wraith *n.* wreith
wrangle *n.* dibber-dabber
wrap *n.* hap-waarm; *v.* wip; wup
wrath *n.* wraith
wreath *n.* (of snow) vreath
wreck *n.* wrack
wren *n.* vran
wrestle *v.* vrastle; warsle, warstle
wretch *n.* vratch
wright *n.* vricht; jyner
wring *v.* vring
wrinkled *ppl.* runklt, wrunkelt
wrist-bone *n.* shacklebeen, -bane
write *v.* screeve, screive; scrive; vreet
writer *n.* vreeter
writhe *v.* wammle
writing *n.* (long piece of) screed
writing-desk *n.* vreetin-dask
writing-paper *n.* vreetin-paper
written *ppl.* vrutten
wrong *adj., n.* vrang; wrang
wrote *v. pt.* vrat; vrote
wrought *v. pt.* vrocht

— Y —

yard *n.* (unit of measurement)
yaird, yerd
yardstick *n.* ell-wan
yarn *n.* (woollen) worsit; (ends of)
thrums
yawl *n.* yole; (used for catching cod
by hand-line) ripper-yole
yawn *v.* gant
year *n.* year; **last year** fernyear;
was-a-year; **year before last**
fernyear was-a-year
yearn (for) *v.* mang for; green
(efter) (B1)
yeast *n.* barm
yell *v.* skraich; skirl; yall
yellow *adj.* yalla
yellow-hammer *n.* yaldie; yeldrin;
yirlin
yellow iris *n.* seg
yellow turnip *n.* yalla

yelp *v.* yalp
yeoman farmer *n.* bonnet laird
yes *adv.* ay; ty; yea
yesterday *n., adv.* (*esp.* evening)
the streen, yestreen
yet *conj.* still an on; yit
Y-junction *n.* split-the-win
yonder *adv.* yonner; yont
you *pron.* ye; *pl.* (in *vocative* case)
you eens
you'll *pron. with v.* ye'll; ye's
your *pron.* yer
yourself *pron.* yersel; **by yourself**
yersel
youth *n.* (abstract term) youthheid;
(young man) halflin
Yule *n.* Eel; Yeel; (the old
Christmas season continuing until
after New Year) hale Eel

Scottish Interest Titles from Hippocrene. . .

SCOTS DICTIONARY OF WORDS AND PHRASES IN CURRENT USE

James A.C. Stevenson

Scots remains a thriving language as covered in this dictionary of the most widely-used words and expressions of today. Entries are arranged within fifteen categories, which express some aspect of everyday life in Scotland (eating and drinking, people, health, law). A key is provided to indicate the various contexts (colloquial, literary etc) in which the words are commonly used. Examples of actual usage in contemporary writing, newspapers, periodicals and conversation are included. This book is a fun and witty approach to the Scots language.

256 pages • 5 ½ x 9 • 1,000 words • 0-7818-0664-X • $11.95pb • (758)

SCOTTISH PROVERBS

Compiled by the Editors of Hippocrene
Illustrated by Shona Grant

Through opinions of love, drinking, work, money, law and politics, the sharp wit and critical eye of the Scottish spirit is charmingly conveyed in this one-of-a-kind collection. The proverbs are listed in the colloquial Scots-English language of the turn-of-the-century with modern translations below. Included are twenty-five witty and playful illustrations. There is something for everyone in this collection.

130 pages • 6 x 9 • 25 illustrations • 0-7818-0648-8 • $14.95 •W • (719) • May 1998

SCOTTISH LOVE POEMS

A Personal Anthology
edited by Lady Antonia Fraser, re-issued edition

Lady Antonia Fraser has selected her favorite poets from Robert Burns to Aileen Campbell Nye and placed them together in a tender anthology of romance. Famous for her own literary talents, her critical writer's eye has allowed her to collect the best loves and passions of her fellow Scots into a book that will find a way to touch everyone's heart.

220 pages • 5 ½ x 8 ¼ • 0-7818-0406-x • $14.95pb • (482)

Language Guides . . .

SCOTTISH GAELIC-ENGLISH/ENGLISH-SCOTTISH GAELIC DICTIONARY

R.W. Renton & J.A. MacDonald

Scottish Gaelic is the language of a hearty, traditional people, over 75,000 strong. This dictionary provides the learner or traveler with a basic, modern vocabulary and the means to communicate in a quick fashion.

This dictionary includes 8,500 modern, up-to-date entries, a list of abbreviation and appendix of irregular verbs, a grammar guide, written especially for students and travelers.

416 pages • 5 ½ x 8 ½ • 0-7818-0316-0 • NA • $8.95pb • (285)

ETYMOLOGICAL DICTIONARY OF SCOTTISH-GAELIC

416 pages • 5 ½ x 8 ½ • 6,900 entries • 0-7818-0632-1 • $14.95pb • (710)

In the Kitchen . . .

Scotland

TRADITIONAL FOOD FROM SCOTLAND: THE EDINBURGH BOOK OF PLAIN COOKERY RECIPES

A delightful assortment of Scottish recipes and helpful hints for the home—this classic volume offers a window into another era.

336 pages • 5 ½ x 8 • 0-7818-0514-7 • W • $11.95pb • (620)

CELTIC COOKBOOK: Traditional Recipes from the Six Celtic Lands: Brittany, Cornwall, Ireland, Isle of Man, Scotland and Wales

Helen Smith-Twiddy

This collection of over 160 recipes from the Celtic world includes traditional, yet still popular dishes like Rabbit Hoggan and Gwydd y Dolig (Stuffed Goose in Red Wine).

200 pages • 5 ½ x 8 ½ • 0-7818-0579-1 • NA • $22.50hc (679)

Ireland

THE ART OF IRISH COOKING
Monica Sheridan
>   Nearly 200 recipes for traditional Irish fare.
166 pages • 5 ½ x 8 ½ • 0-7818-0454-X • W • $12.95pb • (335)

New!

ENGLISH ROYAL COOKBOOK: FAVORITE COURT RECIPES
Elizabeth Craig
>   Dine like a King or Queen with this unique collection of over 350 favorite recipes of the English royals, spanning 500 years of feasts! Start off with delicate Duke of York Consommé as a first course, then savor King George the Fifth's Mutton Cutlets, and for a main course, feast on Quails a la Princess Louise in Regent's Plum Sauce, with Baked Potatoes Au Parmesan and Mary Queen of Scots Salad. For dessert, try a slice of Crown Jewel Cake, and wash it all down with a Princess Mary Cocktail. These are real recipes, the majority of them left in their original wording. Although this book is primarily a cookery book, it can also be read as a revealing footnote to Court history. Charmingly illustrated throughout.
187 pages • 5 ½ x 8 ½ • 0-7818-0583-X • W • $11.95pb • (723) • May

Wales

TRADITIONAL FOOD FROM WALES
A Hippocrene Original Cookbook
Bobby Freeman
>   Welsh food and customs through the centuries. This book combines over 260 authentic, proven recipes with cultural and social history
332 pages • 5 ½ x 8 ½ • 0-7818-0527-9 • NA• $24.95 • (638)

TRADITIONAL RECIPES FROM OLD ENGLAND

Arranged by country, this charming classic features the favorite dishes and mealtime customs from across England, Scotland, Wales and Ireland.

28 pages • 5 x 8 ½ • 0-7818-0489-2 •W • $9.95pb • (157)

All prices are subject to change. To order Hippocrene Books, contact your local bookstore, call (718) 454-2366, or write to : Hippocrene Books, 171 Madison Ave. New York, NY 10016. Please enclose check or money order adding $5.00 shipping (UPS) for the first book and $.50 for each additional title.